CONFESSIONS

Confessions

BARBARA AMIEL

MACMILLAN OF CANADA
TORONTO

Canadian Cataloguing in Publication Data

Amiel, Barbara.
  Confessions

ISBN 0-7705-1841-9

1. Amiel, Barbara.   2. Journalists – Canada – Biography.
I. Title.

PN4913.A43A33   070.4′092′4   C80-094190-X

Printed in Canada for
Macmillan of Canada
A Division of Maclean-Hunter Limited
70 Bond Street, Toronto
M5B 1X3

For George Jonas

Contents

CONFESSIONS

CHAPTER ONE

Encounter with the Thought Police

TORONTO: JULY 3, 1978. "What," I asked my husband, "does
one customarily wear to re-education sessions?" There was
no answer. "Probably something," I muttered, "that allows
one to sweat a lot." As we walked to the meeting, the horns
of midtown traffic and the click of tennis balls on the University of Toronto courts just behind our apartment building
counterpointed one another.

There is a special sweetness and luxury reserved for those
able to live in the middle of a city like Toronto. Commerce
and vegetation seem to co-exist reasonably well. Parking lots,
traffic, and quickie restaurants front onto small parks or
tree-lined streets surrounding the university campus. Perhaps, I thought, it is this pseudo-bucolic atmosphere that accounts for my perennial lateness for appointments. I'm simply in tune with nature's rhythms.

"Stop running," my husband said. "The Rabbi will forgive
you. It's his job."

He did. "Never mind," he said, getting up from the table
at the Courtyard Café, a tall, lean man with a napkin draped
over his business suit. "This is a place to enjoy myself." As
Head of the Canadian Jewish Congress, Senior Scholar of
Toronto's Holy Blossom Temple, columnist for several

1

newspapers, and an author of fiction on the side, Rabbi Gunther C. Plaut probably spent an excessive amount of time at head tables and airport breakfast counters. The Courtyard Café was neither. Of all Toronto's restaurants, it alone had reached the position where the media-cum-affluents who frequented it now also found it fashionable to apologize for eating there. When a place gets to be too In, it's Out.

I've always liked it. Being a rather angular, lanky person I appreciate restaurants with soaring ceilings and room to stretch. The intimate coziness of many continental-style eateries does not appeal to me. I sat down and turned my best pleased-to-see-you smile to the Rabbi.

"Just Perrier, with no ice, no twist. I've never liked liquor," I said with a smile, hoping this would indicate some sort of moral uprightness. The Rabbi smiled too. His was genuine. The three of us talked. We talked of literature – Schnitzler, Hofmannsthal, and Zweig. Of history and culture and art. The Rabbi is a man of considerable erudition, rare among all men, and a quick sense of humour, rare among rabbis. Under any other circumstances I would have enjoyed the meal. As it was, I had a sudden insight that a first-rate tone poem could be written on Judas's feelings at the Last Supper from the point of view of his alimentary canal.

"Well," said the Rabbi, "when this little problem came up I volunteered, as one who was a personal friend of both you, Barbara, and you, George, to speak to you in my capacity as Vice-Chairman of the Ontario Human Rights Commission – and as your rabbi." He waited. We waited. "Now *I* know," said the Rabbi, "that you are both decent people. I explained this to the other Commissioners."

I considered this.

"But," he continued, "we are concerned about the things you are writing. And since I know you are decent people I felt that I could help straighten this matter out and avoid the business of the Commission having to telephone or write to Barbara's magazine again. So, tell me. What are you fighting? Do we not believe in the same thing? Why can't you accept our ideas? What is it that you are afraid of, Barbara?"

I looked across the table at the Rabbi over the plates of mushroom soup and salmon mousse. Not quite the menu of a re-education camp. For a moment I was inclined to dismiss the whole matter with a quick smile, a Semitic shrug of the shoulders, and a return to the easy conversation of three civilized people enjoying a pleasant upper-income lunch. But the very privilege of the surroundings stiffened my resistance. My journey to the land of salmon mousse had not been as difficult or spectacular as that of many, but it had been a journey that had taught me a few things. And along the way I had decided that I was prepared to fight, modestly, for the survival of salmon mousse and the opportunity for it to be sampled by the greatest possible number of people. The Rabbi faced me full of goodwill, well-meaning, his unhappiness with my opinions sitting like a large black crow on his geniality. But behind that unhappiness lay the suasion and – perhaps – the power of the law to shape my opinions, for better or worse, according to his lights.

Of course, if the Rabbi had wanted to simply debate or argue issues he would have written a letter-to-the-editor or gone to lunch with us as a private citizen interested in the play of ideas. But this time he wanted something else. He wanted to establish precisely what opinions my husband and I held, and wanted, further, to make some sort of report – informal and if at all possible in our favour – to the Human Rights Commission on those opinions. As we were later told by a member of the Ontario Human Rights Commission, this interview with us had been approved by a meeting of the Commissioners, who seemed genuinely taken aback that anyone in the media would fail to accept their ideas or methodology on how to make society better.

But I didn't need this confirmation of my fears to understand the implication of the lunch. "Look," I wanted to shout, "I hold these views dear. They have not come easily. They are of no danger to your ideals. What is of danger to them is the idea of a Human Rights Commission. Please, let me explain." But a lunch, wherever it is held, is not the place to explain. And since I knew that whatever I said would be taken down in writing and in some way, somewhere, held against me, I decided that my opinions might as well be filed correctly.

These, then, are the notes I would be signing at the end of my confession. They pretend to no more literary merit than any other notes on a police confession-sheet. They will attempt to answer truthfully the one central question of any interrogation: What, if anything, can you tell us about the occurrence we are investigating?

Though I have as much talent for self-dramatization as any other writer (or any other woman), I will not pretend to horrors I did not in fact feel or expect to experience. I was well aware that I was sitting, not in a dungeon, but in the Courtyard Café. My interrogator was no Red Guard, no jackbooted Gestapo officer, but the kindly and civilized rabbi who officiated at my wedding. I came voluntarily and could have refused to attend, probably with no ill consequences to myself or my family. I did not expect to be tortured, mentally or physically. In this century, when people so much better than myself have been subjected to treatment so infinitely worse, perhaps I should not use words like "interrogation" or "confession", even as metaphors.

But consider this. In spite of all the civility that goes with salmon mousse, a branch of the State, under a law that empowers it to educate, to mediate, and to recommend prosecution, had requested me to explain my opinions. Not my acts, not my misdeeds, but my *opinions*. The liberal impulse that had set up the Human Rights Commission, the impulse that had ostensibly sought justice and liberty for all, had now come full circle. It had, apparently, come into possession of the Truth. It now felt confident enough to outlaw, and, if necessary, to prosecute, Error. However polite and civilized, it had established its own Thought Police, and I was now to answer to them.

I could have refused – as yet – but I chose not to. "What is it that you are afraid of?" asked the Rabbi.

Of you, with respect. Of all of you.

CHAPTER TWO

"The Children Must Be Told"

ENGLAND, 1946. Two topics, always: the war and the Americans. On the radio the BBC tries to maintain contact between families separated for more than six years. "From mother Ethel D--- of Birkenhead to Private William D--- of the Seventh Artillery stationed in Berlin. You may not be an angel, William, but your mother thinks you are and that's the song she's requested for you." The Americans are visible now, no longer confined to their corrugated-iron barracks on the base at the old Hendon Aerodrome where the Germans dropped the largest bomb of the war – 2,500 kilograms – in 1941, about two months after I was born. In fact, the location of the base across the road from our house in Hendon, Middlesex, was said to be the reason for the bombing in this suburban London area. All we have to show for the blitz, though, are some large cracks in the ceilings, and bay windows that are now rather more bowed than before the war. The war and the Americans. Constant reminders that although one should not (a) chew their bubble gum or (b) talk to Yankee soldiers in the park, neither should one forget that (c) they helped us win the war.

The war is visible, too, in the extraordinary ruins of London which one is taken to see as a solemn lesson in the cost of appeasing evil for too long. Fatigue seems to hang over the city after the exhilaration of victory. My mother's face is drawn very often these days as her job with the British Red Cross involves her more and more in the cruel business of dealing with requests from distraught families for information about European relatives taken to the Nazi camps. We are lucky. Virtually all of our family had left Europe for England or Palestine several generations before the war. Still, a distant branch remained in Germany. In England the two members who escaped – a grandfather and his granddaughter – wait for news. The granddaughter goes to my school. She is fat and oily and a target of some ridicule. She is fourteen and I am six, but I feel very much like comforting her on the day I learn that she has no family but her grandfather left.

There is much talk about the camps. In Hertfordshire we visit friends and I am shown a man who has returned from a "camp". He sits in a dark room, though outside the day is bright and bluebells are covering the fields behind the house. He rocks quietly in a chair, never speaking. My grandmother has taken one or two survivors into her home. One of them smells some meat going off in the larder and becomes hysterical. Her face is contorted with dry sobbing. My mother tells me that the odour of meat reminds her of the odour of rotting bodies.

Adults sobered by their brush with the charnel-houses of Europe decide that "the children must be told." At six years of age it is impossible to grasp the full horror of the Second World War but it is not impossible to have a partial understanding. Walks on the open land called "the common" reveal bomb craters, gaping and ugly. I am afraid to go down into them or into the black tunnels I see everywhere – the entrances to bomb shelters. Pieces of shrapnel and a bullet are put into my hand. They were removed from my father's chest after the Italian campaign. War, the adults explain, is inglorious, an ignoble business, but sometimes necessary. This had been a necessary war.

In the east end of London, between Whitechapel and

Stepney, the beginning of England for cattle-boat Jewish immigrants (where on Mile End Road my grandmother still runs a confectionery shop), a street is renamed Amiel Street by gracious order of His Majesty King George VI. It is to commemorate my grandfather's death in the blitz while performing his duties as an air-raid warden rescuing some children. I read everything I can in the newspapers about the war: the story of the resistance heroine Odette, serialized in the Sunday rags between acid-bath murders and the confessions of a child-mutilator. The little I can understand is simple, possibly simplistic, but it becomes an article of faith. The war had to be fought because a man came to power who believed that some races of people could be killed, attacked, diminished, and humiliated simply because of their race. My family emphasizes that, although this happened in large numbers to Jews, a group to which I apparently belong (although I am not at all sure at this point what this means – will I grow up to be a violinist?), this also happened to Poles, Ukrainians, gypsies, and so on. Though life is not a series of fireside sermons and metaphysical discussions but more often trips to the pantomime and blissfully English moments on honest-to-goodness window-seats with Dickens and an apple, the lesson is drummed home. The worst possible evil is racism. It nearly destroyed the world and was responsible for the murder and degradation of millions of human beings.

Thirty-one years later, September 1977, in a rundown house in Teddington, a suburb of London, England, I find myself staring into the lashless eyes of the leader of Britain's nascent neo-Nazi party, the National Front. Facing our television camera, John Tyndall, once known for constantly accessorizing his business suits with German jackboots, finds me quite invisible. I am a non-believer asking him questions and that is like a mosquito asking for a good table at a restaurant, preposterous and to be squelched as soon as the honorarium for the interview is received. Tyndall cites his Second World War military service as evidence of his dissociation with the Nazis and then tells me, without pausing for breath, of his plans for Zionists, homosexuals, and blacks when he comes to power. "Deportation or re-education camps," he explains.

"But surely the war in which you fought was a war to end discrimination and racism," I ask naively. Tyndall's thin lips tighten. (My literary sense wishes, quite irrelevantly, that these Nazis could be slightly less clichéd and boast full, red, sensuous lips.) Tyndall swivels in his chair. He faces our television camera with a posture so relentlessly correct that it seems as if a thin length of piano wire is attached to the top of his head and pulled taut against the ceiling. The sentences are so precise and clipped that I mentally insert pauses and phrasing to eliminate this uncanny element of caricature. It seems unwise to regard a beast as a cartoon drawing.

"World War II," he replies, "was a war fought to preserve Britain and the Empire from outside domination. That was its sole aim." Later, on reflection, I suppose in one sense he's correct. Though Hitler would have been loath to attack "Aryan" England, he probably would have been forced to in the end. And England's *leaders* certainly did not declare war on Germany to save Jews, homosexuals, or gypsies. Only themselves. But at least some Englishmen understood more about morality than their leaders. A good many old men I have met and listened to in England, old soldiers who may never have seen a Jew or understood even their own "Aryan" heritage, went off to war to fight for something called decency. And what a cruel trick this postwar age has played on them. Driven against the wall by the good intentions of people like Mark Bonham Carter, Shirley Williams, David Owen, and many more, these old defenders find themselves, decent and honourable yet, supporting the National Front, whose ideology signifies all that is abominable in human nature and all that they had fought against. "Many of our supporters are ex-soldiers," claims John Tyndall triumphantly, to make his point. You bet.

I could not foresee the sequence of events that would lead to this when I was six, or when I was sixteen. I would see it later, and the chill of that room in Teddington, and the gloom of curtains drawn tight against the bluebells and sunshine in the deadened half-light of a camp survivor, would eddy together in my memory. But at age six or seven life is based on the repeating of the Ten Commandments and a few basic moral paradigms. In those days, next to please-and-thank-you, most conversations about manners and morality were dotted with a curious phrase, "equality before the law". That, explain countless relatives when faced with "the child" asking more questions, is what the war achieved for Europe. Equality, in fact, is described so often and so vividly to me that, since I have a child's limited capacity for abstract thought, it seems to me that equality must be something living – like the girl in class next to me called Verity – probably under the apple tree at the end of the garden where my favourite rhubarb-stalks grow. On a drive down to Brighton, my father, cheerful and academically demanding on his one-day-a-month custody outing, is peppering me with questions designed to make sure I am an achiever. "Name five animals beginning with 'e' within half a minute," he demands. I am confident.

"Elephant, emu, eagle, eel, and equality."

Further complications: equality before the law regardless of one's religion or skin colour, I am told, is the key to a decent country. But when I begin to talk with the lower-class accent of our cleaning lady, I understand, without having to be told, about the limits of equality. If our Doris is accused of stealing the milk money she ought to be treated by the authorities exactly as if she were the Duchess of Gloucester. However, I will get my face slapped if I talk like Doris instead of the Duchess of Gloucester. This, too, is a lesson drummed home.

In Selfridge's on Oxford Street the saleslady helps us with (restrained) British eagerness. "North London Collegiate School," my mother says, and I am immediately dressed up in uniforms of brown and more brown – tunics, cardigans, and horrid little brown-checked dresses which pick up the muddy colour of my hair and complexion. I am delighted. A uniform makes me feel grown-up. The school is located in the seventeenth-century home of the Duke of Chandos in Canons Park, where Handel stayed for some time, composing, we are told, under the great spreading cedar trees and playing the very organ which I can now hear through the assembly doors playing some stirring Christian marches. The school's dozen or so Jewish girls are sent away every morning to their own assembly, where we speculate about the rituals being enacted in the Church of England prayers. I opt for the sacrificing of cats or possibly young Jewesses, but the senior Jewish girls reprimand me severely. When we are admitted into the main hall, whatever had been going on has been cleaned up, and the school announcements are read. Many of them have to do with the support of Bromley House and the Frances Mary Buss Foundation. Miss Buss, the founder of our school in 1850, was one of those genuine pioneers of female lib who believed that women could handle math and science and history as well as knitting and playing the odd (easy) piano piece. Unfortunately she insisted on keeping in the knitting, and I am holding back an entire class in its "helping the needy of Bromley House" by my inability to manufacture a perfect square for the knitted blankets.

Miss Buss, together with her friend Miss Beale, who founded Cheltenham Ladies College, are the women after whom we are taught to pattern ourselves. Madame Curie is a close third, but, alas, she is *French.* That intrepid pioneer of birth control, Marie Stopes, is one of the notable Old Girls of North London Collegiate about whom we never talk, because sex is not on our curriculum. However, we all learn the anon pupil's limerick

> Miss Buss and Miss Beale
> Cupid's darts do not feel.
> Oh, how different from us
> Are Miss Beale and Miss Buss.

By the end of 1946 I have an enormous crush on a middle-school girl nicknamed Sappho who strokes my hair while reading her namesake's poetry to me under the spreading cedar tree. The original Sappho's poetry is not on the curriculum either, so I do not understand why my frequent references to my new idol cause some mild discussion at home.

A tour of Bromley House, which funds lower-class families and an inner-city school in London, is planned to show us where the money we raise goes. "School uniforms will be worn," says the teacher, "and that will include your nigger-brown coat, Barbara." My mother had purchased a white camel-hair coat for me which she insisted I wear one evening to a school play, and the incident has never been allowed to remain unmentioned.

"Eeny meeny miney moe/Catch a nigger by the toe" sing Gillian and I with our skipping-ropes as we line up for Bromley in our nigger-brown uniforms. Such phrases are routine, like the simile "mean as an old Jew". My best girlfriend Gillian and I want desperately to look African or Indian. White (Gillian) and sallow (me) seem so boring. We experiment with Leichner greasepaint which I have for my ballet-school recital. Brown may have been beautiful but it ran, making us look like Appaloosas. It will be twenty-five years before those silly, harmless phrases are made significant, and mythical little black Sambo and Shylock become their real victims.

Sambo and Shylock as victims? How can vicious racial stereotypes ever be called "victims"? Were the horrible pictures of Hitler's war, the death of my grandfather, the jagged piece of lead from my father's chest, not close enough in time to teach me the lesson of where such attitudes can lead? How could little English girls, nearly swept away by the evil of a neighbouring racist State a few years earlier, merrily continue "jewing" each other down or working like "niggers" on their school assignments? How could we not learn?

Perhaps – and it would be many years before I would be forced to address this question in my own mind – we learned no lesson because there was no lesson to be learned. Perhaps we knew, instinctively, that (contrary to what the officious sterilizers of thought and language would now have us believe) there was *no* connection between our stereotypes or adjectives and the gas chambers of Auschwitz. The Nazis were not monsters grown big from our puppy-monsters of caricatures and silly nursery rhymes; they belonged to a different species altogether. The real connection was not between the Gestapo and our little tribal conceits or group-rituals, even when they were expressed by the belittling of other groups. The real connection was between the Gestapo and a State bringing in legislation and regulations about how other groups of people ought to be viewed. Individually held prejudices, though often stupid, and often lacking any foundation in fact or logic, were the benign tumours of liberty; having the unquestioned right to hold our own opinions, we often had very silly ones. The malignancy would have been a State laying down the law about official opinions we were obliged to share.

Much later I heard the difference expressed by an old man who resisted the Nazis with much personal courage. "I wanted Hitler to go," he said, "so that a gentleman could be an anti-Semite once again."

As the cold-war chill set in during the late forties I was often the evil Russian Jewess stealing secrets and hiding them in the school grounds while the rest of the class pursued me. Our game directed no personal antagonism against me, as our nursery rhymes directed none against the African exchange students or the East Indians commonly seen on London streets. It would be some twenty-five years later that the official left-liberal purging of "stereotypes" would claim real victims. But I am ahead of myself.

CHAPTER THREE

Watercress Sandwiches and Socialism

THE GREAT MORAL CONFUSION that was the aftermath of the Second World War never touched my circle of family and their friends. Or at least I never sensed it. For my family there was clearly a proper way to reconstruct a world that had nearly lapsed into total barbarism. It was a black-and-white solution. The road must fork firmly to the left; the only question was how far. Churchill had been thrown out in the General Election of 1945 for Attlee's socialist Labour party. This was a start. I had loved staying up in the evenings towards the end of the war when the blackout curtains made every room seem warm and safe while the radio played the growling cadences and hypnotic rhythms of re-broadcasts of Churchill's earlier speeches. "This is not the end, this is not even the beginning of the end. But it is perhaps the end of the beginning." All the same, the feeling was strong: the need for the "old warrior" was over; one must never fall prey to the folly of too strong a leader again.

My godfather, as he was affectionately called, was a thoughtful, angular-faced man named Sedley who was one of the lawyers for the official newspaper of the British Communist party, *The Daily Worker*. After my parents' marriage had broken up in the high-pitched frenzy of divorce, the

Sedleys became a kind of halfway house in the confusion of custody arrangements, excommunicated friends, and unpleasant scenes. At their home I listened to the songs of the American negro singer and communist Paul Robeson. From the records of Robeson I memorized the first stanzas of The Internationale; I could sing every word of "Joe Hill"; I learned of the plight of the Lancashire cotton-weavers. Robeson's marvellous deep voice would swirl around my head on Sunday afternoons at the Sedleys' as I enjoyed high tea and hide-and-seek and the spirited Sedley family discussions that were the beginnings of my political education.

My father's family ran the gamut of the political left. His younger brother, a lawyer, was a member of the British Communist party, which slavishly followed the Moscow line. Stalin was a family hero, and pictures of "Uncle Joe", together with a small bust of Marx and one of Lenin, decorated the front hall of their home. So did a framed certificate signifying that our entire family had contributed to the Joint Committee for Soviet Aid in 1941 and had purchased a bed in the Maxim Gorky Hospital. This was, of course, a perfectly respectable committee in 1941, endorsed by Winston Churchill as a proper channel for patriotic activity. Later on when Western communists had to deal with such indigestibles as the Doctors' Trial, Khrushchev's revelations at the Twentieth Party Congress, or the treatment of repatriated Russian prisoners-of-war, many would be less happy about any relationship – however tangential – with Stalin, and might not display so proudly a testimony to earlier gullibility. Although the Golders Green home was "shattered" by the revelations and removed Stalin from among the icons, it was not shattered enough to remove the certificate.

My father's sister, a woman of extraordinary beauty and intelligence, first a businesswoman, then an author, and finally, in her late forties, a practising criminal barrister, married a British Jew who was also of the left, but of Maoist convictions – before Mao even came to power. He worked in the British Army's Bureau of Current Affairs during the war which, among other things, was designed to ensure that the proper levels of hatred towards the enemy were maintained. My uncle's job was to inculcate hatred of fascism in any reluctant British Tommy, and as part of this effort he began lectures on Chinese history and culture in order to work up the appropriate antagonism towards the invading Japanese. His study of China led him away from Communism, Soviet-Style, into a lifelong affair with the Great Helmsman (which at last account still placed him squarely behind the disgraced Gang of Four). His close friends, some of whom I would meet, included Edgar Snow, Han Suyin, and assorted Sinophiles. Further down the road, as his relationship with China deepened, would be a lifelong friendship with left-winger and Nobel Prize winner Lord Boyd Orr, and intriguing glimpses of Harold Wilson and a young man named Pierre Elliott Trudeau.

My father, the family member with whom I had the least contact, a lawyer by profession and partner in his own firm, talked little to me about politics. Our meetings took place often under difficult circumstances, and the excitement of seeing one another and catching up on news came first. He had had, as they said in those days, "a good war"; he became a colonel in Montgomery's Eighth Army, and postwar was offered a brigadiership. Sometimes he would joke about the lighter side of desert warfare, but he had been severely wounded in the Italian campaign and was ready for the civilian life. "I'm an East End Jew," he would tell me wryly, mimicking a cockney accent, "wot grew up sleeping in the front room with two older brothers. What am I going to do in the officers' mess with Bannister-hyphenated-bloody-Jones?"

In fact it was the East End that had shaped many of my family's – and later my own – attitudes. In this cramped Jewish quarter of London, the Russian and Polish newcomers worked, argued, and scrambled for a piece of England, bringing with them the socialist ideals and ideas of the *Bund*, the religious-political organization formed in the old country as a beginning of resistance to the authoritarian regimes under which they lived. The spirit of the *Bund* fused with the exhilaration many felt for the freedom of opportunity they found in England, and formed a kind of animus that was a brew of humanism, socialism, and of course idealism. The fact that all four of my paternal grandmother's children, including her one daughter, had been sufficiently upwardly mobile to get scholarships and university degrees did not produce an "I'm all right, Jack" reaction or even an acknowledgement of the flexibility of the society that had enabled them to move up in it, but rather the very opposite. Disraeli's "One may be accepted where many are rejected" was on the table along with the herring and the chopped liver. Some form of socialism, it seemed to family members from Maoist to Stalinist, would be the only means of making their own good fortune universal. On the whole, decent impulses motivated each one of them – certainly in the early postwar years. Later on, when socialists became the quasi-Establishment of England, business and politics would lie in bed together with the inevitable results. But for the time being, even my father's third brother, a gentle, apolitical doctor who cared primarily about his ability to maintain the Hippocratic oath at the lowest cost to patients, held certain socialist truths as axiomatic.

The Amiels were originally Sephardic Jews from Spain. My mother's family were Ashkenazy: her grandmother was an imperious old woman from Kiev, Russia, where she had married Vladimir Isserlis, a direct descendant of Moses Isserlis, one of the most revered names in Ashkenazy scholarship. In a Cracow synagogue built to commemorate his work, a light burned for over three hundred years, till Hitler's foul breath put it out. But as "court Jews" my great-grandparents had permission to live splendidly in Kiev, where Vladimir was an attorney. When his body was found floating in the Dnieper River – under circumstances never explained – my great-grandmother was ordered out of the city and back to the Jewish Pale of Settlement. Being a woman of some independence (and pragmatism), she auctioned off the prayer shawl and phylacteries of the great Moses Isserlis to a wealthy if somewhat impious Jewish family, and on the proceeds of this worldly transaction and the sales of more commonplace family heirlooms bribed herself and her four young children all the way to England, arriving in the East End's Bethnal Green in 1891. Soon she had graduated as a registered midwife and had acquired an office, a shining brass nameplate announcing her profession, a new husband to be supported, and a thriving practice in the slums and dockyard district of London, paid for by middle-class charitable institutions which wouldn't dream of setting up shop in the streets my great-grandmother walked day and night. She walked them contemporaneously with Jack the Ripper and she walked them unmolested. This, it is commonly felt by those who remember her, was due to her ferocious facial expression and an uncompromising female haughtiness. She was fiercely Russian, fiercely socialist, and she imbued her children with the necessity for social service. I am quite sure she would have disowned me, or, more likely, browbeaten me into The Cause. Her daughters became active Fabians. At the end of the Second World War she was still alive, a wrinkled old lady harassing three generations.

My grandmother was a schoolteacher. Her husband, a gentle German Jew, a classics scholar and Francophile, and an actuary by profession, would sit reading Voltaire and Proust in one corner of the room muttering about "the mad Russians". He worked for the Labour party in his spare time, handing out pamphlets condemning inequities and preaching the need for comprehensive social planning. His earliest admonition to me was that "religion is the cause of all the world's ills" and that I should read history with this thought firmly in mind. His own material needs were few: he favoured a particular kind of pipe tobacco and clean handkerchiefs for his sombre three-piece suits. The money he earned went to support the university careers of his three daughters and later on his grandchildren. One daughter graduated as a doctor in 1926 and went on to become the medical assistant to Dr. Edith Summerskill, the lady who gave us the British National Health scheme. My mother left the University of London to work for the British Red Cross, and the third daughter did the unforgivable: she simply *married* a doctor and raised children. Everyone worked for the Labour party.

I decided at age nine to throw in my lot with the British Liberals. This was not because I had the slightest comprehension of the policies of the Whigs or any understanding that, apart from several periods of bloody intolerance, they had been known as the party of moderation and tolerance. It was simply this: a General Election was held in Britain in 1950 and my school decided to give a practical lesson in civics and have an election within the school. By then I had taken to heart the constant concern for the underdog, the underprivileged, and the under-represented which saturated the atmosphere about me. The great Liberal party had been in a state of decline for fifty years, and every commentator on the BBC and every family member seemed to agree that the Liberals were the underdogs in the election. Ergo, I announced for the Liberal party (thank God Sir Oswald Mosley's party wasn't running) and began campaigning furiously on a platform to open up the tennis courts to the lower-school girls on grounds that privileges should be won by merit rather than by inherited position. (A great deal of this had to do with a fairly devastating forehand I had perfected playing alone against our garage wall.) When the election returns came in, the Liberal party, which in 1906 held 379 seats in the House of Commons, had won only nine ridings. At my school, however, it came in second to Labour.

All of this family data is of little interest really to anyone except a few sentimental great-aunts and -uncles. I list it here as an attempt to try and explain the ambience of the time. Along with most people of decent inclinations, some education, and an interest in creating a more just society, my family shared unequivocally the belief that the only route to a better world was through socialism. As I grew older and began not only to mouth the words of The Internationale or the trade-union songs but to actually consider their meaning, I too moved into the social-democratic camp. Indeed, I moved further and further left. Conviction and passion, after all, when alloyed with compassion are highly contagious.

And there was much passion. The full horror of Nazism revealed now in the flood of books and personal accounts, and finally in the dreadful films and snapshots of the concentration camps shown on the cinema screens like some awful parody of a family album, would be an illustration of human depravity that would never leave me. The extreme right was anathema – long before I dreamed of what horrors the extreme left had already institutionalized in the Gulags of the world. Later on, when journalists in Canada would refer to the internment camps for Japanese Canadians in the Rockies as "concentration camps" – or indeed the prisons of America as akin to Auschwitz – I would break out in a cold fury. Outrageous and unjustifiable as the Japanese camps were on many grounds, the comparison with Dachau, Mauthausen, Theresienstadt, and Belsen indicated a kind of historical illiteracy – if not moral bankruptcy – that is a feature of much North American journalism.

Sunday newspapers and watercress sandwiches, the name of Senator Joseph McCarthy and the policies of the then ambassador to the U.N., John Foster Dulles, were filtering across the Atlantic to our parlour political rallies. From the pleasant vistas of suburban London it appeared that the real threat to freedom was once more coming from the right wing and from, of all places, America. And, of course, in a limited sense it was perfectly true – though it was ludicrous to suggest that the prophecies of John Foster Dulles (now, alas, proved true in so many respects, from "containment" and Eisenhower's domino theory on) sprang from the same anti-democratic impulse as those of the Senator from Wisconsin. But McCarthyism, minor though it was (no executions, no exile, and most people getting jobs under pseudonyms till, as actress Lee Grant explained to me, "one day, suddenly, it was all over and we went back to work under our own names"), was a dangerous period in America. Still, it was of some use to such apologists of Stalinism as American playwright Lillian Hellman, whose business it became to turn the bullying tactics of McCarthyism into a creed that made it less than respectable to be anti-McCarthy *and* anti-communist at the same time.

But all this was far away. I had not yet read George Orwell. I had seen little of life beyond the world of Hampstead Maoists and Golders Green socialists. For me, there was school and ballet lessons, piano and speech training, and hundreds of Penguin books lining every available wall in our home. There was Somerset Maugham to read and H. G. Wells and Bernard Shaw and T. S. Eliot. Life was a hundred and one marvellous possibilities with even the prospect, now that I had passed my eleven-plus exam and won a scholarship, of going to the posh girls' boarding-school called Roedean. Then, I supposed, it would be on to Girton and . . . There was nothing that one could not do.

It ended suddenly. One day my mother announced her remarriage and our imminent departure for the wilds of Canada. Since we were wards of the court (a legacy of the divorce), there would be certain problems in taking my sister and me out of England, but she was sure these could be overcome. Why, she asked, would we want to stay in England anyway, where my new stepfather's working-class background would be a liability to him socially and professionally? This had never occurred to me. My stepfather was a handsome, warm man of whom I was enormously proud. I was aware, yet unaware, of the subtleties of the British class system, and was confused by my mother's concern that her new husband's accent would be "embarrassing" on Founders' Day at my school. But she clearly knew what she was talking about.

On a chilly day in November 1952, just before my twelfth birthday, we sailed for Canada.

CHAPTER FOUR

Tobacco Road, Hamilton

LIKE SO MANY IMMIGRANTS we had no idea what was facing us. Canada House in London had given us picture books filled with Ottawa tulips, Mounties, and pictures of Banff. We studied them carefully. Since Hamilton, Ontario, as our Immigration Officer told us, was a city built in the shadow of Hamilton Mountain, we imagined it to be like Banff. Job opportunities in Ontario were marvellous, we were told. Our source of information, apart from the regular authorities, was the owner of a private nursing-home down the road from us in Hendon who was a relative of Ontario's Premier, Leslie Frost. She wrote to him on our behalf and shortly afterward brandished a letter from the Premier encouraging our immigration to "this fast-developing province". During the dreadful winter crossing of the Atlantic the one refrain with which husband comforted wife and vomiting children was the reassurance that if anything went wrong we could contact Leslie Frost.

My stepfather was an electrical draftsman who had done rather well in England but whose career was limited by his lack of university training. In England he had already been given jobs far beyond his qualifications, but the ceiling on his aspirations was clearly visible. His family were about as poor as my East End grandparents, but they were different in one crucial aspect: they were English. Unlike the Jewish immigrants, who could size up the social structure of a society,

21

grasp its rules, and work out a strategy to infiltrate the middle class, the English working class by and large tended to keep to their place. Sending my stepfather to university had just never been considered. (Still, for the record, some of his family did illustrate the relative irrepressibility of talent in those few professions where ability rather than artificial quotas of class or sex count. His cousin Michael Somes became a star with the Sadler's Wells ballet, partnering Margot Fonteyn for many years, and his own brother, Arthur Somes, developed into a classical pianist and teacher of some stature.)

We arrived in Hamilton on a chilly, bleak day, my mother, stepfather, younger sister, and infant half-brother. The early views of Canada from the boat had not been promising. The bleak grandeur of the St. Lawrence in winter with its small communities punctuating vistas of brush and snow was nothing our European eyes had even encountered before. They looked like scenes from a grimmer Grimm's fairy-tale. Countryside meant herbaceous borders and wild cornflowers, meadows and moors; *remote* meant the drizzle and fog of the Lake District where the mountains and stretches of water seemed to enfold one rather than stand at this icy remove. But, Hamilton was where our Horatio Alger ascent would begin. We would become wealthy North Americans with cars that stretched out to marvellous chrome fins, and we would wear fur coats and own television sets.

The difficulties we encountered were not particularly remarkable in the immigrant experience. For the modest frame house rented for us on Tragina Avenue in the east end of Hamilton we were charged $180 a month rent without heating – a rather extraordinary amount in 1952 when comparable homes would have been about $60 inclusive. The job my stepfather had been guaranteed was not there. Canada was entering a period of economic recession and work was hard to come by. As winter inched in we watched the falling snow with utter fascination and no appropriate clothing. Suddenly we were all outfitted in hideous brown storm coats with quilted linings and brown furry earmuffs.

They seemed to cost a fortune. Snow boots had to be purchased, and then the heating bills began to arrive. My mother's new pregnancy was totally unexpected and, of course, we had no medical insurance.

As the weeks passed, the bleakness of our position became apparent. Every morning, long before my sister and I set off for the public school at the end of our street, my stepfather would be sitting in the kitchen going through the employment ads. Every day he trudged out to get a job, anything. He was a quiet, proud man of just thirty or so, younger than my mother, and absolutely determined to provide for this suddenly acquired family of five-and-a-half. His shyness ran deep. The strain of excessive socializing in England in the competitive atmosphere that is comfortable and familiar to many Jews was a nightmare for him; at such events I would sometimes find him upstairs lying on a bed, his breathing laboured and difficult, his face swollen and angry red from the violent attacks of hives that nervousness triggered. Such sensitivity was a luxury that had to be overcome in our situation in Canada. And he did overcome it. He found a job and brought gifts home to celebrate the occasion: a bottle of toilet water, a blouse, a charm bracelet, all carefully wrapped up in tissue paper and chosen from the best counters of the Metropolitan Store.

But our financial situation was grim. We were down to one large meal a day, heavy on potatoes and no seconds. From seven o'clock in the evening, when the meal was over, my sister and I would fantasize about the endless meals we would have when we were rich. Our parents were fantasizing about what they would do if one of the many loan agencies they had approached would help us. Unfortunately for us, one did. A quick course in compound interest rates followed. At that time the sky seemed the only limit on small-loan interest. (Later on, when I was writing the scripts for a television quiz show co-sponsored by the Department of Consumer and Corporate Affairs, I would take particular relish in concocting situations and questions involving finance companies and allowable interest rates. "Usury" was a favourite word that had to be eliminated from my typescript by the lawyer vetting the show.)

But the spirit of the times came to our aid. Hamilton was the site of one of the country's first low-income public housing estates and our dilemma must have been reasonably impressive. Though a bespectacled housing authority officer told us our chances for placement were "very small indeed" since not-yet-completed Roxborough Park had a long waiting list, in the spring of 1957 we were allocated a three-bedroom semi-detached home.

"Tobacco Road," grumbled my mother. This was a good sign. Literary allusions meant that her spirits were picking up. We were doing the weekend walk along the couple of miles between Tragina Avenue and our new house. My stepfather was carrying suitcases, and my sister and I were pulling a wagon borrowed from a neighbour's son loaded with household possessions. "Going up to the estate" was our equivalent of a picnic. There were no sidewalks or roads built in Roxborough Park yet, and the melting spring snow had left thick mud to be ploughed through, but this gave each journey the flavour of a traditional British hike. In our Wellington boots we placed two-by-four planks across the ditches dug in front of our house and wheeled the wagon across the ooze. Inside we'd sit on the newly varnished floors of the house marvelling at the clean North American brightness of it all. No musty pantries, cupboards under the stairs, or menacing lofts. Neat, predictable angles with washable painted walls and gleaming white refrigerators and stoves to match.

My parents would live on the Roxborough housing estate for just over two years. By the time they left they were almost Canadians, familiar with this raw-boned country that was so informal, yet so reserved about subjects that were the matter of greatest informality in England – like sex, scandal, and general smut. My parents were even beginning to see some reality in their dreams of a society based on merit rather than class.

Most of the inhabitants of the Roxborough housing estate worked at the Steel Company of Canada. In the winter mornings you'd see them, small, drab figures hunched around the one old car on the block that was hooked up to an outside heater, trying to get the damn thing started to make the trip down to the lakeshore plant. My stepfather worked first as a labourer in the open-hearth furnaces of Stelco. He'd set off in the morning, metal lunch-pail with sandwiches and safety glasses inside, and come home in the evenings coated with grime like a miner. In the summer he'd take salt tablets and only work alternate half-hours. The temperature, it was said, in his work area was about 130 degrees Fahrenheit.

Soon we learned a new word: layoff. Nineteen fifty-three was not the best of times for Stelco. The men and women would sit on the front steps of the Roxborough houses or on the back porches overlooking the communal lawn and talk about the possibility of more layoffs or even a strike. They all seemed deadly afraid of the union calling for a strike vote, though. They were poor, and a little money seemed to them better than none. The men talked about meeting payments and the women figured how to meet them on strike pay. I remembered, vaguely, the words of "Joe Hill" echoing in the spacious bay windows of the Sedleys' drawing-room.

> The copper bosses killed you, Joe,
> They shot you with a gun.
> Says Joe, "What they can never kill
> Went on to organize."
> From San Diego up to Maine
> In every mine and mill,
> Where workers strike and organize,
> It's there you'll find Joe Hill.
> I dreamed I saw Joe Hill last night,
> Alive as you and me.
> Says I, "But Joe, you're ten years dead."
> "I never died," says he.

Most of the time I was under the back porches listening to the talk, and waiting for the sun to go down and the street lights to come on. Then we'd all meet, panting, inquisitive thirteen- and fourteen-year-olds playing timid games in the dusk, leaning against lampposts and letting the older boys brush against the front of our blouses as if by accident, at which the chill of night would melt in a rush of inexplicable warmth. Back at home the talk was sombre and the fridge was almost empty. But who cared when there were boys to give one such sudden tastes of delight? I did not know exactly what sex was, but if this was any sample I was sure that it would be very nice and that, next to piano concertos and opera, boys were the most wonderful thing that had been put on this earth for the amusement and entertainment of girls.

In fact, Canada, I discovered, was a quite extraordinary country on a number of levels. I have no illusions about the roughness of the mid-fifties for families like ours without medical insurance, without savings, and so on. But those who today depict the Canada of those days – before universal health care, extended unemployment benefits, and improved Child Welfare Acts, just to mention a few of the more recently "improved" pieces of legislation – as a totally unpleasant or thankless place when compared with today's benefit-blessed society either had no direct experience of working-class life or simply refuse to view the facts through anything but an ideological prism.

For example: What was so extraordinary to us, straight from the tender mercies of the British National Health Service, was the attitude of Canadian doctors, nurses, and hospital administrators towards their patients, even their indigent patients. In Hendon we loathed our local doctor, but the National Health Service did not permit us to venture out of his office into the waiting-room of some more friendly practitioner of the healing arts. A common complaint about doctors in England was their apparent reluctance to see patients or have much to do with the sick and diseased, but this was always dealt with by supporters of the National Health Service (our family, of course, firmly in their ranks) as a specific and very minor flaw in a laudably conceived approach to the problem of health care. Our doctor, whose nose was always running and whose complexion suggested the underbelly of a particularly pale fish, looked with total contempt on the patients lined up on the benches of his narrow waiting-room. Though the example of my own uncle convinced me that there must be a number of doctors who genuinely cared about their patients, nevertheless it was axiomatic that going to a doctor in England was regarded by most people with the same degree of enthusiasm as a Canadian exhibits in setting off to see the income tax auditor. Patients were hostages to the system. Doctors were bound by it.

The connection between the "minor flaw" of the doctors' disagreeable attitude to working long hours for fixed salaries and the major theoretical flaw of any state-run salaried health-care system was not made at that time even by the very people who complained quite openly and bitterly about the attitude of individual physicians. English hospitals were a perfect nightmare of regulations and indifference. Patients were regarded with extraordinary contempt by many of the civil servants who operated them. (My mother, who had recovered from tuberculosis, took me with her for her medical check-up and X-rays to accompany our immigration applications. I remember with painful humiliation that, after she had stripped to the waist, she was asked to walk through two rooms full of people without even a robe to cover herself. I walked behind her as she held herself very straight, while interns and male doctors turned around to stare at her. She was very beautiful.) We came to Canada carrying with us this ambivalent attitude to health schemes. We expected to be treated like horrid little pests by doctors and hospitals.

At the same time we also expected that in Canada, should any one of us fall sick, we would literally be left to die in the hospital parking-lot next to the Cadillacs of the doctors. Doctors, we supposed, when confronted with a haemorrhaging patient without funds, would simply make sure they hae-morrhaged in the hall rather than on the carpet.

In fact, our first serious encounter with the Canadian medical profession came in 1953. It was late in the evening when they took my mother out to the ambulance. She had fallen down the stairs in her seventh month of pregnancy. I sat in my bedroom, my sister next to me, looking out of the window at my mother being eased into the ambulance. Her arm fell over the side of the stretcher as they lifted her in, and I could see the thin, white wrist in the light of the kitchen window. I remembered that my stepfather had given her a gold watch for that wrist as a wedding present and she had lost it on the tube train almost immediately. She had cried for a long time because the watch was not yet insured and it was more expensive than he could really manage.

Given our preconceptions about free-enterprise medicine, it is no wonder that the treatment of my mother astonished us. She was critically ill and in hospital in Hamilton for a considerable length of time. Her baby survived, but only be-cause of the sophisticated and constant medical attention – and nearly two months in an incubator. There were innu-merable blood transfusions and when my mother finally came home there were months of medication.

My stepfather, worried sleepless about the expense, mar-velled at the courtesy of the staff. We were offered welfare assistance with the hospital bills but my stepfather was not made for "charity", though clearly much of the real cost was absorbed indirectly by public funds. Still, he budgeted an amount each month out of his salary and paid off all bills re-ceived with great thoroughness. I'll digress for a moment be-cause the health-care issue is so important. These days, when I have to go to a hospital, I am reminded more and more of the wretched English attitudes – so different from my Cana-dian memories of more agreeable approaches.

In 1961, when I was living in residence at the University of Toronto, I was taken ill one night. The private insurance I had tried to keep up had lapsed. Next morning after treat-ment I was visited in my room at the Toronto General Hospital by a social worker, very sprightly and smiling, inquiring about my ability to pay. "Nil," I explained. "Well," she countered, clipboard in hand, filling out the half-dozen questions with quite unsatisfactory answers, "you are in a public ward now and I'm sure you won't mind if the doctor brings in some students to see you?"

I looked around me. The public wards I had seen in England had row upon row of beds. This "ward" had six beds in it, three on each side of a large windowed room. My doctor turned out to be the Head of Internal Medicine at the hospital and a leading surgeon. His students were three interns who were so scared of him that they barely managed to cope with or even recognize the fact that I was female – even though the area they had to penetrate in order to examine my insides ought to have made that crystal clear to them. No, I thought the next day, I didn't mind being in a public ward or having students examine me. What still astonished me was the general attitude to patients that was prevalent in Canadian hospitals in those days. Patients were treated like clients rather than liabilities. I was sure that somewhere down the hall some hideous female with a starched uniform and manner to match was berating a helpless and paralysed grandmother, or a doctor was "unavailable" while his patient paid unstintingly for his services. Still, one had the distinct feeling that such occurrences were most likely to be the exception rather than the rule as they seemed to be in England. In fact, by the time we left England in 1952, long before today's breakdown of the British health system (manifest in its three-year waiting-list for such elective surgery as hernias and the mindless egalitarianism that has abolished paying hospital beds that helped subsidize expensive facilities for the indigent), an informal system of "gifts" as well as the annual doctor's Christmas Box for "special services" was already operative. When I say "mindless egalitarianism" I'm not talking, of course, about a health-care system in which incomes are doubled-taxed in that the better-off are obliged to pay for the same services other taxpayers get free. (The truly indigent, by definition, get it free anyway.) I am referring to the tendency to abolish better services that people can elect to buy, whether private hospital rooms or first-class airplane seats, because the mere existence of such facilities is thought to be somehow offensive to the poor – or the parsimonious.

At the time, caught in the dilemma of state medicine or no-medicine-at-all, it did not occur to me that private insurance schemes could deliver, and *have* delivered, virtually all the services of socialized medicine, at rates not much greater than those of government insurance, *and* at a profit to the entrepreneurs (and therefore to society) instead of a loss to the taxpayers. It is not lack of social conscience, but the exact opposite, for me to ask today: why should the taxpayers give me free health care when I, like most working people in this country, can afford to pay for anything short of catastrophic illness – and can afford to buy insurance against that? Of course, paying is a hardship – it always is – but it is incredibly foolish to believe that we do not pay for what is "free". We pay in taxes. We pay in inflation. (Without Medicare today's 30¢ dollar – who knows? – may still be worth 40¢.) Most importantly, we pay in a loss of liberty.

It never occurred to me then that the process is simple and predictable. When health care becomes a free commodity like air and water it is treated less seriously by people. It is abused in major or minor ways. People go to doctors for colds. My middle-class girlfriends go to see psychiatrists at public expense to cope with the problems of their love-lives. Administrative costs soar, as they do in any State enterprise. The net result is, sooner or later, that medical insurance, which private companies could operate at a profit (and with no compromises in quality of care), becomes an insupportable burden for the community.

When that happens – and it is already happening in Canada today – society responds in the only way it can. Since the attitude of responsibility has been undermined, it is no longer possible to ask individuals to plan and provide for their own future. Reducing administrative costs is hopeless. It is politically difficult – and goes against the grain of the nanny State in any case – to limit the number and kind of complaints for which medical assistance may be sought.

However, coercion not only is possible, but becomes natural and the only way out of the government's dilemma. First, the free-and-easy features with which liberal democracies try to combine social planning are reduced. Gradually, the freedom of doctors to opt in or out of the health-care scheme is replaced by a coercive condition of some kind (which is already being threatened in Ontario by the Minister of Health). Then the patients' freedom to select their own doctors is limited by requirements of residence or work-place. The citizen's liberty to engage in certain practices is curtailed on the basis that it is a health hazard and therefore a legitimate subject for regulation by the community. It is, after all, the community that has to bear the cost of the health care. This argument has already been employed when some provinces in Canada introduced mandatory seat-belt laws. Some advocates have used it in the campaign, as yet embryonic, to outlaw cigarette-smoking. It may yet be invoked to restrict the consumption of fatty foods or to introduce compulsory jogging. *Categories of treatment may be classified to tailor the expense to the citizen's usefulness to the community or the government.* Hospital beds or rare medicines may be allocated on this basis, as in the Soviet Union.

This is why the experience of totalitarian countries is not remote or immaterial when considering the problems of socialized medicine, or other far-reaching social plans. It is a favourite pretence – and perhaps a genuine hope – of left-liberalism that the experience of totalitarian countries somehow "doesn't count". They are far away. They have no liberal-democratic traditions. Studying their systems can teach us nothing about the problems we may encounter when implementing the very ideas on which their systems are based. Often, in fact, a curious note of racial or at least ethnic supremacy creeps into the tone of home-grown social democrats: you can't extrapolate, they seem to say, from the doings of lesser folk like the Germans, the Hungarians, the Chinese, the Russians.

Nonsense, of course, though at the time I didn't see it. But, if you buy it, you don't have to go as far as Moscow for your examples. It was social-democratic England where health-care bureaucrats decided that lab technicians should be paid more than consultant surgeons, while maintenance electricians – and, in some cases reported by Auberon Waugh in *The Spectator*, hospital porters – are paid more than operating-room nurses of twelve years' seniority. It was England from whose socialized health scheme doctors emigrated in droves to Saskatchewan. And it is Ontario from whose government insurance doctors are now fleeing to Arizona.

All the same, my early Canadian experiences scarcely made a dent in my fundamental left-wing views on such matters. True, my mother had not died in the parking-lot with her wedding ring wrenched from her finger. But universal health care was a universal necessity as far as I was concerned. And a universal good. Nor did I question my belief that most people were oppressed by capitalism. All the talk now at home was about how to make ends meet and how to move up in life, which seemed proof to me of the unfair "rat race" aspect of the system. There were bills to be paid off and false shibboleths to worship: the television set, the battered first car, a second-hand washing-machine. Then, in 1955 my stepfather and mother moved with my sister and half-brothers to St. Catharines, Ontario, where a better job and a better neighbourhood waited.

I did not go with them. The inevitable tensions that difficult times bring had built up in our home and I had no choice but to try living on my own – after all, I was already a grown woman of fourteen. This time I moved into a rented room in a house on the Roxborough estate occupied by a garage mechanic and his family. My stepfather did his best during my Grade Ten school year to help pay the $40 a month room and board that this arrangement cost, but it was difficult enough for him to support one household. I began to take jobs after school. And anyway, I reasoned, in Canada with the long summer holidays I could make enough money to support myself during the school year. All I had to do was to avoid coming to the attention of some thoughtful organization like the Children's Aid. If I could stay out of the clutches of a foster home and keep working I was sure that everything would be just fine. The curious thing was that, for once, I was right.

CHAPTER FIVE

Fast-Food Times

EVEN THOUGH ENGLAND was to move further and further to the left in the postwar years and allow power to be shared by trade-union leaders with non-U accents, it was still a country firmly in the strait-jacket of class hierarchy. I didn't know that, compared to most of Western Europe, English society was a model of egalitarianism. At home I had heard only one recurring admonition, to "be more English than the English". And so my ear, eye, and palate were attuned to the nuances of accent, the crustless condition of watercress sandwiches, lupin-bordered gardens, and tweed everything.

For an English girl, Canada, even in the fifties, appeared to be a truly classless society. Alas, that also meant that it had no class. In Grade Eight my Hamilton public school teacher, an admirable woman named Miss Addleton, with steely grey hair and a manner that brooked no interruption as she listed every last lake, stream, and puddle in Canadian geography, would make me the constant object of a humiliating cross-examination each Monday morning at the W. H. Ballard Public School I attended. "Stand up all those who did not attend church yesterday," the devout Anglican teacher would command. Dutifully, I would stand up, the only non-believer in the class, it seemed. "And why not?" she would ask fixing me with the eyes of a thousand martyred Christians. It did not occur to me to mention that I was a Jew. Since no one else in the class was, it seemed pointless to draw attention to this further difference, since I was already the tallest, skinniest, most foreign-accented, and possibly most sallow pupil in her home room. Finally I decided that I would give in.

My conversion to Anglicanism was a most interesting procedure, if somewhat short-lived. Miss Addleton was in a state of apotheosis when I was actually confirmed and came to my ceremony to present me with a beautiful white leatherbound prayer book. Unfortunately, the day that school ended and I was no longer to be subjected to the Monday morning interrogation I went to the minister at St. Mary's and asked him how I could go back to being a Jew. Disappointment clouded his plump face. I had been a real convert brought in from the nomadic plains of idolatry and heathenism. "Why, my child?" he asked plaintively.

"Because," I replied with some honesty, "I'm going to high school next year and Miss Addleton won't be asking me about church any more. And I'm terribly sorry, but I'm afraid I don't really believe in Christianity." This solved the problem for the good father. "When you stop believing, my child," he replied firmly, "you're already a Jew again."

This early example of pragmatism – mine and the Church's – which was to take a far more malevolent turn in the Church proper during the late nineteen-sixties as it embraced the gospel of social justice in order to ensure its piece of real estate in the Marxist-Kingdom-to-Come, was a great object lesson to me. Unlike England, where the best mimicry could take one far, but only so far, in Canada all one had to do to assimilate was to study and adopt the customs of one's new society. Who one's parents were or where one was born didn't seem a barrier to getting into university, acquiring any position, or joining most clubs. One simply had to decide what one was after and go out and get it. The curious thing was that as a left-winger I would have denied this intellectually, but since in my guts I felt it was true, I acted on it. I decided on a university education, to be followed by a career as a writer. Not just any sort of writer: I wanted to be an editorial writer and explain to people the principles of decent left-wing thought. My immediate problem was to finance myself through high school.

By Grade Ten, with my family now moved out of town and money rather short, I had taken a job after school at a drugstore in Hamilton called Joe's, where I ran the snackbar. My working day was from about 4:30 till midnight or so and the pay was $25 a week. I had never cooked anything in my life, so I found the job most instructive. (To begin with, except in BBC Children's Hour skits on Americana I had never heard of such culinary delights as banana splits and cheeseburgers, so having to make dozens of them on my first day on the job with no guidance but Joe's screams from the cash register across the store was a quick education. Soon I was a soda- and milkshake-jerk par excellence, and a not indifferent hamburger lady.)

The drugstore was a popular hangout for the older kids from Delta Secondary School where I was a student, and this enabled me to study North American dating mores. I quickly learned all about flirting, sharing sodas, and other variations on the drugstore gambit. My earlier jobs at the Metropolitan Store and various dress shops in Hamilton (where I was reasonably successful till my age was discovered) had taught me something about current clothing fads and I could pick out a Lansea sweater or a Nat Gordon skirt at about thirty yards on a foggy day. True, the long working-day gave me some trouble with homework and some small problem with fatigue, but I had enough money to pay my rent and even to buy the occasional crinoline.

In the summer holidays I graduated to working in a more expensive kind of ladies' store in downtown Hamilton. I had moved, as well, out of the turmoil of the garage mechanic's home into the basement of a Polish family's house in Stoney Creek, Ontario. And my whole social life had changed. Now I ran with a new crowd. On weekends I enjoyed the vigorous social life of a Polish-Catholic family who invited me to their church picnics where tall young blond men in navy-blue school blazers danced endless polkas in the summer sun. On week nights I was part of a group informally known as the Parkdale gang, consisting of a handful of ex-reform-school youths and native Indian girls. They were friendly and undemanding and adopted me as a sort of mascot. I clearly knew virtually nothing about sex and used long words, while they knew everything about sex and were illiterate. We got along very well. After hanging out at the bowling alley on Parkdale Avenue in the east end of Hamilton we would pile into an old car and drive out to the roadhouses, where the Indian girls would move from booth to booth sitting with various men, drinking and getting lifts "home" with them. I tried it out. On my third attempt a group of men offered to "take me for a ride". I agreed. Then, just as we were leaving, one of them asked how old I was. "Fifteen," I replied. They looked at one another and laughed. "Jail-bait," they said. Rose, the prettiest Indian girl in our group, told me to stop trying to get lifts home and she would see that I was taken back safely each time with the gang. "Then, no trouble," she said. I did not understand.

What I did understand were the couplings among gang members I watched in the back seats of the cars when we finally drove back to Stoney Creek together. It looked clumsy and awkward to me, but obviously everyone was enjoying it. Reality began to sink in when one of the girls disappeared and I was told she had been taken back to the "Centre" because of "bad associations".

I began to understand even more clearly what real problems some people close to my age faced when I saw the home one of the Indian boys had left in order to live in a gutted car near Van Wagner's Beach. His own house was a shack, barely standing, on the main road up to the Roxborough estate. The corrugated-iron roof was tipsy on the walls and the windows were broken. The door didn't lock. Inside I glimpsed his parents, alcoholics given to slugging anything that moved with a bottle, broken or otherwise. The boy had bottle scars on the side of his face. In spite of this I could not quite understand why he had to live in a gutted car. He was two years older than me and there was a job going at the bowling alley which he could have had for the asking. "That's for suckers," he kept telling me, and he would turn up occasionally flashing twenty-dollar bills from some mysterious source when he was not dead broke. I was not anxious to attract the attention of the authorities and find myself in whatever the "Centre" was, and I could see that my evenings with the Jardine boys and Lou and Rose were coming to an end. I was grateful for their company. They asked no questions and never asked for gasoline money.

My limited funds and my home situation made the more routine forms of social activity difficult – except for one brief fling when I spotted a contest in the local newspaper, the Hamilton *Spectator*. The contest was to be "Theatre Manager for a Day" and the rules required an essay to be written explaining why one would like to be a theatre manager. That particular subject didn't interest me at all. What was intriguing was the prize: a year's free movie passes. With those, I thought, I could become the most popular girl in Delta Secondary School. I entered the contest and won first prize. I wish that I could state that my essay was a searing and witty critique of cultural policies of the time, but I can't remember anything about it. My picture duly appeared in the *Spectator* of February 12, 1955; it showed me sitting grinning maniacally in the theatre manager's office. When I was presented with the movie passes I discovered, much to my horror, that they were exclusively for use at the Junior Press Club showings on Saturday mornings. After some negotiations with the Century Theatre I made a deal: two kiddies' tickets for one real movie. That gave me twenty-six free passes to grown-up shows and for a while I *was* in some demand.

In the middle of the summer, Northway's, the store where I worked, laid off a chunk of its temporary help. That presented a problem, since I was part of the chunk. I quickly got a job at the E. D. Smith fruit-canning factory miles away in Winona, Ontario. Since my day began at around 5:00 a.m. in order to meet the factory pick-up trucks, my social life was curtailed. At night I would fall into the camp bed set up for me in the basement under the furnace pipes. Next to the bed I had a portable record-player borrowed from the landlady's daughter and one record I had purchased. It was a 78 rpm recording of Jose Iturbi playing Chopin's Military Polonaise. On those nights when the landlady refused to let her huge red-faced husband sleep upstairs because he was too drunk, the stumbling man would career down the basement stairs and fall into the camp bed next to mine. Sometimes, blind with liquor, he would fall against the blanket strung up on a clothesline across the basement to separate our two beds. He must have weighed close to two hundred pounds, and the blanket did not impede his fall in my direction. There was never any sordid intention in his behaviour, of course. Even if he had been the sort, I think he was too dead drunk to form intent or capacity, but I was revolted by the stink of alcohol and his dead weight on my bed, and I shuddered at the thick, rumbling snores that would follow his collapse. Reaching down to the record-player, I would put on the thunderous sounds of Iturbi. The chords of Chopin would flood the basement; I could see again the hands of my father on the piano, and remember concerts I had been taken to at Festival Hall in London, overlooking the Thames, while the sound of Grieg and the playing of Dame Myra Hess poured over me. The record would come to an end and I would simply start it again. The music shut out all fear, except perhaps the fear of never being able myself to express the power and beauty of the human spirit.

Not that there was no evidence of the human spirit in the Pole's basement; it just spoke a different language. I soon learned that many of the best qualities in people, those very qualities which go into the making of the human spirit, were as often as not to be found co-existing with the stumbling language of a semi-literate Pole or the gewgaw-stuffed apartment of a garage mechanic and his wife. Loyalty came with the mug of coffee brought down the basement stairs for the hung-over husband; love came with the anguished family sessions over how to spend the overtime pay; decency flourished among the most extraordinarily impoverished circumstances – as did moments of imagination and vision. This is all so obvious now, but it surprised me then. I had grown up to believe in some never-quite-articulated way that the human spirit could only be liberated by the force-feeding of a classical education to the poorer-off and the assumption by everyone of the mores and manners of Hampstead.

My independence came to an end suddenly when the cuts and scrapes any newcomer on a peach-pitting assembly line takes in the first few weeks of work became infected. My hands and arms swelled up to an enormous size. I was temporarily but completely disabled. The landlady obtained my mother's phone number in St. Catharines and my stepfather came to take me home. This was the beginning of a brief period of reconciliation which ended abruptly when my clothes were packed into a carton and I found myself living in a house in Grantham, Ontario, with a woman, her daughter, and a female boarder. The three of them all worked at a bar in the evenings, and at night they brought home gentlemen to be "entertained". In retrospect I suppose they were part-time hookers, but then all I was trying to do was write my senior high school exams at St. Catharines Collegiate, and I was too busy to pay attention to the noises around me. I experimented with virtually everything to soundproof my bedroom. Finally I bought earplugs made out of wax which I would knead in my hand to soften and push into my ears to harden.

On my walls I had Scotch-taped the announcements of the newly created Ontario scholarships available to all students obtaining eighty per cent in their examinations. I didn't think I had a chance in Hades of making that score (I didn't), but on those occasions when my mother would phone to suggest that I become an airline stewardess or a secretary or a public school teacher so I wouldn't have to stay at school, the existence of the scholarships gave me some encouragement. Hookers aside, those high school years in St. Catharines were an enormously happy time. By now I was thoroughly Canadianized. My home background was not particularly stable, and certainly in the proper small-town atmosphere of St. Catharines it was difficult to conceal, but I soon discovered that there were ways to get around that. I could construct fairly decent sentences and so between after-school jobs I became the *St. Catharines Standard* high school correspondent with my own newspaper column. As editor of the school yearbook I managed to elicit a certain amount of forelock-tugging – which unlike prettier or wealthier girls I'd never experienced before. Soon I was pledged to the best sorority in St. Catharines where I could write up the minutes and activities of the local chapter in a way calculated to impress national headquarters with our zeal and sense of community service. I made friendships in high school that have lasted into my professional life. In the bourgeois establishment that was the backbone of St. Catharines I discovered a basic decency in people that more than compensated for the odd incident of name-calling or the occasional parent who refused to let her children associate with "someone of her background". When finally I managed to scrape together enough grades to qualify for a bursary to the University of Toronto it was the local IODE ladies who came up with the additional money that actually made it possible for me to pack my bag and get on the train for Toronto.

Trading on a minor knack for writing sentences to get by in life doesn't reveal an especially admirable character. But most societies use barter in one form or another. If I had been blessed with an ability to fish or hunt exceptionally well, or with a face that met the aesthetic criteria of the 1950s, or a skill for sewing, or even some manual dexterity with a cheerleader's baton, I would have bartered that for acceptance. What I could clearly see already was that admittance to what constituted Canadian society was not exclusively based on class or money, that even at school with all its nineteen-fifties saddle-shoe-and-cashmere-sweaters culture the most popular students were not the prettiest or the best-dressed, that in some curious way, even in the self-conscious social structure of small-town Canada, a reasonably agreeable place could be found for almost everyone who wanted one. I also observed, though this came later, that being young meant one could adapt fairly well to virtually any set of circumstances. The only danger to one's equilibrium arose when an adult (or society) began drawing attention to the "difficulties" of one's position. The first time I actually felt sorry for myself was when a well-meaning social worker began quizzing me about my family life and telling me that I was entitled to a secure home. She may have been right, but frankly, as a kid I had never thought about what I was "entitled" to. Things were simply taken as they came.

In fact, since Canada was basically a humane rather than a callous society, all sorts of people were helping me, either indirectly or simply by leaving me alone. The teachers at my high school made sure that I got some student assistance to go to university. My home-room teacher at St. Catharines Collegiate managed to refrain from questioning me when he noticed that my notes excusing an absence on account of sickness were signed by me rather than a parent. Later on, when researching a case at an American university, I would see the havoc that could be caused among reasonable, normal students when a female don, much taken with the then precocious idea of "rap" sessions, would call in students to her room for long discussions about student alienation, the stress of university life, and any special difficulties her girls might be facing – or might not have thought of. Following these therapeutic talks there was a spate of attempted suicides. The don's concern might have been genuine, but as a matter of fact she was a lesbian and managed to impart her own confusion over sexual identity to several of the other girls, some of whom were not quite sure of their own. She also managed to equate confusion with "sensitivity" and to hit on J.V., possibly the one genuinely disturbed girl in the group, who soon took an overdose of sleeping-pills. There was no way of knowing, of course, if she might not later have done this without the don's influence.

There is, no doubt, a Pandora's box inside all of us. But the society that waits for the individual to call out for help when the lid can no longer be kept shut may be doing a greater service than one which insists on prying it open, uninvited. Which is not to say that we shouldn't care: only that caring may mean leaving alone.

The current celebration of young people's problems in endless audio-visual presentations on "young people's suicide", "young people's alcoholism", and the like, seems to have something of a self-fulfilling prophecy about it. It is as if society is insisting that to be authentically young one *ought* to have these problems. I can't help thinking of the Swedish statistics, where, after lavish programs of school sex education with films, demonstration, and much frank discussion to prevent the problems of pregnancy, the illegitimacy rate (which had been declining before the 1956 compulsory programs began) has risen steadily for every group except those too old to have received the special sex education. Illegitimacy may be just fine, of course, but the ostensible reason for the program was to curtail it. Sweeping things under the carpet may not be the best, but at least it's one way of getting rid of things. Bringing them out into the open, contrary to popular thinking, may simply mean that they will seem all right. Sweden now boasts the highest proportion of illegitimate births in Europe (33 per cent of all births) and has a rate of two and a half times higher than that of the United States. A few years down the road, I too would find out just how open to suggestion I was, and it would take me several years to pull myself out of the self-indulgence that followed – though in my case this had nothing to do with illegitimate children.

But at the time I left high school for the University of Toronto I was still full of confidence and my political views were steadily hardening. In our final year of high school, a close friend, Louise Lore (today a senior producer at the Canadian Broadcasting Corporation), had volunteered her house as a meeting-place for David Lewis, then leader of the CCF, to come and speak to us. It must have been pure dedication that compelled Lewis to make the trip to St. Catharines to meet the half-dozen students we managed to turn out. (I think the only reason anyone came at all, besides Louise and myself, was that Louise's father was Chinese and a first-rate cook. His food was legendary in St. Catharines, and while David Lewis spoke to us in the tiny, cramped living-room about the inequities of capitalism, through the paper-thin walls we could smell the tantalizing aroma of Chinese cooking simmering in the great black iron pots.) I admired the warmth and conviction of Lewis, but ironically at the time he seemed to me too soft in his democratic socialism. In spite of my personal delight in the free-enterprise system which had given me the keen pleasure of earning my own way as well as a genuine sense of achievement in so doing, I couldn't shake the almost visceral hold certain phrases and tenets of faith had on me. The basic ideas of socialism seemed irresistible and I was impatient with Lewis's orderly implementation of reforms. Democracy seemed so inefficient. A *people's* democracy was needed to look after the people.

My life was working out, but I simply could not expect that others might also be able to handle their own lives quite adequately. Just because I enjoyed making my own decisions was no basis to give others the opportunity to do so. And so on. I may not have articulated this precisely – it came out and sounded much better in strings of phrases about the social responsibility of looking after the less fortunate – but this was the thrust of my feelings.

At university I quickly discovered that the people I liked and who liked the things I liked – books, music, and philosophy – all held left-wing views as well. This seemed one more proof that left-wing ideas were correct and that socialism could be equated with enlightenment. We may have had prairie populist John Diefenbaker at Canada's helm, but on campus my friends were writing about the need for a planned economy with universal pension plans, universal free medical care, free post-secondary education, and income redistribution. It was all blowing in the wind and I was puffing along with them. Given these views, it was not surprising that my political sympathies would lead in an unwavering line to my becoming a member of the British delegation to the Communist World Youth Festival in Helsinki in 1962.

CHAPTER SIX

Shocking Pink

IN MY THIRD YEAR of university my grandfather died. He left me four hundred pounds sterling with the stipulation that I claim it in England. The University agreed, though not easily, to continue its financial aid for 1962 in spite of my taking time off work that summer in order to collect an inheritance.

I arrived at Heathrow Airport in London and was picked up by my Maoist uncle's chauffeur. The car took me to their Hampstead home, an exquisitely furnished house full of Chinese antiques and lush Chinese rugs specially woven to their design. Only the household help was home. I wandered through the rooms looking at familiar photographs and the occasional memento associated with my childhood. On the grand piano several dozen long red roses were carefully arranged in a cut-crystal vase that threw splinters of violet-tinged colours on the Wedgewood blue walls. The furniture was plump and inviting. The neo-Georgian bookcases reached up to the ceiling, and as I sat looking out over the terraced garden the maid appeared with tea. (Years later the American journalist Tom Wolfe, who was an acquaintance of the family and had spent some time in this house, would describe to a friend my "fantastically English background". On being told that it was barely one generation removed from East Europe and currently financed by Mainland China, Wolfe lapsed into a stunned silence. Which, I suppose, goes to show that an American can see through Park Avenue pretensions more easily than Hampstead ones.)

My correspondence with my relatives in England had been rather sporadic and they had no knowledge of my personal or financial circumstances. Only my late grandfather had known, and for a few months during my high school years I had gone to live with him in England. But a spirited sixteen-year-old girl and a seventy-six-year-old widower present a conflict of socio-cultural values that is difficult to reconcile.

Now I had arrived back in England at an appropriate time. My cousin was coming down from Balliol College, Oxford, and had arranged a suitable date for me so I could witness his graduation rites. My date was called Tommy Platts-Mills, son of John (Faithful Fortescue) Platts-Mills, a well-known Communist sympathizer who had been expelled from the Labour party. "Lend me a Kirby grip, could you please?" asked Platts-Mills on picking me up for the Balliol dance all decked out in his pink Leander blazer. (Tommy rowed for Oxford.) He took the bobby-pin and pulled back his chin-length forelock and secured it behind his ear, and then the 6'4" shocking-pink apparition led me off to my cousin's rooms in Balliol College for an evening during which I discovered that absolutely any statement could be satisfactorily answered with "quite" or "gosh". By now I was beginning to develop a serious interest in the Communist party and I found Balliol positively stuffed with grads all exhibiting a similar interest. "Gosh," I thought.

My one problem was reconciling the redistribution of wealth and ownership of the means of production and so on with the extraordinary amount of money that was obviously present. Later on, back in Hampstead, my uncle helped me out with one of the golden nuggets of free-enterprise Communists. "What we want to do," he explained as we fished about in the wine cellar for something he was sure I would like, "is to bring *everyone* up to our standard of living."

"Quite," I thought.

The following week I went to stay at the Sedleys'. The Paul Robeson records were still there but the children were not. Their son was in Moscow getting ready to leave for Helsinki, where he would be doing simultaneous translation from English to Russian at the upcoming World Youth Festival.

The World Youth Festival is the Soviet-sponsored bash held every four years for "young people" from around the world. In effect, it is the communist version of an international Scout jamboree and in 1962 it was the turn of the reluctant Finns to host the red-flag delegates. The Sedleys helped me get onto the British delegation to the festival about three days before it was to leave. I was very keen to go. The cost was forty-two pounds and that included fare and board for almost three weeks of travel through East Germany, Poland, and the USSR, and over to Helsinki. At Victoria Station I waited for the boat-train on a platform loaded down with back-packed young communists and whispers that "one of the Redgraves is here." (One was, but I don't think it was Vanessa. This one was too chubby and too nice.) My Canadian passport was viewed with much suspicion by the committed, but as we stood eying each other at a distance of about six inches I tried to look proletarian and did my bit by whistling "Joe Hill".

I have no excuses but I have some shame. This was the summer of 1962, only six years after the Hungarian Revolution, only six years after the revelations of Nikita Khrushchev at the Twentieth Party Congress, twenty years after the show trials and the purges, thirty years after Western fellow-travellers first tried to suppress the truth about the millions starved to death in the famines of the Ukraine. There was no need for the journey I was about to make – which in the end would take another ten years to complete intellectually. Other travellers had charted the terrain with devastating accuracy – Orwell, Muggeridge, Koestler, Camus. But there I stood on the platform, ready and anxious to learn from the People's Paradise.

The forty-two pounds sterling I paid for this privilege would not give any monetary boost to the regimes I was about to visit. But my presence, along with that of the thousands of others who regularly tour the totalitarian states, snapping pictures of Great Walls and statues and carefully moving to avoid blurring their Instamatics with the shadows of such stone walls as Leningrad's Peter and Paul Fortress where Solzhenitsyn was imprisoned once, this presence would help give these dreadful and murderous regimes the appearance of approval and respectability.

West Berlin. "What's that?" I asked the blonde bus guide as we came to a dead halt. It was the Berlin Wall. Less than a year old, the bricks were still bright red. It stood there firmly planted at the end of the street, cutting through houses, topped by barbed wire. As we got out of the bus to take snaps of it, I thought, my god, we can walk up and touch it. It was like going on a tour of a prison and coming to the gas chamber. Look, see the leather straps on the chair.

Next day, in East Germany, there were hot potatoes at every meal for the festival entourage, but when I went on a (prohibited) prowl by myself the shops had none and the housewives were lined up with the omnipresent string bag to get their ration of three a week. "Shortage," said a surly man to me. "Razor blades, too." At first I was amused. "A provocateur," I thought. Then I discovered that my legs needed shaving and the man seemed to have been right as far as razor blades went. Now I became righteous. "Capitalism saved by Toronto girl's unshaved legs". Tomorrow, I decided, I will go on the scheduled tour of the communal factory.

On the platform of the East Berlin train station we said goodbye to the girl in her early twenties who had been our translator. I had required her less than most, since, happily, my high school German had quickly returned. She was a pleasant girl, restrained, but with an intelligent face and what appeared to be genuine competence in sorting out the inevitable bureaucratic confusion that accompanied plans to take us by bus to this Second World War memorial or that example of communal enterprise. We had all grown to appreciate her ingenuity in unearthing out-of-stock items such as safety-pins in moments of considerable need. When others became frantic after apparently losing passports or getting locked out of the hideous Railroad Transport Workers' Hall at which we were staying – and into which martial music and jolly announcements were piped at 6:30 a.m. until I disconnected the loudspeaker in our room – Gertie, our translator, was always a model of calm assurance. Which, of course, made her behaviour at the train station all the more disconcerting.

Tears fogged her glasses and trickled down her face. She was crying helplessly and hysterically with all reserve gone. "Take me with you," she cried, "please. My sister, my brother are there. Take me too." I was astonished. In my shoulder tote-bag was a Canadian passport. I had been born in England, a subject of Her Majesty Queen Elizabeth II. Borders were there to be crossed and ticked off in one's mental landscape as another country visited. Some countries might not let you in, but that was their problem. I had never actually considered what it might be like not to be able to leave one. Gertie was draped over my shoulder, I stood her up and held her very tight and she pulled her navy-blue suit jacket straight.

"We're not going back," I said stupidly, "we're going on to Leningrad." She looked at me and smiled, the tears still coming evenly down her face.

"Over there," she pointed to another platform. "That train goes to the West." She caught my puzzlement. "You could go on it any time you want." I was naive but I was not stupid. I had not expected to see such numbing greyness in the streets and faces of East Germany, or such sullen rudeness of one citizen to another, or such terrible shortages of basic household needs fifty-five years after the revolution and seventeen years after the war. But, unlike stupidity or malice, naivety is a treatable condition and it does not affect one's eyesight. Here in front of me stood a girl, only a little older than myself, weeping for the right to get on a train. It was, I believe, at that moment that I began to understand that one simple way to measure the desirability of a society is whether people can leave it when they want to – and whether more people want to get into it than want to get out.

But on that platform Gertie had no ideological blinkers to obscure her vision. All that obscured it were the tears that seemed independent of her jerky movements with hair and jacket and notebook.

"Let me talk to our immigration department," I said desperately, trying not to look at the corners of her mouth, which were threatening to cave in again as she tried to smile. She started writing something down. Two uniformed men approached her and began talking to her in German. The train station was nothing but confusion and noise, but Gertie's noise and confusion were quite distinctive. She said something I couldn't catch, shrugged a few times, and nodded in my direction. The two men looked at me with disinterest mingled with distaste. One of them muttered "fascist" and then all three set off down the platform. Gertie was gone. By now I had heard the word "fascist" so often in East Germany in reference to the enemy that after a while I had begun to think that the Second World War was really the story of the Germans fighting the Italians. Still, this was the first time I had heard the word "fascist", even in an offhand way, directed at me. I did not know that it would be in Canada that the word would be appended to my name with some actual seriousness.

And since my train of thought has taken me forward, let me insert, out of context, a further story about the Berlin Wall. It is an angry story because of Gertie, and the millions of Gerties I have not met.

It would be some seventeen years later that I came across the following lines in a foul little treatise written by an associate professor of the Department of Philosophy (*sic*) of the University of Toronto:

> The *primary* purpose in putting up the [Berlin] wall was to stop a U.S.-backed campaign of economic sabotage by the capitalist Federal Republic of [West] Germany. Like all countries devastated by the war, the [East] German

Democratic Republic faced terrible problems building up its farms and industries to provide food and other necessities. As in other socialist countries, these goods were offered at much lower prices than in the capitalist countries of Europe. In a campaign of economic sabotage people were encouraged to go into the GDR each year before it finally constructed a wall to stop it.

This is the most important fact about the Berlin Wall, but it is almost impossible to find it discussed in bourgeois news reports or histories of the wall.

Now, I hasten to say that the author of this passage, one Frank Cunningham, is not (and would not even describe himself as) a liberal, or a social democrat. He is a crypto-Communist, simple if not pure, and he is writing plain, unmitigated propaganda. His pamphlet (which we are told "grew out of lectures he has given, both at universities and high schools") is a press-release from the land of walled-in people. But that is not the point.

The point is that this man teaches and publishes undisturbed at the University of Toronto. Before anyone pounces on me, my point is not that Cunningham should be prevented from lecturing. Far from it. As long as liberty as I understand the word is part of the ethos of this land, Professor Cunningham should be able to lie unmolested, if he chooses.

But in the mid-seventies, as in the sixties, fifties, or indeed thirties, the liberals' watchword is still *l'ennemi pas à gauche.* There's no pernicious, ridiculous lie, even as blatant as Cunningham's, to which today's liberals would not lend the protection of free discourse – providing it comes from the political left. Similarly, there is barely a view, no matter how careful and responsible, to which they would if it comes from the political right. Professor Banfield's example at the same university, of which more later, is a case in point.

The trip to Helsinki via East Berlin, Warsaw, Minsk, and Leningrad was made on a long train specially allocated for youth festival delegates. Each railway car was supposed to carry one delegation, but when my passport was returned to me with car and berth number attached, I found that for some reason my berth was in the section reserved for Arab delegates. There was nothing I could do about this. I argued, demonstrated, remonstrated, and tried to point out that five days of sleeping in a car full of Kurds, Iraqis, and pan-Arabs of various sizes but, apparently, one sex – male – might not be the most convenient way for a nice Jewish girl to travel. No. It could not be changed. My ticket number was *assigned*. Nein, nyet, and again, no. On I got.

The sleeping arrangements were primitive. Open berths in each car stacked up to the ceiling. There was one toilet and one sink per car for about forty occupants, and I soon discovered that my fellow passengers used the bathroom facilities in a variety of intriguing ways, none of them familiar to Westerners. Changing into bed clothes became somewhat like running the gauntlet as I dashed for the bathroom clutching my toothbrush, cleansing cream, and Eaton's pink quilted robe. I soon gave up on this and changed in my upper berth under the blanket. In fact, apart from the odd genocidal outbreak between the Kurds, who wandered around with curved daggers stuck in leggings and waistbands, and the Iraqis (who had a rather excitable reaction to the singing of Kurdish anthems), under the circumstances everything went remarkably well.

It seemed foolish to remove the small mezuzah I wore around my neck, and anyway my Sephardic name was immediately recognizable to the Arabs, so there was no point in lapsing into Miss Addleton's High Anglicanism. On the first morning of the train journey I woke up to a strange sound and discovered my blanket had been neatly folded away from my berth, my nightgown was up around my neck, and I was lying on display to a rather curious but totally passive group of Arabs who were sitting on neighbouring upper berths singing some sort of ghastly song. And smiling politely.

For a moment I froze. Then I gently pulled my nightgown down, the blanket up, smiled sweetly, and told them to fuck off. The idiom may not have been universal but the tone in which it was delivered was perfectly clear and the singing ensemble disbanded. From then on I slept in shorts and a tee-shirt, which was about all one could stand in the unbearable heat of that packed train in August.

A few earnest Western intellectuals insisted on discussing the Arab-Israeli question with me and pointing out that our camaraderie was an indication that Arab and Jew could sit down together and talk. I said yes, of course, and privately thanked Allah that the Communist organizers had no such idealism and had refrained from putting any of the Israeli delegates in that car – or we'd all be dead. The only places that were cool, in fact, and allowed tempers to ease, were the one or two box cars that were between the sleeping-compartments. In the boxcars the side doors could be slid open and lucky riders could sit with their legs dangling in the breeze as the train rattled along at a slow crawl through the flat farmland of Poland. We were told that this was a train route that was rarely used any more and it certainly seemed to attract much attention from the labourers in the fields. Most of them were women, indistinguishable in their kerchiefs and lined, dark faces, their hands sometimes held out so close to us that we could touch them as the train passed.

We approached Warsaw from the north-west, the afternoon sun beaming down on the massive Palace of Culture that dominates the city. Suddenly I was cold. It was affectation, of course, but it seemed a betrayal to be sitting in a boxcar tanning my legs on the way to Warsaw. For *what* had this now disused railway line originally been used? What other human cargo had these boxcars seen besides subsidized students? The motto of the festival was "peace and friendship". Had others ridden these tracks from Germany to the beat of "Arbeit macht frei"?

The trip fell into place in a series of tableaux vivants: The girls crowding around me in the locker-room of a school in Dresden, East Germany, desperate to buy my lipstick, face powder, handbag, or anything that I had with me that I would sell. The sudden chill on the school dance floor when I began doing the twist with my young partner and everyone edged slowly away till my shoulder was tapped. "Not here. Not done," whispered the voice. "Verboten." My frozen smile on the front page of an East German newspaper as I accepted some dreadful confection of handiwork made of string and sticks and wool from an eight-year-old wearing a Young Pioneer scarf who had marched forward from the ranks of hundreds of other Young Pioneers all drilling and wheeling on the square as far as the eye could see. Stiff handshakes with Yuri Gagarin and Yevgeny Yevtushenko, and the inevitable we-clap-you-clap line-up (the socialist form of applause, not a venereal disease) on the platform at the end of public performances of any kind. In the streets of Helsinki, Finns watching, hostile and suspicious: quickly one learns to say very deliberately "me (pointing to one's chest) t-o-u-r-i-s-t not c-o-m-m-u-n-i-s-t." All the same there is tear gas in the streets and there are crowds of anti-Soviet Finns to quell.

Finally, the discussion period in the USSR delegation head-quarters in Helsinki (tables laden with pamphlets outlining the gallant struggle in Vietnam/Cambodia/Laos and pictures of Mao and Stalin together), where Western students are invited to stand up and give their frank impressions of the East. I listen in fascination as glowing accounts of material affluence in the people's democracies are contrasted with the stark poverty and oppression (sic) of the West. Then, my turn. A narration of a Westerner's feelings at the sight of the Berlin Wall and a country that refuses to let its people emigrate at will. My horror at all the "forbidden" activities and "forbidden" books. Nobody interrupts, nobody discusses, nobody comes to march me away. But everyone is very silent. I don't get the clap.

On the beaches of Helsinki in the August night when there is no night and the northern lights illuminate the sky in pale flickers, I sit on the sand with a friendly Arab who can speak nothing but Arabic and therefore refrains from discussing the problems of surplus value or Tel Aviv. We sit and watch the sky. And what if I could not get on that train any time I liked, I wonder? What then? Would I resist the endless barrage of propaganda and psychological coercion? (I cannot conceive of the physical aspects of the Gulag yet.) How long would it be before I too would praise the empty food shops for their plenitude and Pravda for its openness?

No conclusions, only perceptions challenged and the beginning of a fundamental abhorrence of coercion. But at that moment coercion seemed the tool of totalitarianism only. It would not be so long, however, before I was to see that the coercive society was the creature, just as inevitably, of democratic socialism as well, and a notion about to be enthusiastically embraced by the West.

Still, Canada obliged my lingering left-wing instincts by bolstering them with a timely display of political wrongheadedness. I returned to the University of Toronto campus from Europe in the fall of 1962 to find the newspapers full of stories about RCMP files on student activists. The start of one such file, it was claimed, had been some printed material a Vancouver student had received on the World Youth Festival. Eventually the student, who did not attend Helsinki, discovered that the RCMP had begun a dossier on him. Why, no one has ever discovered. I read this with some apprehension. After all, I had actually been *there*. Now, each day the news was full of more revelations about dossiers and security checks. Even the grumpy old ladies who gave out the mail in the women's residence where I lived were beginning to joke about all the letters I was receiving from Russia and Poland as my summer's worth of exchange addresses began to make good on correspondence promises.

Obviously the sensible thing to do was to find out if the RCMP was keeping a file on *me*. I contacted Perry Ryan, the Liberal MP for the riding in which Whitney Hall girls' residence was located, and after some hesitation, he showed up in the lobby of the residence. I explained my concerns to him. Ryan seemed unimpressed, but he had a quick solution anyway. "If I were you," he said, "I'd get on the phone to the RCMP and volunteer myself as an informer on Communist activities on the campus."

I was more confounded than shocked. I would have liked

to explain to Ryan that, much as I had come to loathe the
Communists, I had not extended my loathing to political liberty. In fact, I said nothing. I would have liked to explain to
my Member of Parliament that I detested Communists precisely because they had based an entire society on a system of
spying and denunciation, and that I had not the slightest interest in emulating them. But I said nothing.

I said nothing, I suppose, partly because I foolishly assumed that a Liberal was a liberal and, somehow, in spite of
his suggestion to me, would regard these truths as self-evi-
dent. Though I was beginning to learn something about the
Far Left, I had at the time not yet learned anything about
the Near Left and the Centre.

I knew nothing about the party that, though called by the
name that would make it an heir to the ideas of John Stuart
Mill, was about to be led by a man who would inform the
Canadian public some twelve years later that, if people were
disturbed by the Royal Canadian Mounted Police opening
mail or burning barns illegally, he would make the opening
of mail or the burning of barns by the Mounties legal. Like
everyone else on campus in those days, or nearly everyone
whose voices were heard, I assumed that some form of socialism was not only inevitable, but desirable and moral. In
fact, along with other left liberals, it never even occurred to
me that quasi-Marxist thought may not have a monopoly on
morality. Even less did I see – though I was no longer a communist sympathizer at all – that there might be any connection between the fine progressive sentiments I and everyone
else espoused and the deadly reality of the Berlin Wall.

"You always were a right-winger, even at university,"
claims Rosemary Speirs, the *Varsity* review editor for whom I
wrote book reviews then and who now writes on labour and
politics for the *Globe and Mail*. Whatever the perception of
others, I saw myself clearly as a left-winger. It was also clear
to me that, welcome though such views were on the campus,
I was not talented enough for an academically distinguished
life. This was crystal clear to the University, who regretfully
informed me in a discreet note that I was debarred from the

School of Graduate Studies on this, the occasion of my second failure in Anglo-Saxon grammar.

But I had caught a glimpse of the new class and the new power in our society. They were, like me, clothed in the mantle of the left. And since I didn't want to be a civil servant, I headed quickly for the media.

CHAPTER SEVEN

The Opiate of the Self-Indulgent

NOT EVERYTHING YIELDED TO POLLYANNA. "You're addicted," said the doctor to me at the Addiction Research Foundation in Toronto, "and you're going to have to get off it." He looked down at the questions and answers in front of him. "Overdosed once." He looked up. "You know how it kills you, don't you?" Yes, I knew. It had started in 1959 when I discovered that the muscle fatigue of long hours could be eased by taking drugstore remedies with codeine in them. At university I began to take more and more. I took it in the form of 222's or the cheaper C2's which I bought at drugstores. In the sixties those preparations still had phenacetin in them, a substance which combated fever at the price of literally eating up the oxygen in your blood. After taking more than a dozen or so at a time you could lapse into unconsciousness. It was best not to wear nail polish or lipstick so that the distinctive blue tinge of phenacetin poisoning would be quickly seen.

By the end of university I hated those tablets and the physical disabilities they brought with them. My intake was up to twenty a day, and while that wasn't so extraordinary, it was presenting considerable problems. One of the problems was psychological as much as physical. Codeine aggravated fear.

Since early childhood, fear of empty rooms had been something of a problem for me. In adolescence, when I was very often alone, I stayed out of a house or a building even in the sunny afternoon until there was someone else there. Otherwise I could find myself sitting in the middle of a room, stranded, sitting in my own urine, sitting for hours, too frightened to cry and too frightened to move. I soon devised routines to circumvent this problem. But in university, as the codeine intake increased, so did the fear, even now with normal, flesh-and-blood students in the room next to me in residence. There were hallucinations and voices (imagined), and unfortunate scenes (real). Eventually the Dean of Women insisted on an appointment with a psychiatrist. The psychiatrist, after asking a number of simple-minded questions, decided university would have to take a back seat for a while in favour of appointments with him. Fat chance. I went back to residence and stuffed an old nylon stocking with washcloths, making it into a big sausage which I could bite at whenever faces appeared at my residence window. My fellow students were no longer disturbed by my terrified cries, and I never saw the psychiatrist again.

The doctor at the Addiction Research Foundation was a far more practical man than the psychiatrist. Dr. Danoff carefully wrote out a prescription for a very small amount of Librium and Valium that could only be renewed at the ARF Hospital, told me he would prefer me to kick the codeine habit in their hospital, but since I wouldn't, the drugs he was prescribing might help the muscle spasms. That was it. He was as near as the phone – if I needed him.

It was in 1963, my final year of university, that I began to move into a much trendier world, centred in Montreal, where real drugs were being played with, used, or at least celebrated by golden and glamorous people. There was the poet and singer Leonard Cohen, the up-and-coming film-maker Claude Jutra, exquisite mulatto girls with high cheek-bones, beautiful and clever Indian women fighting for improvements on the reserves they had left behind, sculptors and painters and writers and businessmen. And cocaine and heroin and hash and marijuana. Not all of them took it, but it was part of the culture. It was chic. My entrée to this group was a wealthy businessman who financed Jutra's *A Tout Prendre* as well as the ambitious literary magazine *Exchange*, and who took a brief liking to me.

It was all very glamorous. Attending the opening night of Jutra's film in a Rolls-Royce with television cameras rolling as one stepped out. Listening to impassioned discussions on the future of Canadian culture in the coffee shops on Crescent Street in Montreal or amid the white-washed walls of my friend's rambling apartment on Pine Street. Watching Leonard Cohen as he ambled up the rain-drizzled streets of Westmount with his Scandinavian lady Marianne in tow, plucking poetry out of the air, while I wondered why, when he could have lived so well, he chose to live so sparely. For someone like me who had spent a fair amount of time worrying about how to make ends meet, it was difficult to understand people of means who celebrated the Spartan life.

And the air was too often filled with the smell of drugs, and the beautiful furniture at the apartment on Pine Street was too often littered with human debris. My businessman friend had a stronger addiction than mine – heroin. With fascination I would watch him go through the ritual of cooking his drug and filling the syringe. Then I had to avert my eyes. It disturbed him that I would not "try" any of the drugs, didn't drink, and found that ordinary cigarettes, if inhaled, made me sick. I promised that I would try to "become more sophisticated". But my codeine intake was down to half a dozen a week, and between school and work there was little time for the kind of somnambulance I could see all around me in the expressions of the drugged. It was also increasingly clear to me that the artists who were actually producing any work of merit were not doing it under the influence of narcotics or even of the "soft" drugs they might take for pleasure. The mindless ramblings of the stoned faces I saw would never have been published. The beautiful girls with heroin shot into their veins lying on couches or arched on beds could never have modelled, acted, or raised money for worthy causes. They were good for only their own stupor.

It was on a visit to New York with the businessman and Cohen that I discovered my reaction to drugs. In a large room at the old Hotel Astor on Times Square a pipe was passed around the half-dozen people gathered together. "Go on," said my friend, "it's just grass." After two hours I was still unable to come down. Time and sequence had blurred into a terrifying jumble. Sentences would begin in my mouth only to disintegrate in my mind. Faces like plasticine models melted and dissolved in front of me into grotesques. In the early hours of the morning Cohen and my friend, despairing and exhausted, marched me out into the Square for some fresh air. The streets were packed. It was summertime. Everything was neon-bright. Shrieking, I huddled against the shop fronts. "She tried to pick my pockets," I screamed at the waitress in the coffee shop. It was an eight-hour nightmare for everyone. Whether it was hash or marijuana I never knew. I tried marijuana only once more with similar, though less prolonged, results after two puffs.

I did not need any laws to keep me away from drugs. A few years later my businessman friend, still young, was found dead in an alleyway in Hong Kong.

Drugs did not become a public issue in Canada till at least three or four years later. Haight-Ashbury had not yet bloomed, and only rounders and a select group of middle-class sophisticates were inhaling white powder through rolled-up dollar bills. Films like *Easy Rider* and *Panic in Needle Park* were still a good five years away. At university, students got high on beer or wine, and under-age purchasers of aeroplane glue were not regarded with suspicion. Still, perhaps because of my Montreal associations, I found myself getting into arguments about the use and abuse of drugs and debating the issue of marijuana and cocaine a little time before it appeared as a major social issue.

The various ups and downs of the legalize-marijuana movement in Canada and the United States have always seemed to me very much beside the point, as those on either side of the controversy muster information about the relative harm or harmlessness of the drug, and much is made of comparisons with narcotic drugs and their physically addictive properties. During the early 1970s when Canada was in its "greening" stage, such institutions as the Addiction Research Foundation would be more interested in amassing data on the harmlessness of "soft" drugs and preventing research on their harmful aspects than they would be in the late seventies when the bandwagon seemed to be going in the other direction.

The only *practical* arguments I heard about drugs at that time were made by the New York doctor-lawyer I interviewed for the CBC. Her name was Dr. Judith Densen-Gerber and she founded Odyssey House, a group of homes on Manhattan for young addicts. I interviewed her in the late sixties. "Give me a heroin addict any day over someone on speed or even hash," she said. "A heroin addict just nods quietly away and if you fill him up with his drug he'll nod his life away without bothering anyone. The others may go out and kill or attack someone who they think is about to kill them." And as for legislation: "Well," said Gerber, "if you're going to legalize another intoxicant in addition to liquor, then you'd better be prepared for the same kind of casualties that you get from alcohol. And that means putting money into a whole system of rehabilitation for drug victims."

In the early seventies the only man in Canada who was prepared to speak about drugs with the same kind of no-nonsense approach was the Addiction Research Foundation's Dr. Andrew Malcolm, who was fired in 1970 for his trouble. The then-very-liberal ARF, all caught up in putting its staff through various consciousness-raising techniques and keen on "rap" sessions with addicts in drop-in centres, couldn't tolerate spending any money on a doctor who believed that marijuana may be distinctly harmful and wanted research funding to investigate this. And they showed, what I would later come to recognize as the trademark of *contemporary* small-l liberalism, that they would brook no dissent.

But when it came to my own view on the legalization of marijuana – or indeed any drug – I found myself diametrically opposed to the hard-line approach of Drs. Malcolm and Gerber, though not from any sympathy with the soft-drugs-are-harmless devotees. Soft drugs could clearly be harmful to some people, and the simplest kind of empirical observation indicated that they were taken in fact to produce a state of intoxication which made the drugged person unable to perform or indeed want to perform any sort of work. To use Dr. Malcolm's phrase, they produced an "amotivational syndrome". But it seemed to me that the key to this problem was not to penalize everyone. Some people, perhaps most, manage to handle liquor on a sensible scale. They restrict its use to appropriate circumstances and generally refrain from driving cars when drunk or bashing in the heads of friends whom they suddenly see in a flash of alcoholic wisdom as enemies. Most people do not become drunk when they drink – and if they do, they vomit nicely and go to bed. Since it would never occur to me to prevent all those people who enjoy their two gin-and-tonics a day from indulging in this little vice in order to protect the minority who can't stop at that, it would similarly seem improper to prevent anyone who wishes to use drugs from doing so in order to save the drug abuser himself. This seems an inappropriate principle on which to make social policy in a free country. All one can do is legalize everything, then hold everyone responsible for their behaviour while under the influence of an intoxicant. Liquor, for example, would not be a mitigating circumstance in the case of a criminal act. Rather than saying alcohol prevented someone from forming intent, so that the murder committed in a drunken rage becomes manslaughter, one ought to say that the voluntary taking of alcohol constructs liability in itself.

A drug-befuddled mind would not be accepted as a "sickness" in the event of a ruined career or inadequate schoolwork, but as a cause for dismissal or failure. If we have anything to learn from the communist countries it is not their economic systems, but the draconian way in which they hold an individual responsible for his acts. Anyone driving in Hungary, for example, who is found to be drunk has his licence lifted on the spot. Of course, with responsibility goes freedom – but the communists don't acknowledge the second half of this equation.

The drug that was to be my undoing was not hash, or heroin, or even the morphine-derivative codeine that had caused me so much trouble. No, it would be a drug properly prescribed for me after hospital tests in a medical climate all infected with the new enthusiasm for mental chemotherapy.

The hospital was modern and comfortable and I was resting when my doctor brought another doctor in with him. I had been in for "tests" to help determine the best therapy for a common cystic condition and the results had indicated some gross hormonal imbalances. Hence the endocrinologist, who began asking questions. Did I perspire a lot? Yes. Did I get frightened? Yes. What drugs had I taken? Codeine. Under what circumstances? I explained. By the end of the session the doctor was elated. It would not be till much later that I discovered he had recently become interested in research on the chemical underpinnings of emotional illness. He would prescribe a dose of 200 milligrams a day of Elavil (an anti-depressant) and advise me that I would probably need to maintain that dose for the rest of my life. (Later I would find out that 200 mg was a *maintenance* dosage given only to severely disturbed psychiatric patients.) "Why?" I asked. The doctor smiled benignly. "You do still get frightened *sometimes*, and you do still take codeine *sometimes*, and of course there's your *background.*"

Background. Ah, yes. Among the routine questions the hospital had asked were the cause of my father's death in 1956. He had committed suicide. This saddened me greatly, and occasionally I would dwell on it. But it was not until my sessions with the endocrinologist that I began to think of it as a significant factor in my life.

Society, you see, was moving into a new phase. This was

1965 and the threshold of the great era of self-elevation. The environmentalists were explaining behaviour in terms of the spots on a child's rocking-horse and the Spock generation was about to flower. A psychiatrist for every psyche would be the goal of the prosperous, self-involved sixties. The most simplistic and sentimental answers to truly disturbing social problems were about to be made into public policy. Crime would become a product of poverty. Or, in the words of Canada's trendiest solicitor general of all, Warren Allmand, "the result of lack of love at home".

In this world – which it would be unfair to call Allmandian because he was far from being the only, or even a particularly significant, exponent of it – certain left-liberal hopes, or hypotheses, or suspicions, or superstitions, were elevated to the position of scientific truth. No individual and no group was to have any responsibility for his, her, or its position any longer. There was no room for inherent factors, fate, fortune, character, or natural ability. Achievements could be seen only as results of unfair advantage, and failures, of course, as results of unfair disadvantage. Words like "poor" or "illiterate" were replaced, not with mere euphemisms, but with accusatory adjectives such as "deprived". A person could no longer be lazy or diligent or talented or stupid. Such distinctions, being more difficult to vary by social action, would have formed no basis for planners to plan and bureaucracies to regulate.

It became a heresy to suggest that, where opportunities are equal, results may still be different. To say that one couldn't argue backwards from disparity to prove the existence of discrimination could have cost a person his or her licence as an intellectual. For instance, it became an article of absolute faith that if a group was found to be under-represented in a profession or an income bracket, this proved that its members were discriminated against. If an ethnic minority had some statistical difficulty meeting certain standards, it was the hidden bias of the standards that had to be called into question. To this day the suggestion is being seriously advanced that the height requirements of some police forces exist mainly or solely to discriminate against Orientals or women.

If people from poor homes couldn't spell, correct spelling became a class-conspiracy on the part of the affluent. If others couldn't think straight, it was "linear" thought that was declared to be discriminatory and outmoded. Rewarding ability or hard work at school came to be thought of as "elitism" and "competitiveness", something that would ill-prepare students for the "co-operative" society of the left-liberal future. In this society rewards and punishment would, presumably, no longer be distributed according to merit (as determined by such objective standards as numbers or such impersonal ones as supply and demand) but according to policy goals set out from time to time by the ruling social engineers, who had a monopoly on virtue.

Meanwhile, any vestige of value judgement, any habit of mind that would have viewed an act or a person as "good" or "wicked", "able" or "inadequate", "beautiful" or "ugly" – thereby removing it from the social manipulators' jurisdiction – was pronounced to be reactionary and mean-spirited. If people stole or murdered, if they couldn't read, write, hold down a job, get their poems published or their loves requited, it was due to nothing but psycho-social conditions or, perhaps, the slanted, racist, sexist, capitalistic way in which vested interests persisted in defining crime, literacy, or sexual attractiveness.

And these benign theories (and self-serving lies) were not merely favourite dogmas on the leading edge of intellectual fashion. They were implemented in binding government regulations. They were – and are – acquiring the statutory force of the law, as we shall see later in my argument.

Admittedly, this left-lib approach often made the vicissitudes of existence easier to face, which was very convenient for me. In this climate any personal shortcoming or emotional or career setback could be blamed on external forces such as an inequitable society or a deprived childhood. In essence, one of the most potent motivations for social democracy was getting ready to surface: the need for individuals to find a collective scapegoat for all their inadequacies.

Now it was explained to me. My bouts of irrational fear, my inability to completely rid myself of my dependence on codeine, my uneven academic career, and my erratic emotional life were not the products of any personal deficiency but the effects of an unstable childhood and the trauma of my father's death. This was all compounded by the chemical imbalances in my system that exaggerated my feelings. It was never made clear to me, and indeed I don't think that it was clear in the doctor's mind, what caused what in this chicken-and-egg situation; whether, for example, the symptoms of fear were caused by the childhood experiences or the chemical imbalances. No matter. *Nothing was my fault.* If I would just depend on these little yellow pills for the rest of my life I could be (almost) normal.

I swallowed it – and them. Not because I was intimidated by the position of authority the doctor held (today's popular excuse for the sheep-like attitude of patients to society's witch-therapists), but because I wanted to. It made me sound, well, so glamorous and hard-done-by. And it explained away so much. Now I could be moody to my sister or fickle to my boyfriend whenever I felt like it and take comfort in the fact that "I couldn't help it." I could stop fighting that urge to take codeine because it wasn't my fault. I could continue to work myself up into a hysterical frenzy late at night in the CBC offices, where I now had a job, and tell myself the reason I was unable to leave the desk was because people hadn't loved me enough as a child. I swallowed the suggestion, believed in it, and with those eight little pills per day I did indeed enter the wonderful world of equilibrium.

I never realized quite how drugged I was for those seven years until I decided in 1972 to stop the cycle. I had been away from Canada for four years. When I returned in 1972 I visited the doctor and asked him in the presence of George Jonas, whom I was about to marry, just why I had to be on the pills. He was sorry, he replied, but in spite of my request he had been "unable to locate the records". Offices had been moved, old files had been thrown out, etcetera, etcetera. (Probably, as an endocrinologist always on the leading edge, he was by that time "into" gland transplants.) However, he confided to my companion, "She's probably looking for an excuse to stay on the drug and it's probably just as wise." Jonas said something impolite and I began withdrawal that day. It took several weeks and was an excruciating process in which I scratched virtually every shred of skin I had off my body. By the end of it I was a wreck but I was free of the drug. About five months later, in order to see what on earth the medication had been doing for me, I took two of the Elavil pills. The effect was astonishing. I slowed down to about half my pace. My mind felt as if it were on vacation. Like a cow, I thought, I've been chewing cud for seven years.

I'm not suggesting in all this, of course, that every mental disturbance is mere self-indulgence. It may well be that genuine psychiatric disorders are caused by hormonal imbalances, or a particularly deprived childhood, or hereditary predispositions, or indeed a combination of the three. There is equally little doubt that in some cases, or in many cases, they may be cured or controlled or alleviated in their worst symptoms by chemicals. Or psychotherapy. Or falling in love with the archbishop of Cologne.

As I am not a doctor, none of this is my concern. My sole concern is the blind, total, all-embracing assumption, which was the coming thing in the sixties and before, and a virtual orthodoxy today, that a person's own will and character play no role in his or her equilibrium. The orthodoxy that everything is socially or chemically determined, or set into motion by too much or too little parental love. The notion that nothing, ever, is a person's own damn fault, and he or she can do nothing, ever, to snap out of it.

Or that my only choice should have been between shaking with fear in a darkened room or becoming a turnip on Elavil, worthy, in my eternal dependence on hormones, society, or family, of neither reward nor punishment.

CHAPTER EIGHT

The Media Gliblibs

BUT PERHAPS HAVING a state of mind somewhat akin to that of a turnip is the best way to begin a media career in Canada. The small-l liberal views and opinions I held certainly raised no hackles, only my job status, and with some speed I worked myself up from my first task as a typist on the Canadian Broadcasting Corporation's *Juliette* show to being a script assistant on CBC's *Take 30*, which was at the time introducing a new hostess, Adrienne Clarkson, to co-host with regular Paul Soles. I soon discovered that what was actually *said* in an interview seemed to count for less than what the story format planned the interview to say. On one occasion I watched a flabbergasted Clarkson (who hid her surprise with professional competence) interview a maniacal, giggling Dr. Humphrey Osmond on his experiences administering mescaline to Aldous Huxley, and on the suggested new uses for LSD as therapy for certain forms of mental illness. The interview revealed a seemingly senile and wretched old man. It certainly called for a story about the use to which the Saskatchewan government was putting the work of Osmond and his colleague, Dr. Abraham Hoffer. But we were all caught up in the wonderful new world of altered consciousness, and that sort of story would not have been in vogue among the more-with-it-than-thou people behind the cameras. For we were liberal arts graduates with solid backgrounds in sociology, anthropology, political science, and graduate English. We had, therefore, unshakable opinions on the chemical effects of pollution (bad), the physical and mental effects of intoxicants (harmless), and the effectiveness of the free market (vicious). Our television experts on these subjects were chosen to coincide with our opinions. We were always frantically busy writing up treatments on the deficiencies of society's social service programs or the abuse of the blackfly. We could be spotted by our preference for lunch-at-the-desk while chatting with researchers and secretaries *endlessly* about the latest corporate power battle – or office affair. Male or female, in this we were all alike – what we lacked in hard knowledge we made up for in soft sciences and soft thinking.

Later on, when I was working for prime-time public affairs television, I sent a letter to Dr. Hoffer asking him for the test he sent out on request to ascertain schizophrenic tendencies in individuals. The test duly arrived at my home address. It was the HOD test, a list of sixty-seven questions to be answered "True" or "False", consisting of statements like: "My body odour is now much more unpleasant"/ "I can no longer smell perfume as well as I used to"/ "Cigarettes taste queer now"/ "Very often friends irritate me".

The test seemed more able to detect malfunctions of the olfactory nerve and the taste buds, and whether the subject had moved next door to a glue factory, than to indicate schizophrenia. According to Dr. Hoffer's accompanying letter, written on the letterhead of the Department of Public Health for Saskatchewan, "The HOD test is a very simple crude card sort test, badly designed in comparison with standard tests. But, unlike them, it works. A crude instrument which measures accurately is, I believe, preferable to a fine tool which does not measure at all." Well, maybe. Maybe not. This seemed to me a situation well worth investigating.

But the program I worked for was interested in the subject only if I could pull together a story on the *usefulness* of the test in detecting schizophrenia and controlling the following therapy (together with some punchy footage on those unfortunate victims of LSD who had been foolish enough to "drop acid" without taking the test). By contrast, the program was not at all interested when I talked about investigating the dangers of any faddish solutions being subsidized by Saskatchewan taxpayers. Soon I came to understand that in CBC Public Affairs television we muck-rakers (a decent and honourable occupation) had to have a definite point of view. We did stories on union busting, welfare mothers, skid row derelicts, and native peoples. We did battered wives/battered children/battered animals and battered environment. We were fearless critics of government (provided it was not an NDP government) and of business and America. I entered into this with some enthusiasm and much culpability.

One of the earliest projects I worked on was a film on Toronto's skid-row derelicts being made for the CBC. My job was to pick out two or three appropriate derelicts as stars in this epic. After some days of wandering around the Scott Mission in Toronto and similar organizations, I came up with Charlie and two friends. Charlie became the blight of my life.

The day before shooting was to begin, Charlie took the cash advance we had given him and spent it on a binge that culminated in a charge of disorderly conduct and many broken windows. My unit manager put through the necessary papers, and I went off to pay Charlie's bail and get him out for the shooting. A repentant Charlie, a Newfoundlander of about thirty-five who looked fifty, was installed in a room in a house in Toronto's Cabbagetown and I was turned into his guard. I unlocked Charlie each morning at 7:30 a.m. and locked him up in the evening. But Charlie loathed this new rooming-house. He wanted to be back in his flop-house.

"Put him back where he wants to be," I was told. "We'll be filming there anyway." Armed with DDT and wearing Saran Wrap inside my underwear, I marched Charlie off to his favourite flop-house. Even without close inspection it was clear that the bed sheets were alive. I sprayed the DDT vigorously about, much to the loud dismay of the occupants, and refused to sit down. The day filming ended, Charlie celebrated in his customary fashion and was back inside. Then, a telephone call. Charlie was out and had decided to reform. This was greeted with much enthusiasm, and like Major Barbara I sallied forth with a scrubbed and dried-out Charlie to one of the little shacks that hires hourly labour. Charlie was off to work for the first time in about ten years.

When I returned that evening to my bachelor apartment Charlie was waiting there. No more work; he preferred being on-camera. Was there any more filming that he could do for the CBC? I said no, although deep in my heart I was sure he could get regular employment as the CBC's own authentic derelict. While I made tea, Charlie drank my cooking wine, not by invitation. When he left he also took with him a small number of sterling silver items which I supposed I could pick up at one of the local pawnshops if I wanted them back. Since we were still in the editing stage of the film, I thought it might be amusing to include the actual lives of the participants in the script: surely there was *something* to be learned from Charlie. I wasn't sure what, but I was damned sure that the film we were going to show, much of it in soft focus and silhouette lighting, of the lonely, tough life of the skid-row derelict, and society's callous attitude to him, would miss the essential con-man aspect of the real Charlies of the world. But Charlie's off-camera unscripted reality never hit the screen.

To avoid any misunderstanding: Charlie did not offend or disappoint me. I was no do-gooder brought up short by reality, ready to vent my anger on the object of my misplaced compassion. I simply thought that if Charlie was to teach us anything, it was less about society's nature than about his own. But this was and is taboo in the world of left-wing media. Charlie, went the litany, was the product of society's wrongs, not his own.

My own chance to say something came when I was given the funds to make a film on the case-history of a battered child. The story was dramatic: Peter had been sent to a foster home. The foster mother's first child was found dead in

an outhouse. She was acquitted of infanticide and under-
went a short period of confinement in a psychiatric institution. This minor hitch did not stop the Children's Aid Society from sending her more foster children. Peter was abused
for several years. The methods were unspeakable: the child
was suspended from a shower rail and beaten with a wooden
stick studded with nails; he was dipped in scalding water,
whipped, lacerated, and tortured. All the while his teachers
and neighbours politely averted their eyes from the blood-
stained clothes, the bruises, the scars, and even the small
pools of bloods forming at the foot of his desk at school.
Eventually Peter ran away and was found by the police, who
took one look at the child's battered body and sent him back
to Children's Aid. Meanwhile, the Children's Aid branch in
question made plans to fill the vacancy at Peter's old foster
home by sending yet another child off to the convicted
mother. "We think Peter may simply have been a beha-
vioural problem for the mother and we'll look after him till
he's eighteen," explained the CAS director.

My executive producer at the Canadian Broadcasting Corporation, Ross McLean, was very pleased with the show. But
another producer, Ken Lefolii, was angry. "The show," he
said, "says very little about the inefficiency of this branch of
the CAS. It fudges and lets them off the hook. They should
all be fired." He was right, of course, in a limited way. And
McLean was right, in so far as the show *was* an effective hu-
man-interest story. Except that the real story was staring us
all in the face but our automatic liberal reflexes were dulled
and predictable. It never occurred to me, or to Lefolii or
McLean, that the question was not the replacement of a particularly inadequate Children's Aid Society staff *but the very
existence of such organizations as the Children's Aid Society.* Any
organization that requires victims if it is to survive has a
vested interest in maintaining the dependency of its clien-
tele. In the United States journalists would soon uncover the
shocking story of children kept from adoptive homes by social workers whose jobs (and grants) depended on having a
good supply of non-placeable kids to administer. In Canada,

various pieces of legislation designed to limit the wardship period of children under the Society's care tried to alleviate this aspect of the problem. But today, as we shall see in a later chapter, the militancy of many social workers inside government organizations for such hideous pieces of legislation as a Children's Bill of Rights is clearly directed at expanding their own power base. At any rate, in the media in 1967 none of us could conceive of questioning the fundamental institutions of our budding welfare society, except in terms of an individual or two falling down on the job. Anything more basic would have been taboo.

Incidentally, there would be much to learn in a negative sort of way from the dreadful abuse of parents and children in Sweden by the all-powerful Directorate of Social Affairs, whose authority to remove any child from a parent's custody is absolute (and where, incidentally, in the spirit of the International Year of the Child, it is now forbidden for a parent to spank one). Indeed, there would be much to learn from the Swedish experience on many levels, but although we referred with approbation to the Swedish experience in many of our scripts and always in comparison to our own callous society, during the past ten years that I have been in contact with the media no one has ever responded with any interest to my suggestion that a critical look be taken at this "model" welfare state.

I settled down happily into work at the CBC as a story editor and interviewer. At first I was dreadful on-camera. A lacquered apparition with bouffant hair, glazed smile, and detachment bordering on the unconscious often reinforced by the mandatory dosage of Elavil.

"Can't you try to be just a little *warmer,*" my producer would plead. But gradually one learns. By the second season I had mastered enough to graduate from doing interviews on visiting perfume exhibits to more flashy stuff. I knew how to get wrestler Gene Kinisky to show me his grip on-camera and twist my arm down to show off my best profile. I could ask actress Monique Van Vooren how a sex symbol deals with the problem of crow's-feet and the approach of old age.

I could make John Cassavetes approach tears and go into spasms of anger by asking him if his method of making films was not exploitative of ordinary actors who were subsidizing his whims. All in all I learned to be a reasonably smart-ass interviewer and was gaining some respect for this skill. In fact, one day, getting up from the set in CBC's Studio Six after hosting a live show with Warren Davis, I looked up at the lights strung across the ceiling, the abandoned cameras shunted to the side, the shine on the painted and re-painted studio floor, and thought in a classic moment of triteness: "*This* is what I've always wanted."

There were moments when things were not quite so smooth. One day I was called in to do an interview with American folk-singer Phil Ochs. I went to the library and got out his records. I noted with some interest that Ochs had chosen the poetry of Mao Tse-tung for the back cover of one of his albums, and as I read the research material on him and listened to the words of Ochs's ballads about how "the marines have landed in Santo Domingo", I could see that this was a man who did not wish to be known simply for the quality of his high C's, or the mellowness of his guitar strings. The interview became quite stormy. "If you hate America so much, why do you stay there?" I asked. "Aren't you having the best of both worlds?" Later, as we walked off the set, the argument continued: "Why don't you stay in America, then, and put your money into a non-profit foundation to help the exploited?" I demanded, conceding that a committed man might well want to stay in his country and try to change it for the better.

Ochs and I parted friends – he giving me free tickets for his concert that night – but my executive producer was furious. "That's not the sort of interview you should be doing," said Ross McLean. "Ochs is not a political interview. He's a musician." Having listened to his album, I could not agree. Nor did I think that a man who put a note on the back of his album under the poems of Mao asking "Is this the enemy?", and above such songs as "Cops of the World" and "Ringing of Revolution", would agree. But Ross McLean, not that it would help him in the long run, understood the CBC better than I.

By the time of the emergence of Pierre Elliott Trudeau early in 1968 I was chugging along at the CBC in a fairly enviable position. I was appearing on-camera several times a week and working on the major Sunday-night public affairs program. As the Liberal leadership convention approached it was clear that "our pet, Juliette" had been replaced by another P.E.T. at the CBC. I was put in charge of a massive project to contact every one of the delegates to the Liberal leadership nominating convention and ask them how they planned to vote. We had installed all sorts of electronic computers in the studio to announce the results of our survey days before the convention was to begin.

Several researchers and I divided up all the delegates and began to spend our lives at the telephone. It was an impossible job. Delegates were difficult to contact; if reached, they hadn't the slightest intention of telling us their choice. But we had a new and eager producer – now CBC's Vice-President and General Manager, Peter Herrndorf – and he was determined that the computers were going to light up in Studio One. We tried again. A trickle of answers began to flow in, and the stencilled charts we all had finally began to have some markings on them. The producer came to my office on the Friday before our Sunday show – and the week before the convention. "Well," he said, all cheery and confident, "how goes it?"

"Slowly," I replied.

"Oh, come on, Amiel," he answered. "Stick at it. You can get those figures if you really try."

On Saturday I appraised the situation. There was no way I was going to continue this madness. I simply couldn't get enough answers from enough delegates to establish a trend, and I knew that Herrndorf would not find the impossibility of the task a sufficient excuse. After all, having sold *his* superiors on the idea, if it did not pan out it would be his head or mine. I somehow suspected that, given this choice, he might prefer mine. I wasn't going to find out the hard way.

The only solution was to select the winner off the top of my head, but which one was I to select? Just about everybody at the CBC, indeed all the media, preferred Trudeau. I knew that if I chose anybody else my prediction would go against the grain. My figures would be checked and double-checked, and of course found to be wanting. But I thought, if I went for Trudeau, there would be no questions asked.

I was right. My "results" were greeted with ringing cries of enthusiasm even as I was filling out the charts. Eventually I gave up on the charts and began typing out summaries instead: a strong margin in favour of Trudeau. This was greeted warmly by my producer, and my regional "summaries" were fed into the computers and the excitingly flashing lights. That Sunday night the CBC gave out the news, in a triumph of scientific analysis: Trudeau would win the nomination! His fellow contestants protested to the CBC in vain, rightly worried about how this might influence the delegates, and demanded to see how we had reached our totals. But by the time memos started trickling down from head office requesting an investigation, Trudeau had been nominated. After that, every Liberal in sight was eager to confess to having confided to us that Trudeau was the one they were going to elect.

Over the past ten years I have gone through periods of bitter remorse for inflicting P.E.T. on the country, but of course my little fraudulent poll had no such significance. Trudeau would no doubt have been nominated without it. It is doubtful, however, whether he would have been nominated without the universal endorsement of the media. He gained this universal support because the left-libbers – that is, the near-absolute majority at the CBC and the considerable majority at all the other networks, newspapers, and magazines – considered him to be one of them. (Though they soon concluded that they were wrong, I believe that they were quite right, except that Trudeau, possessed of much intelligence and good instincts, could combine ideology with the art of the possible, which is after all the definition of politics.) But I do not wish to suggest – as Trudeau himself was moved to do later – that there is some deep and dark left-wing conspiracy afoot at the CBC. The problem is far worse than any conspiracy, which, being something conscious, would be limited by its nature to a number of conspirators. What afflicts the CBC, and to an only slightly lesser extent the entire Canadian media, is *a syndrome*. The syndrome can be identified quite easily as soon as a viewer or a reader of the Canadian media tries to find any coverage of an issue that departs from the basic premises of democratic socialism. Friends, you see, quite understandably hire friends – or at the very least fellow-thinkers – and left-libbers in Canada are not only friends with other left-libbers but consider it downright pathological or immoral to hold any other point of view. This is not the United States, where William F. Buckley sails and holidays with John Kenneth Galbraith. This is Canada, where no magazine or television network departs more than Very Occasionally from a sentimental socialist's look at the issues – whether it is our own venerable *Saturday Night* magazine or the trashy weekend newspaper supplements. (With the exception of *Saturday Night* editor Robert Fulford's own "Notebook". Fulford is, I think, one of the last real liberals.)

Of course, there are a few Canadian journalists who share some of my ideas and often express them considerably better – like history teacher and author John Muggeridge or my husband, George Jonas. But they are rarely asked to submit to magazines. Except for their own newspapers, hardly anyone ever asks Robert Nielsen, Peter Worthington, Richard Needham, and other veteran but non-socialist journalists for their views in the media. This is particularly tragic in Canada since, unlike the U.S., we have no alternatives to the small-l liberal publications. The result is that some of our best journalists have nowhere to publish in Canada, or at best are forced to write about more "acceptable" topics. George Jonas is always asked for pieces on motorbikes or women – but hardly ever for articles on social issues, which are reserved for journalists of a more "correct" political persuasion.

In television the situation is worse. This is in part because television is an expensive – and therefore highly commercial – medium, less concerned with ideas than with entertainment. Still, in the U.S. (and cable-Canada) viewers can turn to the Public Broadcasting Service, which sometimes examines more than one side of an issue. In Canada, the entire CBC hasn't a single conservative/neo-conservative/classical liberal – call them what you will, the CBC doesn't have one – producer on its public affairs staff. If they do have any, they're tucked away in farm programming or serious music, where they have neither the budget nor air time to do any harm. In fact, the CBC has yet to give us a single examination of any issue that is not seen through the lens of what Lionel Trilling called "the adversary culture", which is just about a synonym for the standard left-lib line. TV Ontario, which is the Ontario government's (or rather the Ontario taxpayers') contribution to enlightenment, seems all geared up for the revolution to come. Sometimes as I watch yet *another* TV Ontario program on the horrors of sexual stereotyping or the need to redistribute wealth, I suspect that, having fewer stations and a smaller budget than other broadcasters, TV Ontario is up for the Leftest of All Stations Backpack Award. (It will be neck-and-neck with CBC.) This is fair enough in a private broadcaster, but a bit thick in a fully tax-supported one. Only rarely, in those local stations which rely on direct support from the public, does any deviation from the party line occur. The best example of this is Toronto's CITY, which consistently demonstrates that even with such *a priori* subjects as Native Rights, Homosexuality, and the Energy Problem there may be two sides to be heard. Even three.

Many years later, on reading George Orwell's and Malcolm Muggeridge's accounts of London in the pre-war thirties, I was struck by how much Toronto – and New York – of the late sixties resembled that period. The Canadian media seemed caught in a dizzying love affair with every faddish idea that the vegetarian and sandal-wearing left described by Orwell had embraced. Our media thundered out anti-American, anti-business, anti-free-enterprise diatribes.

I have yet to see any time devoted to any one of a whole

range of subjects in the national press or the CBC, ranging
from South Africa to multinationals, that gave serious consideration to any side of the problem but the standard left-
lib line. This problem does not exist in the U.S. to the same
extent. The U.S. offers comprehensive coverage on most issues, as does England. But in Canada there is a stranglehold
on the media, no less absolute for being unconscious. In fact,
when Henry Champ of the CTV program *W5* dared question,
let alone analyse, the appropriateness of the World Council
of Churches supporting the Rhodesian guerrillas, the CRTC
received fifteen petitions against him, including eleven from
the churches themselves, asking that he be banned, cen-
sured, or forced to apologize.

But in the thirties, the times of Orwell and Muggeridge,
people had some excuse. The ideas of the left were not entirely discredited. The idealistic lure of Marxism was not altogether tarnished. People had not yet had the benefit of the
knowledge that de-Stalinization brought. Such events as the
Berlin Wall, the Cuban missile crisis, the invasion of South
Vietnam and Korea by the North, were all to come. One had
not seen the dreadful collapse of character that democratic
socialism would bring (epitomized in the immortal words of
the English cleaning-staff supervisor on the picket line at
West London Hospital in the 1978 strikes confronting a
frantic husband whose sick wife lay inside: "Why should I
apologize? I'm enjoying myself. I've certainly got no regrets
for what might happen to the patients. That's management's
fault.") One had not heard such voices as those of the Swedish Directorate of Schools' Mrs. Maj Bossom-Nordboe explain: "It's useless to build up individuality, because unless
people learned to adapt themselves to society, they would be
unhappy. Liberty is *not* emphasized. Instead, we talk about
the freedom to give up freedom." Ah yes, "the freedom to
give up freedom". But at the CBC and in the Canadian media
in general, only one set of opinions was acceptable, even
though by the end of the sixties we ought to have learned at
least to give a hearing to another point of view.

But perhaps none of this would have dawned on me, except that after I had refused an assignment to cover the campaign of Pierre Elliott Trudeau during the 1968 election I had time to begin to read again. Cautiously and outside the curriculum. This coincided with a period of mutual unhappiness between the CBC and myself, and so, with Orwell, Camus, and the *actual* works of Marx (rather than commentaries on him), I set off for the States with film director George Bloomfield, who had been hired to direct an American movie. I was a camp-follower, I suppose, but it came at a good time. I was tired. I had been working for some time now and had a good deal of growing up to do. Canada had been good to me and I had come to love it as a sometimes dull, often awkward, but remarkably generous country. Of the United States I knew little. And much of what I thought I knew turned out to be quite wrong.

CHAPTER NINE

Jane Fonda's Headache and Other American Crises

THREE WOMEN. First, Ann-Margret. We drive up to her home at the top of Benedict Canyon, past the mock foliage and the little English street lamps marking the end of each enormous dark driveway, and turn in to the cluster of buildings. "It's the old Humphrey Bogart estate," my boyfriend whispers gleefully, smoothing down his Savile Row casuals and his Los Angeles handbag. Inside, half a dozen people are waiting. Husband Roger Smith walks nervously up and down the foyer, which appears to have been modelled on the proportions of Versailles. He is talking to a huge man called Alan Carr, who is Ann-Margret's agent-cum-manager with Roger. Carr rolls across the room to meet us, three hundred pounds of ebullience. "Welcome, welcome, the drinks are on the sideboard. Everybody help themselves." Everybody, except me, does. The two or three other people waiting for her entrance seem to be television critics or agents or possibly heads of studios. It is hard to tell, but they know everything about the business and are telling all in hushed tones audible in the cottage at the end of the famous Bogart black swimming-pool.

Ann-Margret enters. She has just had a bath and washed her hair and is in a bathrobe sashed loosely at the waist. I

long to take a bath immediately and sash a terry-towel bathrobe at the waist. Except I know that it will not look the
same. It is clear that everyone in the room suddenly feels
very grubby and wants to take a bath. Her face is scrubbed
absolutely clean, her hair is soaking wet and revealed to be
short and red and barely there, and she is really not very tall,
and the room is mesmerized by her presence. She falls to the
floor on her knees. I wonder if this is a Hollywood cult, because suddenly everyone is falling to the floor on their
knees. I remember the week before when my boyfriend and
I went down to the Hare Krishna Temple on La Cienaga
Boulevard with Alan Alda and his wife because I wanted to
check into the financial background of cults (I was beginning
to think about freelance journalism) and suddenly I see the
derrière of Alda in front of me bobbing up and down together with his wife Arlene's, and I realize we are all about to
dance and pray and knock our temples against the floor, and
frankly I'm not sure if journalism is worth it.

Still, I sink to the floor in Ann-Margret's den and then,
thank god, I see that we are all on comfy pillows or low furniture in order to watch the screen which is descending at
one end of the room to preview her upcoming television special. There is absolute silence in the room for the entire program in which Ann-Margret sings, dances, and speaks (a little). She is a superb performer: her sense of timing is
exquisite. First, twenty-eight boys come out and dance as if
the Queen of the Willis were the director. They spin and
click their heels and jump and twirl on the floor and keep
smiling and go on for six minutes or so, and then they part
to each side of the set pointing towards heaven and Ann-
Margret appears between them to thunderous applause.

At the end of the special the screen rolls back up and the
lights go on and we applaud as thunderously as six people
can. Ann-Margret smiles and looks even further down towards the floor. Her little-girl voice is perfectly sincere: "I
only hope," she says, "that I will have pleased America." She
means it. Then she smiles, talks briefly, and goes to bed. She
has a dance class at eight in the morning, a Vegas act to get

ready, and a movie starting to shoot in a week. That little-girl voice is coming out of a cast-iron moulding. Roger Smith and Alan Carr back out of the room as she leaves, begging her not to exhaust herself. Sweetly she smiles and says tomorrow she'd like to talk over "certain business things". They look terrified. She is feminine and beautiful and a sex symbol, and every man in that room is working for her, on her payroll, or dying to be.

(2) Marlo Thomas: On the windy New York Street Marlo is getting ready for a scene in the film *Jenny*. She is supposed to be pregnant and distraught. Marlo is hoping this film will finish soon because she wants to commission Gloria Steinem to do a script for her about a Real Woman. Soon Marlo will be very active in the women's movement. Meanwhile, my boyfriend the director is calling for her on location, and the hairdresser and the make-up lady she brought to New York with her from Los Angeles (it's part of her contract) have not finished with her appearance. The director explains that it is no use doing all that to her hair because it is very windy and everyone else's hair will be blowing. Marlo doesn't care. She has the hairdresser hold her hair in place till they get her in position, and spray it down like rolls of wire, and then just as the director yells "Action" the hairdresser springs out of the scene. Her hair blows everywhere and they do it all over again.

Marlo has just ended her long-time television series *That Girl* and is still in her wholesome all-American frame of mind. For the film she has made a major concession after some pleading by the director and producer. She has abandoned her bangs and allowed her hair to be teased back off her forehead. The writer is frantically trying to inject some oomph into Marlo's part. "You know," says co-writer Martin Lavut of Toronto, "I think she could be a really groovy chick." He has an idea for a scene in which the eight-months-pregnant Marlo will be accosted by a lonely middle-aged salesman in a New York convention hotel. The salesman will be very kind and sweet and Marlo will feel very sorry for him as he spills out all his troubles to her. Then she will go up to his room with him – where he will spread cream cheese on her tummy. Marlo is deeply disturbed. "Go up to his room? I can't go up to a *room* with a man," she says. "What would my fans think? Couldn't we do the cream-cheese bit on my tummy in the lobby?"

The script with Gloria Steinem falls through but Marlo does become very involved in the ERA movement. "It's the most important thing there is for both the men and women of the U.S.A.," she says, bringing Shaw's remark about America to mind. Bernard Shaw, who did not know Marlo Thomas, once described America as a country that moved from barbarism to decadence without an intervening period of civilization. Marlo evolves from Doris Day to Gloria Steinem in much the same way.

(3) Strange, now I can't remember her name. She lived in a small one-bedroom apartment in a very modest area of Los Angeles and she had a job as a receptionist in some nondescript office. Real estate or insurance. Her apartment was crammed with mementos, though, all over the walls and inside the big trunk. She had been a bullfighter, one of the first – she thinks she was the first – female Americans to fight in Mexico. She still had the ears and a tail. "Look," she says, holding them up, "you see. I got them given to me." They are horrid, dried-up, pale-brown pieces of something. But she is so proud that I hold them with much awe. It is an achievement, measured tangibly, that few of us will match.

She has been gored very badly and she shows me some of the scars running bright red down her pale belly and side and legs. "Afterwards you have to go back in the ring at least once," she explains. She talks very quietly and not easily. But she is very pleased to show all these things – the cape, the sword, the hat, the write-up in *Life*, and finally the book. "They wrote a book about me," she says. I look at it. "It's not about you," I say, "it's *by* you. An autobiography." She shrugs. "I can't write. A man came and asked me questions and took notes and he wrote it."

I am to do an interview with her for the CBC radio *Matinee* show. I put my little cassette recorder on the table and try. But she can't answer questions and the day ends with very little on the tape except the questions and pauses where she has nodded. I take her book home with me. Next day I have her read underlined passages from the book in answer to my questions. She reads hesitatingly and it sounds perfectly natural. I know they will like it very much in Toronto. I tell her she will be sent an honorarium and she is very happy because money is a little tight at the moment. I ask her about the women's movement and she doesn't know exactly what it is. "Is it to get more women in bullfighting?" she asks. I want to say yes, but then I remember that most of the libbers I have met think bullfighting is a cruel, bloodthirsty sport, and that seems a cruel thing to say to the gored lady in the one-bedroom apartment with her scrapbooks, two ears, and a tail. So I smile and get ready to leave. She asks only one question: "Did you get to read about going back in the ring afterwards at least once so you're not afraid?" Yes, I reply. "That's why you fight bulls, you see," she says.

Ann-Margret, Marlo Thomas, the lady bullfighter: I have never been in a country of such extraordinary contrasts. Not disparity. Contrasts. In New York I hover around Fifth Avenue and watch the new black upper-middle class in Bendel's buying furs and jewellery with the same taste and glee as the new white upper-middle class. They recognize one another, trade fashion names and tips, and meet on the pages of *Women's Wear Daily*. A good friend in those days, Marlene Clark, a black girl married then to actor Billy Dee Williams, lives with him in a one-room walk-up on Broadway. The two of them have an expensive answering service and the largest empire of cockroaches to be found in the city. One day Marlene goes to an audition and everyone is excited when she walks in, slim, full-breasted, high-cheekboned, a presence that knocks the director out of his current girlfriend's clutches. Marlene sits down to read, puts the script on the table in front of the director, shrugs off the crocheted suede jacket she scrimped to get on sale at Bendel's, and opens the script. Three large black cockroaches walk out of the pages towards the director. He screams and runs out. "I have never been so embarrassed," weeps Marlene in our living-room.

Our cleaning lady comes from Harlem. She comes to the residential hotel we live in called the Hyde Park on Madison and 77th Street. Every other day she insists on changing the toilet-paper rolls. I have not yet learned how to cope with help – have never had it before – and I don't want to offend her. She is stealing the toilet paper from the hotel and she is doing it for us. At the end of two weeks I have run out of space in my bedroom drawers for the unused rolls she proudly gives me. Soon I start putting them in the suitcases under the bed. At the end of two months I change cleaning ladies. It is cruel and cowardly and I give her two weeks' pay, but I can't cope with all the toilet paper.

Before she goes we talk about the economics of her situation. She is drawing unemployment as well as the money I pay her – which is a cash payment, not taxed. Life is not easy for her, with three children and no husband, but she is paying a rent that would get her an apartment in Queens – a far better district than where she lives. I ask her if they would rent to her there. "Oh yes," she replies. But she doesn't want to leave her friends, the people who give her support, and the neighbourhood she has known. The journey to work, since she lives way uptown, would be about the same if she uses the 59th Street bus. I ask her if it would not be good for her children and she acknowledges that the schools would be better. I don't know if she is typical. It is not until I am in Newfoundland that I encounter this attitude again – people who could make better lives for themselves, and especially for their children, if they would only move to where the better jobs and housing are. But they won't.

I remember my stepfather and my mother. My stepfather never got to own racehorses or design tall buildings, and my mother never did get diamonds or a mink. But in the course of twenty years in Canada they managed, largely by their willingness to move on to the next city and the next job, to achieve a pleasant, comfortable existence. My half-brothers would have the university education that eluded their father, and my mother would ski, sail, and holiday under circumstances that would have been quite beyond her husband's reach had he stayed in England – or Hamilton, or Niagara Falls, or Montreal, and so on – among his friends, his neighbourhood, and the people who loved him. Like hunters, sharecroppers, pioneers, explorers, they went to where the game, the jobs, the opportunities were. All they asked for was the freedom to do so. They never expected to have their chances brought to them at public expense.

But it is in Los Angeles, sitting around the swimming-pool on a bleaching hot day, that my perceptions begin to crystallize and take shape. It is May 4, 1970. I am lying in the sun next to the pool at the Sunset Marquis Hotel off the strip. It is not idle luxury: artists wait here for work like longshoremen before the Union Hall in San Francisco. Everyone on the way up – or down – stays at the Sunset Marquis once. Screenwriters like Frank and Eleanor Perry, directors like Jacques Cousteau; old actors live here, like Van Heflin (till he died), and new ones, like Tiny Tim (till he went broke). There are always sort-of-famous people here who have just split from spouses and taken up in the Sunset Marquis. There are paranoid film people waiting for a call about that big new project, and they can always see a cameraman – if they're a cameraman – or another director – if they're a director – in the room across the way who is on the phone probably to the head of the goddam project they are waiting to hear about.

I had spent the evening before with pop singer Joe Cocker, who was on tour with his entourage and would come and sit outside our room and play his tape deck endlessly, asking "Does it sound all right?" He was a shy boy and he kept saying that he didn't understand America, it was really "weird". I felt very North American next to his British confusion. "No," I replied, "they're really very easy people."

Now I listened to the radio on the patio between my chaise longue and the blonde girl all greased up next to me and wondered what the hell was going on. Everyone was listening suddenly. The small talk had stopped. The radio was announcing a riot at Kent State University in which four students had been shot to death. The tanned, white-whiskered man who was always talking about the Hollywood Ten started crying. Great big tears rolled down his cheeks, and his large torso with the golden chain was shaking. I was horrified. Four students dead. Was America living by the rule of the Wild West again? I went back to my room and began to think.

I do not know what happened on that day in Kent State University. After reading Michener's book, the Justice Department's investigation, and a considerable amount of other material, I am inclined to think that a nervous, inexperienced group of guardsmen pulled triggers when there was no need. It was a terrible tragedy, a waste of four lives that had every right to expect protection from a system based on the rule of law. They even had a right to expect sane, appropriate responses to students' mild infractions of the law. But what astonished me was that the very proper outrage over Kent State was coupled with the most improper silence on far more extensive – if not as dramatic – events that had been taking place on campuses all across America. Events we all knew about. For several years a consistent pattern of intimidation by left-wing groups in the name of all sorts of causes had been practised on faculty and, most especially, on uncommitted or conservative students. In Stanford, for example, the situation had peaked with the discovery of a cache of stolen bicycles and a truck loading them up from the Chicano House on the campus. When an investigation was carried out, the Chicanos cried "racism" in an article published in the student newspaper, and the administration was mau-maued into refraining from pressing charges. At the same university the conservative Free Campus Movement (FCM) was fire-bombed and attacked time after time. The FCM had hit upon the tactic of photographing any incidents of looting or assault and using the photos to force the administration into taking action. This particular bit of activism drew the wrath of the leftists, who indicated their disapproval by shooting at unarmed club members and wounding two of them, as well as smashing a few heads. The incident was noted on the inside pages of the student newspaper. At the university's clinic the nurses and doctors bandaged the FCM's and treated them with much sympathy – thinking they were victims of police brutality. When the error was noted, doctors and nurses finished their bandaging in silence and walked away in cold disapproval.

"I learned a lot about my liberal friends and colleagues," says Dr. John Bunzel of the Hoover Institution at Stanford University, a man who was featured on the front page of the *New York Times* in 1969 as "the moderate" and crowned "the liberal in the middle" in the NBC special "What Happened at San Francisco State?" Bunzel, a Democrat, was Chairman of the Department of Political Science at San Francisco State in the late sixties, on a campus that had all the black-power heavies before they made it to national prominence – Eldridge Cleaver, Huey Newton, Stokely Carmichael. "Our campus was literally hijacked by the Black Students' Union," says Bunzel with a rueful air. Bunzel made the unusual decision to remain a liberal in a period when most were quickly converting to a voguish radicalism or keeping very quiet.

On November 5, 1968, the Black Students' Union (BSU) made public a list of ten non-negotiable demands. Two days later the Third World Liberation Front (TWLF) added five more similar ones. The University offered to discuss the demands with the students, but was refused. They were "non-negotiable". The demands included one that the college accept all blacks who might apply for admission in fall, 1969, without regard to their academic qualifications, and another that a black-studies department be established at once with twenty full-time faculty members independent of college authority. The black studies the group intended to teach were spelled out quite clearly in a meeting between Stokely Carmichael and the BSU and the TWLF. It was to be revolutionary black nationalism taught *to* blacks exclusively *by* blacks in order to help them go back to their communities and organize the black revolution.

This was too much for liberal Bunzel. He wrote an article for Irving Kristol's magazine *The Public Interest* criticizing the content – not the idea – of this approach to black studies. As a result Bunzel was labelled The Enemy by what he describes as "the avenging furies of the left". A bomb, still ticking, was found early one morning outside his office door. His car tires were slashed. The graffiti on his car read "Fascist scab". Disrupted classes and round-the-clock police security became part of Bunzel's life. "My liberal friends said, 'Stick with it, Jack, we're with you,' and I said, 'Hell, why don't you *do* something, sign a petition'; but they'd just slip away. But you learned certain things from it. I learned very quickly the difference between being afraid and allowing myself to be intimidated."

Not everyone did. From Columbia to Berkeley the intimidation of the majority of apolitical students by the radical-left Students for a Democratic Society, the Weathermen, and various black groups became routine. The radicals no longer bothered to cloak their intimidation in pacifist rhetoric. At Harvard, writes democratic socialist and activist Steven Knelman in his book *Push Comes to Shove*, students signed the anti-war petitions and became on-the-spot radicals as the unmistakable odour of violence enhanced the smell of grass and granola. According to Knelman, it was a case of radicalize or else. Knelman's examples included the blond-haired and bronzed surfer caught in the unlikely act of signing a Negotiation Now petition who explained: "Fuck, man, I just don't want to get my ass blown off, not for nobody. That's all."

The heroes of the left became not only the foreign terrorists in national liberation movements far away – the "correct" national liberations, of course, not Croatia or Latvia or Tibet or the Ukraine – but home-grown ones like Dwight and Karleton Armstrong, whose bombing of the University of Wisconsin physics lab killed one researcher and injured three other people. Professors were harassed, and sometimes beaten, if their views were disliked by the left. This

happened from Eysenck at the University of London to
Teller at Berkeley to Edward Banfield at Harvard. The Chicago Seven were heroes touring the country as media stars,
advocating theft and violence. Yippie leader Jerry Rubin
would later confess that he was drawn to the movement because of the sex, publicity, and money. "During the five-and-
a-half-month trial [for conspiracy to riot in Chicago]," he
wrote, "I agreed more with the government's analysis of our
behavior than with our defense. The government held us responsible for what happened in Chicago. Our defense saw
us primarily as victims." Still, the Chicago Seven were acquitted of the charge of conspiracy. Bobby Seale tried to sabotage due process and the rule of law by yelling obscenities
during the Chicago trial or hurling himself (and any handy
furniture) about the courtroom. After he was gagged and
chained to enable him to be present at his own trial instead
of being removed from the courtroom, these measures were
depicted as "victimization". And as students across America
closed down classes, bombed buildings, looted and ram-
paged like Nazi thugs (and shed crocodile tears over the
tragic victims of the intemperate police response they had
deliberately provoked in their "politics of confrontation"),
the small-l liberals made cowering noises.

"Basically," says Bunzel, "my argument was that if the university had been attacked by the right-wing from off campus
the faculty was perfectly prepared to stand up and unite.
But once there is an attack from the left, the moderate liberal ranks split within the academic community and become
fractionated." Or paralysed at the prospect of taking a stand
against any indignity originating from the left.

Together with the phrase "black power", the words "racist" and "fascist" would be thrown about by the left with a
promiscuity that made the late witch-hunting Senator from
Wisconsin seem almost benign. In Canada, American draft-
dodgers became local heroes. It seemed to me at one point
that every public affairs television show at the CBC and every
magazine had its favourite draft-dodger to interview and
profile about the "difficulties" encountered in making the

courageous flight to the Bloor Street Siberia of Toronto. And while I personally thought the U.S. involvement in the Vietnam War was a mistake, I had little sympathy or respect for draft-dodgers. I had much of both for the draft-*resisters* who stayed behind in the United States serving prison sentences. It wasn't that I had any illusions about myself. In the same situation I would probably have sneaked off in the night and escaped to Kuala Lumpur if necessary, rather than pay the price of my ideals. But I wouldn't have expected to be admired for it. I found it unlikely that I'd be on the various media cocktail circuits discussing my sneaking across an unguarded border as some sort of brave political act, standing tall in my denims and Viet Cong mock-up, being lionized by Canada's journalism set as I heaped abuse on the fascist regime in America.

Ah, Canada. The mindless anti-Americanism that had become so fashionable among the cliques of left-wing intelligentsia that ran such publications as *The Canadian Forum*, or formed committees to protect the resources – both natural and urban – that we would never risk developing, had a field day with the mindless rhetoric of the left. (A telling anecdote comes from Harvey Kalles, a Toronto real estate man who as a beginner managed to get his hands on a block of land at Toronto's Bay and Bloor streets. "It was in the fifties," says Kalles today with much regret, "and I couldn't get a Canadian to put a penny into developing it. They were putting their money into the States. Finally we lost it. We couldn't hang onto it, and some Swiss and American investors were ready to take the risk. Today that may be the richest piece of real estate in Canada.") At the CBC program I worked on we paid routine obeisance (and honorariums) to Stokely Carmichael, Jerry Rubin, Rap Brown, or whoever we could get to come and lecture us on the oppression south of the 49th parallel. We did not try to get interviewers that could challenge them. We had mass love-ins, courtesy of the Canadian taxpayer. Our media seemed to lament only that we ourselves had little slavery and discrimination in our past, or that we lacked the political astigmatism that involved America in a war against her own strategic interest. If anything, in true Canadian fashion, we were even jealous of American guilt.

We did our best, though, under these trying and competitive circumstances. We rediscovered our native peoples, drew all the wrong conclusions from their conditions, and tried accusing ourselves of at least small-scale genocide. Peter Gzowski took an appalling but isolated incident in North Battleford, Saskatchewan, in which an Indian was murdered by a middle-class gang of white thugs, and wrote a moving but quite-beside-the-point article which claimed with a hopeful note: "This is Canada's Alabama. In the next few years we may have there, on a lesser scale, what the U.S. has had in the past few years in the South." Canadian writers like Heather Robertson and Harold Cardinal rose to success thanks to best-selling books aimed at white guilt. And, as the seventies moved on, we would resurrect the spectre of racism and fascism. Only this time those who yelled "racist" the loudest would have more in common with the Third Reich than with the eminently respectable and concerned victims of the remarks.

In the States, meanwhile, some of my most cherished prejudices were breaking down under the sheer weight of empirical evidence and personal experience. The Watts ghetto in Los Angeles was not a hellhole of rat-infested tenements but a perfectly standard lower-middle-class community of blacks with most homes well kept – and some homes disastrously run down. Looking for an apartment in L.A. for a black girlfriend and her man revealed that blacks could rent in virtually all areas if, like whites, they had the money and a job. Nor were jobs hard to get for those who would match their expectations to their qualifications. Poverty in *urban* America – I have never seen rural Appalachia or sharecropper Mississippi – seemed a misnomer to me. How could poverty mean families with television sets, cars, and money for the numbers game? Surely people were free to choose whether to spend their income on luxury consumer appliances, liquor, drugs, or food? How could this be compared to the frightening hardships which faced the involuntary poor, like many of the elderly? How could unemployment mean an illiterate and belligerent youth refusing to take a delivery job on account of "Man, I don't have to do that crap," as one said so eloquently to the manager of the First Avenue D'Agostino's store where I grocery-shopped in Manhattan. What sort of insult was the left dishing out to the vast majority of working-class blacks who managed to survive their economic and social status without mugging and raping, when left-wingers called violence an *inevitable* by-product of a racist society, and practically exhorted black youths to prove them right at the cost of ruining their own lives.

Friends of ours had their children in an uptown public school in Manhattan where most of the youngsters were Hispanic or black. The friend, Trevor Williams, a brilliant set-designer who worked for the CBC and went on to design and produce films in the U.S., shunted his relentlessly blond and blue-eyed children from school to school each time he did a new project or film. One of the children was a thalidomide child, bright, sensitive, and with an arm that ended in a flipper at the shoulder. The child would go from elementary school in Manhattan to the Bahamas, taking the new taunts and new environment in his stride. Only in Spanish Harlem did his parents have to be sure that he had "muggers' money" in his pocket.

"Otherwise," said his father, "he'd fight the kids with his steel arm and claw and they wouldn't have a chance." But 99.9 per cent of the school left the little Williams children alone. What kind of an insult was it to all those street-wise kids to say that the 0.1 per cent trouble-makers "couldn't help" being criminals?

But America was not asking these questions. At least not mainstream America or policy America. Money was being pumped into programs that perpetuated the idea that people were not responsible in any way for their own behaviour. It was all society's fault. No one was in the streets protesting the dawn of the moral relativism that was to shine so brightly in the sixties: violence by the Viet Cong was OK because, even though they had invaded the South, they were progressive. Self-defence by the South was not OK because they were capitalistic and corrupt. No one in the streets was carrying signs suggesting a pox on both your houses.

So there they were, lined up in the streets of America, the anti-war demonstrators watched suspiciously by grim-eyed police and occasionally attacked by rabid groups of hardhats. Or sometimes it was the tea-party revolution set, like aristocratic John V. Lindsay, Mayor of New York, taking his celebrated walks down a pedestrianized Madison Avenue and a security-swept 125th Street to "meet the people", while aides and agents ran cover around him as he strolled into the Pierre Balmain shop to buy some ties.

The anti-war movement brushed my life three times and left no mark. Once in Los Angeles with actor Alan Alda and his wife, we met on the streets a long, winding column of students and plump, happy, middle-aged men and women; the men all holding very moistly the hands of stringy-haired braless peaceniks, and their wives reaching out with smiles for the hands of shirtless, bearded fellows with tight-tight jeans and the glazed look of dopers. We joined that long, winding column, the Aldas, my boyfriend the director, and I, he in standard tie-dyed blue safari suit and omnipresent handbag now tucked into his waistband, and I in an expensive combination of Bloomingdale's casual and L.A. funky. Perhaps my concern for or attention to what we wore indicated an exclusively personal shortcoming. I think not. In all the rap sessions around L.A. I have never heard more attention being paid to anything, apart from the next demonstration, than the swopping of expertise on where to get the tightest jeans or how best to dye them.

The line wove around City Hall in downtown L.A. whining monotonously "All we are asking is, give peace a chance. All we are asking is, give peace a chance." I recognized the Jewish trombonist who was living down the strip from the Sunset Marquis. He was trying to pass himself off as black because the anti-Zionist imperialist number was getting "very heavy", but meanwhile he had to borrow my bonnet hair-dryer to keep redoing his Afro, since the salons hadn't yet got into the Afro perm business.

The second time I was preparing breakfast in our apartment on East 57th Street, just up from Sutton Place and the hidden townhouses of the truly rich, like Onassis and his entourage. Jane Fonda was sitting in our rented furnished apartment waiting for the croissants to warm up and the orange juice to be freshly squeezed. I kept sneaking looks at her from the kitchen. She was quite lovely, fresh-looking and with a voice as throaty and coloured as it sounded on screen. Her manner was warm and generous. There was nothing shrill or polemical about her. Briefly she discussed the kind of scripts she was interested in doing. They sounded much like the kind of script every actress from Ellen Burstyn to Ruth Gordon wants to do: "A real role that cares about what a woman really is . . . or something like that," the key question being, of course, how the individual woman sees the generic woman.

Suddenly the flow of conversation was broken. Fonda had asked a question. A political question about Canada. My boyfriend was nonplussed. His interests did not extend to Canadian politics, except, perhaps, to who would be running the Film Development Corporation. "The War Measures Act," Fonda was saying, "that Trudeau has just passed. Do you understand what that means?" My boyfriend looked towards me in the kitchen. I did not understand what it meant. The Act had been imposed very recently and I had absolutely no idea whether it had been legitimately invoked. The true situation in Quebec was about the last thing I could comment on. However, Miss Fonda's question appeared to be rhetorical. "Trudeau is a fascist," she remarked, biting into the croissant. "Canada has become a totalitarian country. It's terrible. They're rounding up political prisoners and throwing them into jail without trial. God, who would have believed it could happen in Canada. You're worse than the States."

Later on I would agree with her in aspects that would simply be beyond her comprehension, but in so far as her specific charges went, what nationalistic feelings and common sense I had rose to the surface. I protested. We simply didn't know what was going on yet. Kidnap and murder were involved. Bombs in letterboxes. Canada was not "a totalitarian country". I kept squeezing the orange juice. Fonda complained she had a headache.

Eager to steer the subject away from the murky land of Trudeau's record as a war criminal in Vietnam, which was beginning to be exposed in the apartment on East 57th Street, I offered Miss Fonda some 222's. They were taken, and fifteen minutes later a serene Jane asked me with some eagerness just what I had given her. "Codeine," I replied, "with acetacylic acid. It's available over the counter in Canada." Wonders. It turned out Miss Fonda was off to Montreal to give a speech at some university or other, hence her vital interest in linking Trudeau and the War Measures Act to the spirit of repression that was behind the Vietnam War, and if I would just write down the name of the pills she would pick up a bottle or two in Montreal.

It was about a week or so later that I read in the newspapers that Miss Fonda had been arrested at an American airport on her return from Canada for attempting to transport narcotics into the U.S.A. The "narcotics" turned out to be the 222's which contained codeine, a controlled drug in America. She was released after some discomfort and harassment. I was filled with a warm glow. It was my contribution to the war effort.

The last time was in 1972, in Ottawa. My husband-to-be, George Jonas, and I were on Sparks Street admiring the newly opened Mall. Suddenly a screech of voices, and jeers, and the sound of boots on the asphalt began to fill the affluent air. Up the road a long line of protest marchers appeared, waving placards denouncing the U.S. incursion into Cambodia, praising the peace-loving Chinese, the peace-loving Viet Cong, the peace-loving Cambodians, and demanding an end to U.S. imperialism. By now I loathed the sight of pretend-moralists of all placards and no brains latching on to second-hand causes. By now, whether one approved or disapproved of the war, it was scarcely possible for anyone but an idiot to describe the Viet Cong or the Khmer Rouge as "peace-loving". I turned my back on the demonstrators but Jonas was gone. His face bright with enthusiasm, he stood in the middle of their path. As they were cautiously winding their way around him, he jumped in front of one of them, a weedy-looking youth with a large placard that read "Kill the fascist-imperialist Pigs". Jonas smiled. "Here I am," he said to the youth, who stood looking at him, his jaw still open from chanting "Ho, Ho, Ho Chi Minh". Jonas let his hands fall limply to his side. "Go ahead," he said, blocking the marcher from slipping by, "let's see you kill. Please. I'm an imperialist. I don't like the peace-loving Viet Cong. Put down your placard and kill."

There was a moment's stillness in the cacophony. Terror took hold of the marcher's face. He looked around at his fellow protesters. "He's mad," he said. "He wants to fight." And with a quick, rabbit-like movement he lowered his placard and ran sideways and up Sparks Street.

It took me several minutes to calm Jonas down. "Stop treating me like one of your Hollywood actors," he said. "I'm not suffering from dizziness, just disappointment." It took him several days to get over the disappointment. Though the militant left included a few terrorists and thugs, the immense majority were well-fed, well-protected middle-class youngsters, who never really had to face the plain consequences of their slogans. Jonas, who came from Budapest in 1956, always dreamed of finding a left-winger in North America who would be willing to live up to the militancy of his words, not when mobbing a lone liberal school administrator, but in a hand-to-hand encounter with a large, unpleasant Hungarian. "It's a little guerrilla theatre they need," he'd say. He was forever out of luck.

CHAPTER TEN

Quail's Eggs, Red Guard Style

"WE'LL EDIT IN LONDON," said producer Ed Sherick of Palomar Pictures jovially. "We'll edit in London," I replied happily. We had shot the film on Grand Bahama Island for Sherick's New York film company, with my director-boyfriend giving it the required whiff of Canadian content, and now, naturally, we would edit it in London. I had no idea how many government subsidies this qualified us for (three, I think), but it was sufficient to put us into a posh flat on South Street in Mayfair that was, the London agent claimed, the pied-à-terre of the chairman of the Italian Olivetti Company.

The chauffeur announced he had just finished driving for John Schlesinger. "A very nice man," he said, "easygoing, but knows what he wants." I knew what I wanted. To be dropped at Selfridge's or Harrods to pick up fresh salmon, and search for quail's eggs. This seemed to me the ideal set of circumstances for learning how to cook properly and be the compleat hostess, and so I learned. I gave dinner parties for twelve and managed to serve at least four courses. Only rarely was the Charlotte Malenkov less than a roaring success. The masseur came every Thursday, in between pounding the exquisite back of Nureyev and the wealthy one of

Lady Weidenfeld. Walking from room to room in the luxurious apartment overlooking a small square with stone balconies off the master bedroom and the drawing-room, I took to heart my uncle Bernard's dictum: "It is not a question of giving up what we have. We simply want everyone to enjoy our standard." Uncle, I thought, I'm on my way.

Except. Something ominous was afoot in England and all the quail's eggs and Bill Gibb dresses wouldn't drive it away. The chauffeur loathed blacks and his small talk was sprinkled with constant derogatory references to them. The masseur would stay discreetly off the subject, wiping his ex-sailor's hands on a small white towel as he flipped me over on the table, preferring to concentrate on catching a quick glimpse of something and asking regretfully if that was "all" when the routine massage was finished. He was, however, moved to comment one day when he arrived late and perspiring that the "wrong sort" were coming into England cluttering up the streets and making things very unpleasant. The cockney couple who came with the apartment and cleaned it three times a week quickly established that I was not a *bona fide* anything and would barely talk to me at all. Listening to them clean the silver, though, in the kitchen, I could hear them constantly sniffing about "them foreign types" and how the only person who understood it all was Mr. Powell. "Good old Enoch," they would say.

Even over in Maoist Hampstead there were *sotto voce* references made apologetically to the "problems" massive Commonwealth immigration was causing. I thought, naively, that this meant sturdy types from New Zealand and Australia, drinking too much and singing rugby songs and throwing up in the streets. I did not yet know about the official classifications of the British Government Census Office, which had decided to euphemize the whole subject of race and now had blacks classified under the heading of New Commonwealth Citizens. In Golders Green, at the Soviet branch of the family, there was barely disguised glee. "England is turning into a vicious racist society. The workers will unite against it." Except that it was the workers who seemed most "racist" of all, and the Marxist orthodoxy explaining that this was caused by the ruling classes fostering race hatred to divert the attention of the toiling masses from the class conflict sounded pretty thin in England. The "ruling classes" – that is, the government and the media they were supposed to control – did nothing but foster good liberal values day and night. They even legislated them. But the unhappy workers couldn't seem to understand that they ought to be unhappy about the British factory owner rather than the alien customs and culture of their new Commonwealth neighbours. Though all the left-wing members of the National Union of Journalists preached class, it was the *tribe*, which nobody preached, that seemed to be the more jealous master.

By now any semblance of the communist international had evaporated in my family. No more campfire sing-alongs in the dining-room. Brothers and sisters still cared deeply about one another, so their spouses had to be blamed for unspeakable deviations in political thought. Hard-line members of the Moscow–Golders Green faction would not cross the doorstep of the Hampstead Maoists. My grandmother, bewildered by her children's material success and radical views, surveyed the political schism with a small Yiddish moan: "Nu. To this they came? How did I manage to raise *communists?*"

Private – and not so private – conversation was scathing. Much was made of the capitalist spirit of the Maoists by the Soviet faction. After all, my uncle was buying up half of London, it seemed, and then he was hopscotching over to Zurich and Geneva for financial "consultations" afterwards. By the early seventies he owned property all over London, had renovated a country house in Little Tew, Oxfordshire, for his eldest son, and had bought up a corner of a square in Islington in order to provide a pleasant home for his younger socialist-doctor son. His Trotskyist daughter had been established in a correctly "working class" district of London distinguished by the solitary row of renovated town-houses in which she lived, protected from the dilapidated neighbourhood by an iron railing fence.

On the gracious lawns of the Hampstead home the talk about the Moscow wing was equally bitter. "Bloody butchers," said my uncle. "They don't understand the purity of the Chinese or the Chinese sense of morality. The Russians are just a bunch of shitheads, more interested in their country dachas and big cars than the wretched buggers they rule." (It is said, by those who know me, that I get my propensity for always using a swear word where a nice proper noun would do from my uncle.)

Bernard's interest in trade with the communist world had begun soon after the war. It did not begin with China. True, China excited both his imagination and his sympathy. It was a civilization that had suffered, he felt, on a scale barely equalled in history. But at that point the real market for a businessman was China's great ally, the Soviet Union. In 1950 at a dinner that included the then president of the Board of Trade, Harold Wilson, and another couple of prominent Labourites, such as John Silkin, the group made plans to send a trade delegation to Moscow to open up the market. The presence of Joseph Vissarionovich Stalin as head of state didn't seem to dampen their interest. "We didn't know about him then," explains Bernard, "and anyway, we were thinking of how to better everyone through trade."

A lot of people, of course, did know about Stalin very well then and had written to that effect. The record was set down by no lesser ex-idealists than Gide, Silone, Koestler, and Orwell. My uncle was not alone, though, in his wilful blindness. At the end of the war the millions of Russian prisoners of war who were lucky enough to be in the West, including émigré Russians, Ukrainian nationalists, and plain civilians, had been forcibly "repatriated" by the British – with some American acquiescence – and sent back to death and the Gulag. (Some of the most callous accessories to this cold-blooded mass murder, members of the British Home Office and Foreign Office, went on to continue their fine work: Sir Samuel Hoare personally intervened to help the Soviets get back a sixteen-year-old boy who was a civilian and clearly not legally eligible for repatriation. The boy escaped and Hoare decided that it would be dangerous to pursue him further because elements in Britain "might protest". Hoare, fittingly, became a member of the Human Rights Commission of the United Nations. Another high official, who masterminded a good chunk of the return of three million men, women, and children to the camps and death, went on, just as appropriately, to play a major role in a politicized charitable movement.

My uncle, to his credit, sent no one to the Gulag; all he wanted was trade. Of course, history has an unfortunate way of making mincemeat out of those comforting theories that bettering the economic lot of a totalitarian regime will help the people. In this sense it makes no difference whether the "helpful" trade goes on with a right- or a left-wing autocracy – which the liberal press is quick to recognize when the proposed trade is with, say, the one-time Shah of Iran. No progressive intellectual suggests that we should pacify or make more humane the generals of Chile or the apartheiders of South Africa through trade. On the contrary, we are urged to follow a policy of economic sanctions or total boycott – and, often, we do. But this recognition of futility does not extend to the equally inhumane Marxist tyrannies of Africa, or the infinitely worse ones of the Soviet block. In Africa, for instance, we have by the mid-seventies helped to establish a new tribe called the Wa-Benzis in Swahili, after their shiny new Mercedes-Benz automobiles. They are the new socialist-bureaucrat rulers of "developia", whose people continue to do no better economically (and often much more poorly) than in the openly imperialist days of the nineteenth century and who are probably worse off politically.

Meanwhile, in 1950, plans for the British thrust into the Soviet market went ahead. Arrangements were made through Harold Wilson, although it seemed that Wilson preferred all the official contacts on the matter to be made through his special assistant, Marcia Williams, who in 1976 would be christened Lady Fork Bender after her honours-list elevation to Lady Falkender. Wilson asked my uncle, via

Marcia Williams, to draw up a list of names that would be representative of British industry as a whole. At this point Bernard was a joint managing director of Richards' Shops, a chain that sold ladies' goods and lingerie.

In March 1952 Bernard was in Moscow at one of the Soviet-sponsored economic congresses to which sympathetic observers, fellow-travellers, and the committed are invited. It was there that he heard the emotional speech of one Pierre Elliott Trudeau addressing the delegates in what Bernard described as "a torrent that came from his heart, not his head." Remembers my uncle: "It was all about the need for the people in Canada to help the Chinese. And how the poor of the world should work together." His impression of Trudeau? "An obvious dilettante. I was asked to recommend him to the Chinese for a visa there, but I wouldn't because I didn't think he was serious politically." Later on, my uncle revised his account. "I didn't recommend him because I would only recommend people to go into China that I knew. I didn't know him and I couldn't be sure that he would be objectively friendly." Since my uncle used the word "objective" in the sense of scientific socialism – i.e., "subjective" – in his evaluation of Pierre Elliott Trudeau, he made a rare error of judgement. Trudeau would later reveal himself, at least vis-à-vis China, to be either a fellow-traveller or a politician entirely devoid of the constraints of "bourgeois" morality. (The only other alternative is a fool, but since Trudeau is clearly not that, the choices narrow to limits that ought to be acceptable to men like my uncle.)

At the 1952 meeting Bernard's group signed a memorandum of agreement to exchange forty million pounds sterling of trade. It was big money for those days. Now he would concentrate on the needs of China. He would buy steel for them in one country and sell it through another. Planes here and bauxite there. And China's exports – the beautiful rugs, the handicrafts, the mass-produced textiles and cheap clothes – would start to flow to the West. His activities did not endear him to the board of Richards' Shops. "You either work for us or the Communists," said the chairman one day.

The timing of the ultimatum was exquisite. The Chinese had been pressuring him to start a business of his own. And anyway stubbornness is a family trait. "If ever I'm given an ultimatum," claims my uncle, "I go with the 'or'." My uncle's import-export firm was born. For the next dozen or so years much of China's western trade would filter through his firm.

Sitting in the sunshine-flooded dining-room of the Hampstead house I tried to sort it all out. "What about the cultural revolution?" I asked. My uncle had been in Peking at its height. "Exuberance," he replied. "You know the West bloody well exaggerated the whole thing. Mao was only trying to get those damn puffed-up bastards off their asses and back to reality. Trying to prevent what's happening in this blasted country with the fellows in their big offices and lording it over everyone."

The clichés bounced off the cut crystal and the concerned faces; off the Rover cars in the circular driveway in front of the house, the summer home being built in the South of France, the ski holidays in St. Moritz. I tried again to put all this talk about the need for the ruthless bloodshed and philistinism of the Cultural Revolution into some sort of rational framework. "It wouldn't work here, of course," he said. "But we don't need it. Anyway, the Chinese are different." It was an argument I was to hear again and again. I would hear it from respected journalists like Charles Taylor, and from apologist diplomats like Chester Ronning. *You don't understand the Chinese. We do. They are intrinsically different. Your concepts of freedom and individual liberty are meaningless to them. They are beyond that.* Of course, if people had used a similar "intrinsic difference" argument about the blacks of South Africa, the same intellectuals would have cried "racism". I toyed with my leg of lamb.

It was about this time, the beginning of the seventies, that the Chinese vogue began to flourish. The Soviet celebration was on the wane, what with the dissidents, that damn Gulag, and correspondents of the *New York Times* suggesting it wasn't *all* perfect. There was the appearance of Russian soldiers in unlikely places and Euro-Communists being sticky about the way they did things over there. It was time to find a new and better Ideal Society. China loomed – primitive, puritanical, and adorable in plain blue Mao suits. (Bloomingdale's would sell the first batch. I was greatly amused to discover that for a brief while the radical-chic crowd all turned blue after wearing their authentic Chinese outfits. The dye, unfortunately, wasn't fast. For weeks one could recognize members of the radical-chic set on the beaches from the bluish tinge of their skins.) My uncle gave me Edgar Snow's *Red Star Over China* to read, and I synopsized it for my director-friend. That did it. He became a Sinophile. His single goal in life was to make a film of the Long March. (I did not recognize this as an early symptom of CBC-itis.) This seemed like a good idea to everyone, and my uncle got on the phone to his old friend Edgar Snow, who was living in Geneva. My task was to research China.

We returned to Montreal to sort out our financial affairs. China, it seemed, that fall of 1971 was Very Hot. It, as they'd say in Hollywood, had legs. "You want to do a film of the Long March?" said producer Martin Bregman (*Serpico*) to my companion, George Bloomfield. "That's a fantastic idea. Could we shoot it in China and get Chinese co-production money?" I elbowed my boyfriend. "Tell him I don't think so. Not up front."

"OK. OK," said Bregman. "I think we can get development money from the studios. You've got Edgar Snow in this. Can he get Mao to give us the go-ahead?"

"That's what we're hoping," said my boyfriend.

"Well, you've got money from me to do the initial work," said Bregman. "Let me see a treatment *soon!*"

I got down to serious research. From this point on I kept a diary of the events. It tells all about my state of mind.

Monday Aug. 16/71. Returned to Montreal from London clutching two books on China Uncle B. lent me plus a reading list.

Aug. 23/New York. *Great enthusiasm* from Bregman & Co. about China project. They are willing to finance meeting with Snow. I am to go on a weekly salary to prepare research for project. Bloomfield and I somewhat stunned by enthusiasm for what we had considered an impossible project. Must call Bernard when we get back to Montreal.

Aug. 25. Call Bernard's London office. He is still in Cannes.

Aug. 27. Partial success. We get cleaning lady who says Mr. & Mrs. B are on the beach. She will get them. We are to call back in 15 minutes. Great excitement. We replace call and get cleaning lady who couldn't find them. Suggest we call around supper time.

Jubilance. B on phone. Feel as if we've got Mao himself. B promises to have Snow very receptive to phone call from us. Gives us Snow's private home number. I copy it into GB's Mark Cross address book. It displaces David Steinberg and Roger Smith as celebrities under S. Bloomfield begins to visualize himself with megaphone telling 250,000 Chinese to charge bridgehead. I secretly think of intimate evenings with Mao.

Aug. 31. Cable arrives from B. "Snow agrees meeting in Geneva Oct. 20. Am writing." Call friends to drop Edgar's name and trip to Geneva.

Sept. 1. Serious research. I am to get map of China with provinces on it. Bookstore lady says to go to the Automobile Association. Explain we want map of mainland China. She says AA will have best driving map.

28 February 1972
Dear Barbara:
Last December when I spoke to Ed Snow, I suspected the worst. Since then I had been in weekly touch with his wife Lois and whatever could have been done was carried out. Chairman Mao and Chou En Lai sent 3 doctors and 4 nurses to stay with Ed. They were in Geneva 5 weeks on 24 hour duty. Lois was so moved and so grateful, as you can well understand. The Swiss doctors and surgeons who were excellent, showed the Chinese doctors that it would

only be a matter of days, but most impressed by the Chinese method of nursing and said that it saved pain and prolonged life for a while.

R and I went to Geneva for the funeral memorial service. The Chinese Ambassador to Switzerland and entire staff attended. Han Suyin, K. S. Karol and some American writers and doctors paid touching tributes. Ed's son Christopher and daughter Sian – in University of California were model children.

. . . I may be coming your way early April en route to China, but it is possible that I would first go to China. When arrangements are fixed I will of course let you know so that we can meet.

I think politically, artistically and commercially, any good film on China is a potential spinner, so let's think about it seriously. We really must discuss it. I keep coming back to it, because I think it could be terrific.

It was only a few months later that I separated from my boyfriend. I don't know if it was this or Edgar Snow's death that ended his interest in China. Anyway, he went on to make another film – a Canadian love story all about the difficulties of leaving one's husband without alimony. So much for the political, artistic, and commercial potential of The Long March.

There was one footnote. My boyfriend's political consciousness had been raised. Years later he would be chosen to direct the CBC's best left-lib effort of revisionist history: the deification of Louis Riel. Yes, Mao, the best journeys begin with a single step.

CHAPTER ELEVEN

High Marx for the Nanny State

DUES MUST BE PAID. In preceding pages I have made snide remarks about everyone from my own family to my boyfriend, from the film people I met to the CBC executives for whom I worked. It is only fair to say that I was guilty of everything for which I sneer at them – and more. This is scarcely a revelation to anyone who has read this far in my account, but it is necessary, I think, to make the mea culpa unmistakable.

More guilty, I think, because while Bernard was ultimately interested in making money and Bloomfield was basically interested only in making films, I aspired to something higher. I wanted to pontificate on the world – when not hankering after its goods. And by now I no longer had the excuse of naivety or ignorance. Like the New Philosophers of Paris, most aptly summed up in Bernard Henri Levy's book *Barbarism with a Human Face*, I not only ought to have known, but *knew*, the reality of the left. I had read Solzhenitsyn, and before that Camus, Orwell, Silone, and Koestler. Even reading some Gibbon might have been enough, since nothing can demolish the rabid "new" findings of today's ideologues like the historians of yesterday. I *knew* that the world of scientific socialism was awash in blood. And I was beginning to see, even before I read the works of Hayek, von

Mises, Hazlitt, Ravel, and other fine American and European political thinkers, that systems of democratic socialism lead as surely to the spiritual oppression of totalitarian regimes as does tyrannical socialism.

The end of illusion began in fact with the reading of Marx, Engels, and Lenin. For years I had haunted the left-wing bookshops in London, in New York, in Toronto. I had a credible library of theorists ranging from Hungary's Lukacs to America's Marcuse. And ever since the Twentieth Party Congress had revealed the barbaric nature of Stalin's Russia, I had listened to apologists tell me that the tragedy of the Soviet Union was caused by the *corruption* of Marxism. Corruption by Stalin, of course, or at most Lenin, who after all had personally created the dreaded Cheka, the secret police.

It was time for me to go to the sources: Marx, Engels, Lenin. Painfully, ponderously, I ploughed through the books I ought to have read long ago; ideas I had embraced secondhand through commentaries, critiques, and the slogans of the left. The experience numbed me at first and then its implications terrified me. How could so many embrace such open and unambiguous oppression of the human spirit? The Soviet Union was no aberration of Marxism: it was its fulfilment. Indeed, at times I felt as if Stalin represented a humanistic moderation of his masters' views. The classics of scientific socialism depressed me to such an extent that for some time I could quote some of their passages by heart.

"Your bourgeois notions of freedom, culture, law, etc.," said Marx in the *Communist Manifesto*, "are determined by the economical conditions of existence of your class." But if my notions of liberty sprang from the capitalist mode of production and not some eternal verity, I thought, it followed that the Soviet system of the Gulag sprang from the socialist mode of production. If Marx and Engels were right, the communists' ideas of culture – the deadly prose of Pravda, the tendentious, unreadable novels of socialist realism, the mock-heroic paintings, the dreadful revolutionary operas – stemmed inevitably from the abolition of private property, which, according to Marx, was the simplest definition of socialism. And law – if fair jury trials or presumption of innocence were mere conventions of bourgeois enterprise, the secret sessions of kangaroo courts could have not been Stalinist aberrations but the very essence of socialism. And what provisions of the Communist Manifesto did Stalin break? Number 4: "Confiscation of the property of all emigrants and rebels"? Or Number 6: "Centralization of the means of communication and transport in the hands of the State"? Or maybe Number 9: "Combination of agriculture with manufacturing industries; gradual abolition of the distinction between town and country, by a more equable distribution of the population over the country"? It seemed that Marx and Engels would not have been remotely disturbed by such "Stalinist" sins as the forced resettlement of the Volga Germans or the Tartars of Crimea; the murder and imprisonment of millions of "Kulaks", or successful peasants; or the forced and bloody collectivization of agriculture.

I also wondered if the group of Toronto intellectuals who took out a huge ad in the *Globe and Mail* in support of the communist-dominated Armed Forces Movement in Portugal at a crucial moment in the evolution of Portuguese democracy had ever read Marx's *Address to the Communist League*. The *Address* tackles the delicate problem of what to do immediately after bourgeois democrats have tossed out the oppressors. "From the first moment of victory," exhorts Marx, "we must no longer direct our distrust against a beaten enemy, but against our former allies." To keep the revolutionary ball rolling, Marx then encourages excess, vengeance, and brutality, with the proviso that it should be the revolutionary workers who stage-manage the gore. And, as a *coup de grâce* to democracy, Marx urges the workers to exact guarantees from the new government that are so onerous and demanding that they will have to be compromised. "Manifest open distrust of the new government," writes Marx, "and set up a revolutionary workers' Government." Or, run an ad in the *Globe and Mail* in support of the workers' revolutionary councils – no matter what form they happen to take.

More reading. More questions.

What would peace-loving, ivory-tower liberals have said about such pronouncements of Engels as those in his seminal *Anti-Dühring* which mocked those who regard brute force as "absolute evil . . . the original sin"? In fact, according to Engels, force is "in the words of Marx, the midwife of every old society that is pregnant with the new . . . it is the instrument by the aid of which social movement forces its way through and shatters the dead, fossilised, political forms." Lenin himself was particularly taken with this rhapsodic view of force and sneered that while most people only remembered Engels' passage in the same work on the "withering away" of the State, it was the panegyric on violent revolution that was the real grabber. Writes Lenin: "This, of course, 'no one remembers'; to talk or even think of the importance of this idea is not considered good form by contemporary Socialist parties. . . ."

Not good form, indeed, for those who to this day are trying, blindly, desperately, in spite of all available evidence, to reconcile the ideals of ordinary justice, peace, and the rule of law with the ambitions of the militant left. And it is cold comfort to those of us who loathe these parlour socialists that the legacy of Marx and Engels will make sure that, come the revolution, the parlour pinks will be the first lined up against the wall. Or as Engels put it in his own warm way in *Conditions of the Working Class in England*: "the very people who from the 'impartiality' of their superior standpoint, preach to the workers a socialism soaring high above their class interests . . . and tending to reconcile in a higher humanity the interests of both the contending classes – these people are either neophytes, who still have to learn a great deal, or they are the worst enemies of the workers – wolves in sheep's clothing."

But the "neophytes" and "wolves in sheep's clothing" were not deterred – not in the 1970s, writing for the *New York Times*, *The Observer* (to be reprinted in the *Toronto Star*), or *The Canadian Forum*. Why should they be? They were not deterred eighty years earlier, in 1892, when Engels exposed their disguises: "There is indeed 'socialism again in England', and plenty of it – socialism of all shades: socialism conscious and unconscious, socialism prosaic and poetic, socialism of the working class and the middle class, for, verily, that abomination of abominations, socialism, has not only become respectable, but has actually donned evening dress and lounges lazily on drawing room *causeuses*. That shows the incurable fickleness of that terrible despot of 'society', middle-class public opinion, and once more justifies the contempt in which we Socialists of a past generation always held that public opinion." But Engels was not about to throw the baby out with the bath-water. Keeping in mind the CBC-ers of his day, he shrewdly concludes: "At the same time we have no reason to grumble at the symptom itself."

No reason at all. Before communism can come into being in liberal democratic societies, it is first necessary to hammer home certain basic ideas with such consistency that they become accepted without question. Repeat a lie long enough and it will be believed, said one (National) Socialist many years after Marx. Our armchair socialists have by now hammered home with such force the idea that it is man-made injustices *alone* that create disparities in our society that we no longer balk when intellectuals set up committees to regulate and correct these disparities by the force of law. We have long ago abandoned the idea that people may in *any* sense be responsible for their own shortcomings or needs. By now the coercive state, the regulatory mechanisms of democratic socialism – the anti-this board, the review-that board, the control-this committee – are firmly entrenched in all our political parties. Should full-fledged scientific socialism ever come to Canada, it could as easily be under the guise of Joe Clark's Progressive Conservatism as under Communism. The regulatory spirit has become triumphant.

Other left-liberal movements, from peace to civil rights, or from women's lib to the protection of the environment, also followed a pattern outlined by Lenin in such works as *What Is To Be Done?* Peace movements, explained Lenin, are often the "beginning of a protest. . . . It is the duty of all Social-

Democrats to take advantage of this sentiment. They will take the most ardent part in every movement and in every demonstration made on this basis." Lenin goes on to emphasize the necessity for getting his "own Men" inside every organization to stir things up. "We would be Social Democrats only in name (as very often happens) if we failed to realize that our task is to utilize every manifestation of discontent, and to collect and utilize every grain of rudimentary protest." Perhaps, I thought, on reading CLC President Dennis McDermott's anguish over Marxists in the Canadian trade-union movement (and not, I must emphasize, knowing to what degree Marxist-Leninists have infiltrated the unions), perhaps he's been reading the source material and knows it's a question not of *numbers* but of tactics.

But it was in Lenin's *Socialism and War* that I discovered what seems to be the handbook of our most respectable left-libbers – particularly in their curious dichotomy of standards for such problems as separatism in Canada or third-world nationalism. It has always seemed strange to me that the principle of self-determination for the French in Quebec or the blacks in Africa – at the expense of immigrant groups or other tribes among them – is enthusiastically embraced by progressive social democrats, but is a principle that is viciously denounced when it emerges in the form of a Canada for the white liberal culture. But Lenin understood. He carefully outlined the proper course for left-libbers to take in such situations as, say, the separatist movement in Quebec.

English- and French-speaking activists were to have slightly different roles – in practice this is followed far more closely by English fellow-travellers than by French. The Anglo-Canadians, being members of the *oppressing* country, should, according to Lenin, "recognize and defend the right of the oppressed nations to self-determination in the political sense of the word." But not so the fellow-travellers in the oppressed group. They should "unequivocally fight for complete unity of the *workers* of both the oppressed and oppressor nationalities. . . . The idea of a lawful separation between one nationality and the other (the so-called 'national cultural autonomy' of Bauer and Renner) is a reactionary idea."

It is interesting to note how two Canadian left-libbers from the same political cradle, Trudeau and *séparatiste* premier René Lévesque, have been playing their various roles according to the first *and* second paragraphs of Lenin's dictum – unconsciously, no doubt.

Such tactics sound like the blueprint for such extraordinary writings as Professor Stephen Clarkson's introduction to the University of Toronto Press's book on the Déné nation entitled *Déné Nation: The Colony Within*. In his introduction, Clarkson, who would no doubt consider himself a supporter of parliamentary democracy – or maybe not, by now – argues the case for a separate and independent Déné nation to be carved out of a chunk of Canada.

True, he qualifies this scheme as one that should be worked out within Confederation. But this book, to which Clarkson gives his "explicit support", destroys Confederation as any of us understand it. Perhaps if the term "sovereignty-association" had been more current at the time of its writing (1977), Clarkson and Professor Mel Watkins, who edited the book, would have used it instead.

Says Professor Clarkson in his introduction: "The aboriginal right to self-determination claimed by the Déné is a universal human right; Canadians must therefore accommodate these demands within Confederation."

Says Professor Watkins: "The Déné have recognized the extent to which they have become a colonized people and they have begun to move down the long and difficult road to decolonize themselves. In their striving for liberation, they have understandably found sustenance in the increasingly successful struggles of colonized peoples elsewhere in the world."

What amazed me was not only how it was invariably the most extreme, inhuman, and cynical of contemporary leftist positions that seemed to resemble most closely the classics of Marxism – though I admit that it shocked me, indicating that at the time I must still have had some illusions left. But my real surprise was how precisely Marx, Engels, and Lenin predicted the views and actions of the *non*-communist left around me. It was almost as if those writers, activists, teachers, and students were following a prescription, a reflex that seemed truly knee-jerk, even while being ridiculed for it by their Marxist puppeteers from the grave.

But mainly I understood from the views of Watkins and Clarkson, along with most of Canada's "liberal" intelligentsia, that there could be no painless, democratic, liberal route to socialism. The *degree* of repression might, of course, vary significantly from time to time and from country to country. The bottom line, however, would always be the same: a coercive State, enforcing its singular idea of virtue in every human sphere. In this, at least, Marx *et al.* seemed absolutely right. And in a curious way their open insistence on coercion – as in the closing lines of the Communist Manifesto – seemed somehow more sympathetic than the hypocritical snivelling of the Western apologists in power from Sweden to England to Canada.

Once people decide that they have come into possession of a formula that enables them to determine what is a "fair" distribution of wealth, the "best" way in which a nation's economy is to be planned, and which individual or group ambition deserves to be elevated into a "historic" or "human" right, it is almost impossible for them not to proceed to regulate their society to correspond to this knowledge. People are good after their own fashion – as the great philosopher Spinoza pointed out in his *Ethics* more than three centuries ago – and they do not, knowingly, withhold that which is fair or deny that which is a right. The only safeguard against people acting (usually rather mercilessly) on what they believe to be the common good is the classic liberal assumption that, the common good being completely unknowable, everyone should be free to act as he pleases within a law that protects his person and property as it protects those of others, and guarantees him no right except life, liberty, and the pursuit of happiness, in return for the same warrant to his fellow citizens.

Even the gentlest, most democratic socialist state cannot be satisfied with this, for it has to plan and direct; fix, distribute, and expropriate; tax, guarantee, stimulate, and educate according to whatever social goals it may set itself from time to time in order to promote what it regards as the public good. Whenever the scales are not evenly balanced – and they never are, at any given moment – the state has to put its own weight on what it deems to be the lighter or more deserving side. If a group or a region is lagging behind, the rest have to be held back. If one side has less, it must be taken from the other. Why? Because a state as such is incapable of generating either wealth or prestige or status or knowledge, and it must do the only thing it can, which is to interfere in its distribution and dissemination.

True, the state may do so with greater (Yugoslavia) or lesser (Albania) efficiency. It may do so corruptly (Hungary) or honestly (Sweden). It may acquire its mandate through guns (China) or even the popular vote (England). It may perform with hysterical tyranny or some civil sophistication. It may try to murder its opponents or merely attempt to re-educate them.

But it cannot do without coercion. It cannot co-exist with liberty.

And why is liberty important? Liberty itself, of course, doesn't solve any of the problems of existence. It doesn't even address itself to their solution. All it does is to leave each person free to find an answer to a pressing human need, lack, or iniquity. It does not attempt to substitute a party's, a dictator's, a saint's, or a philosopher's view for the goodwill and ingenuity of millions of free individuals.

Does liberty have a price? It certainly does. When people are free to act well, they are also free to act badly. When they are free to hold humane and accurate views, they are also free to hold inhuman and stupid opinions. But the safety-net of classical liberalism rests on the not unreasonable belief that free people will act for the good with at least the same frequency as they act for the bad, while excesses of malice and greed can be held in check by ordinary criminal laws guarding citizens against injury, theft, fraud, libel, and the like.

Does liberty *work* better than the planned society? For millennia centralized kingdoms, empires, and religious states have planned diligently for prosperity which eluded them (or was theirs only temporarily as a result of bloody conquest) until the ideals of classic liberalism allowed a small part of the world in which they took hold – North America and Western Europe, mainly – to create undreamed-of riches. Of course, the technological advances of the Industrial Revolution played an immense part in this – but were themselves largely produced by this freedom.

The wealth created by a relatively undirected, uncanonized, untheological, un-feudal, free-trading supply-and-demand economy was, of course, not distributed equally among citizens, but who can deny that it was distributed increasingly more equally – and more equitably – than the wealth of any centrally regulated system, monarchy, or dictatorship, before or since? And while justice in such free societies was far from perfect, who can deny that it was far more perfect than justice meted out in any regulated state?

Socialists who concede this still say that we can't go back to the ideals of the nineteenth or eighteenth century because society has become far too complex for that. Meanwhile, they themselves are going back to systems based on beliefs commonly held in the twelfth century and before. Only they substitute for the divine rights of kings the divine right of the state and its bureaucracies.

Some might say – and many have said, in fact – that the practices of official communism do not discredit theoretical Marxism, but if they did, this would still not discredit the ideals of democratic socialism. People who say this, of course, would be astonished if someone suggested in reply that the practices of Franco or Mussolini had done nothing to discredit the ideals of fascism, but if they had, this would still not have compromised the tribal myths of D'Annunzio or Gobineau. But while one cannot resist such below-the-belt analogies, one need not rely on them to demonstrate the links by which the practices of the Kremlin or the teachings of Marx are tied to even the most idealistic forms of socialism.

There is, of course, a difference between orthodox communists and democratic socialists, but it boils down chiefly to this: the communists are ready to liquidate everyone who stands between them and total power, while the democratic socialists would not go that far. The socialists are asking for a licence (renewable every four years or so) to bring the same coercive state into being that the communists would establish and maintain at the point of a gun. The communists, for their part, find the democratic socialists' preference for the continuing consent of the people they propose to coerce quite ludicrous. They say it's a sign of illogical bourgeois qualms. This may be so, but much as I admire consistency in logic, I would prefer the social democrats if my only choice were between the two. In this world it's only illogical bourgeois qualms that stand between life and death.

Still, both communists and socialists would be as one in disentitling the individual to the "unfair" portion of, not only his property or earnings, but his conscience and opinions. Some examples from socialist England and Sweden – not from the Soviet Union or China – might illustrate the point.

England
- Writing in *The Spectator* recently the Right Honourable Lord George Brown, former Foreign Secretary and Deputy Leader of the Labour party, described the predicament of the dissenting worker in Britain's closed-shop society:

  If a worker – trade union member – were to resist the Union Official or shop steward's call, his union card could be withdrawn. And when it is, the employer will co-operate in the punishment for standing up to be counted by sacking the worker. The government will then further join in by refusing the victimized citizen recourse to Law Court or Industrial Tribunal. Such is the sickening degree of double-talk today – that the resister of disruption becomes labelled as the disrupter and is put beyond the pale of legal protection. You can steal your employer's or your fellow worker's property and yet go to an Industrial Tribunal and, as like as not, be greatly compensated for getting the sack for it. You can poke the foreman in the eye and be similarly rewarded. And if you sleep away the nightshift, the Tribunal will give you tax-free more than you could earn in a couple of years by staying awake. I imagine these things not. All have recently happened. None could have happened without Trade Union, Management, Government and Parliamentary authority.

There is, however, one last avenue of recourse for the British worker. In a number of recent cases where British workers were fired or refused employment because they did not wish to join the union, the European Court made what some observers described as "legal history" by deciding to hear their cases. Essentially the Court was to decide whether the British government's closed-shop policy went against Article II of the European Convention on Human Rights. The Court ruled against the British government. Being an international court, it had no jurisdiction in Britain. But it was a firm rebuke to the democratic-socialist policies that violate the most basic rights of freedom of association.

• At Glasgow University in 1977 a campaign was mounted for amalgamation of the two Students' Unions, one for men and one for women. The student body voted against amalgamation in a recent referendum. They decided, on balance, that they preferred having separate unions. However, the British Equal Opportunities Commission stated that both sexes were being discriminated against by this decision and wrote to the University authorities suggesting the amalgamation would be the best way to bring this "offence" to an end. The Commission offered to back any student who would take the matter to court.

- The fight against private business and the self-employed in Britain is waged with astonishing bureaucratic oppressiveness. Self-employed citizens were recently told that they would be taxed an *additional* 8 per cent of their profits up to £4,900 under a new "Class Four" contribution which would go to support the British pension scheme. However, the self-employed – who already contribute to various social schemes for which they are ineligible – were reminded that they would still not be eligible for benefits. The pamphlet which accompanied the new tax explained: "Class Four contributions will not entitle you to any extra benefit; their purpose is to ensure that the self-employed as a whole pay a fair share of the cost of pensions and other national insurance benefits." Since the self-employed in England have no guaranteed employment, no pension beyond what they provide for themselves, no holiday pay, no sickness or unemployment benefits, etc., this new contribution was seen as a further attempt to eliminate the minuscule number of workers – tradesmen, typists, editors, piano teachers, and so on – who prefer to work for themselves.

- The Capital Transfer Tax in England makes it virtually impossible to pass on a family business, estate, or farm. These tax rates are the highest in the world, the idea being that wealth should not be inherited. (See #3 of the Communist Manifesto.) Similarly, estate duties break up inherited homes. Since most businesses rarely have loose cash around, the high tax most often means the business cannot remain intact. A business worth £100,000 will have to pay nearly £20,000 in tax; on £200,000 more than £105,000 tax has to be paid. If the business is worth £450,000 a tax of nearly £600,000 would be paid, and figures are only this lenient if the transfer is made more than three years before death. If the owner dies unexpectedly, and his business or farm is transferred at death, the rates would be far higher.

- Most serious crimes require intent in order for an individual to be convicted. I may be convicted of speeding without its having to be proved that I *intended* to speed, but in British criminal law I can't be convicted of burglary or murder without its being proved that I intended to do the evil act. However, under the British Race Relations Act of 1977, intent is no longer necessary in order to be convicted of "inciting racial hatred" and being liable for imprisonment of up to fourteen years. It is enough to show that the words or actions were "likely" to incite. The intention of the speaker is of no account. In spite of this, in the first prosecution under the new Race Relations Act, a jury acquitted John Kingsley Read of the charge of inciting racial hatred. Said Judge Neil McKinnon at the conclusion of the trial: "In this England of ours at the moment we are allowed to have our views still, thank goodness – and long may it last." This sentiment was too much for one hundred democratic-socialist Labour MP's, who demanded Judge McKinnon's dismissal.

As to Sweden, the following might be instructive.

- Crime: Since the progressive Swedes have decided that all crime is produced by emotional or environmental causes rather than simply by the deeds of inherently unpleasant individuals, it is a simple extension to conclude from this that the accused is not in possession of his full faculties – or full civil liberties. In Sweden any offence that carries a sentence of one year's imprisonment or more requires a compulsory psychiatric investigation of the *accused* (not the convicted). This may also be invoked where terms of only six months are involved.

- In Sweden all professors at the universities are appointed by the government. In his book *The New Totalitarians*, the London *Observer*'s Scandinavian correspondent, Roland Huntford, wrote: "A professor at Uppsala University once talked very freely to me about political bias in the Swedish academic world. Before he parted, he earnestly requested me not to couple his name with his complaints. 'I'm not a very brave man,' he ended up by saying, 'and my position would be seriously jeopardized if it got about that I had been criticizing the government. You see, I am only a bureaucrat – all Swedish professors are bureaucrats – and I must *not* antagonize my masters. If you want somebody to quote, go to X (mentioning a certain historian), he's not a university man; he's free, the lucky devil.' "

- Swedish law: Except for libel cases the jury system is not used in Sweden. Judges sit alone or with assessors. The defence lawyer is not necessarily there to argue for an acquittal, but to "help" the court. Writes Hartford: "The function of a Swedish court is not to decide whether a suspect is innocent or guilty, but to put evidence on record and decide on a penalty for guilt established by preliminary enquiry. The only alternatives open to a judge are to hand down a sentence or to refrain from delivering judgement." In Hartford's view: "To the Swede, the law is not a protector of the citizen, but an agent of the State." This view seems confirmed by a court official, who told Hartford: "The law is *not* there to protect the individual. I feel that very strongly. It is a norm for civil servants and it has got nothing to do with guaranteeing one's freedom. Somehow it seems *natural* to me that the law is there to put the intentions of the bureaucracy into practice. It never occurred to me until you brought the point up that it was there for the protection of the individual. The whole of my training suggests the opposite." Said Mr. Carl Lidbom, a former judge of appeal, cabinet minister, and social-democratic theoretician: "The purpose of the law is to realize official policy. It is one of the instruments of changing society."

- Swedish education: Mr. Sven Moberg, deputy Minister of Education: "Education is one of the most important agents for changing society. It has been integrated into our scheme for changing society, and its purpose is to turn out the correct kind of person for the new society. The new school rejects individuality, and teaches children to collaborate with others. It rejects competition and teaches cooperation." In a speech touching on the importance of ideology in education, and the necessity of eradicating reactionary tendencies from the schools, Mr. Olof Palme, former Prime Minister, quoted a passage from a textbook that displayed a non-socialist viewpoint. "That book," he said, "had not been investigated by the textbooks commission." The implication was, of course, that if it had been investigated, it would not have appeared in print.

• The oppressive and humiliating nature of the democratic-socialist state does not go unobserved by the people forced to fill out innumerable forms if they wish to leave their jobs, sell their houses, or pick up their milk subsidy for unmarried mothers. But, even in Sweden, a mild public outburst was occasioned by one of the census-takings which, rather than guaranteeing individual anonymity, requested not only name, address, sex, and birthdate, but also the most personal information about state of mind and motivation for occupational choice.

But the intractable problem of social democracy is that it appears to cause character changes that seem virtually impossible to reverse. The Swedes may throw out Olof Palme and the British may wave goodbye to James Callaghan, but most of their social programs will remain intact. The nanny state is addictive. Social democracy, which teaches you that nothing is your fault, *is* more comfortable than liberal democracy, which suggests that you bear a large measure of responsibility for your lot in life. For the Swedes the untranslatable word *trygghet* implies a kind of warm, embracing security that protects the individual from everything that might disturb, or frighten, or penetrate the womb of gentle equilibrium that he has come to expect. No Swedish politician can avoid promising the continuance of *trygghet* if he wishes to survive. And Canadian Conservative leader Joe Clark said, even while criticizing oppressive government, "One of the ironies with which we have to live is that people have become accustomed to a state apparatus." The germ of *trygghet* has crossed into North America.

CHAPTER TWELVE

"Fascist Bitch"

THE MOST BASIC SYMPTOM of the grip of Marx on contemporary Western thought is the laundered lie. In Marxism, I learned, this lie is referred to as "objective truth". Objective truth is an assertion that "serves the needs of the people", whether or not it is in fact true. In the early seventies as I moved steadily into a career in journalism, I would see just to what extent the syndrome of "objective truth" had permeated Canadian "liberal" thought, from the view of the women's movement to the aims of the Human Rights Commissions. Laundered reality to "suit the needs of the people" would become the very ether of Canada by the mid-1970s.

In the winter of 1973 I sat down at my typewriter and bashed out a television game series that was shown on the CTV network. The series, designed to educate consumers as painlessly as possible in the perils of the marketplace, was fairly easy to write, and mind-boggling in the clearance procedures required by its co-sponsor, the federal government's Department of Consumer and Corporate Affairs. For every script I would receive page after page of notes objecting to such details as how to contact the department's complaint bureau.

Memo: Re Show #12. Please delete "Write for advice to Box 99/Ottawa." Replace with: "Write to Box 99/Ottawa for advice."

Somewhere, I thought, there is a real live person making an actual salary doing this. But my job paid rather decently as well, and when the series was over and dutifully translated into French – just in case – I had accumulated enough money to take a gamble on myself. In the spring of 1973 I set about writing my first piece of feature-length journalism.

My decision to move into print was taken after some thought. In television there were at least two or three other people who always came between a writer-interviewer and her views. Television required "punchy", "snappy" footage that would entertain visually. Television producers loathe "talking heads" or any item that is too long or too complicated. ("What you don't understand," I was told later at the CTV network, "is that a viewer can only assimilate one idea per item.") While I wasn't convinced, I didn't wish to fight. Print offered the opportunity of examining issues in some detail and drawing conclusions. And in print there was nothing between myself and the reader except my own limitations.

In the next six years I found myself covering a wide range of subjects, writing articles, columns, book reviews, and news reports. It was the opportunity anyone who has some interest in the condition of society would like: a paid education in contemporary issues and concerns.

But the conclusions were not happy.

I do not think it is too late to save this country from socialism or statism, but it is certainly late in the day. I do believe it may be too late to rescue it from the spiritual and moral bankruptcy into which it has fallen. Bankruptcy, you see, is a delightfully comfortable state once you have declared it. You no longer have to worry about paying debts or evening matters up with creditors. And our legislators have declared moral bankruptcy over and over again. We bully the little villains like South Africa and Taiwan, whose economic patronage we do not need and whose guns are pointed away from us, in order to placate the big villains like China and the Soviet Union. We allow our Prime Minister to declare *a priori* that this country will not take in white refugees should a bloodbath erupt in Rhodesia. We watch our leaders embrace Fidel Castro and simultaneously refuse to take in refugees from the Colonels' Chile. At the United Nations we abstain on tricky resolutions concerning Israel, the PLO, and Zionist "racism". We declare that we will not be victims of blackmail and will move our embassy from Tel Aviv to Jerusalem – which nobody was particularly fussing about anyway – and then, having brought the fuss upon ourselves, promptly get fussed and blackmailed into remaining in Tel Aviv. At home we condone illegal actions by our police and propose new laws to aid them in further eavesdropping and regulating the private lives of citizens. And worst of all, having revealed ourselves as the masters of pragmatic politics, we insist on clothing ourselves in virtue and describing these actions as the stance of a moral leader of the West.

My own allegiance is to a liberal democracy which sets the commendable goal of equality of opportunity for all. What I see in Canada is a country that has all but rejected liberal democracy in favour of social democracy; a country that no longer believes in the goal of equality of opportunity for all, but only in special privileges for some. It is a country held hostage by small cartels of special-interest groups who have seized on certain popular buzz-words to justify their intolerance and their special demands.

It is also a country that has been very good to me. I happen to be a *woman* – which is In, in itself. I also happen to be tall and considered shapely and attractive, and that makes me "very merchandisable" – as one agent put it. I may have shuddered at the phrase but how can I deny that this "packaging" has made my "right-wing" views not only forgivable but intriguing – and given me access to forums that would be closed to those of similar views but more standard appearance. I can exist quite comfortably while being described as "the red-neck in a Givenchy dress", a phrase that Alan Edmonds at CTV once applied to me. I can pin up on my bulletin-board the letters denouncing me as a reactionary Queen Bee and grin all the way to my office at *Maclean's* magazine. Once, when theatre director Leon Major seriously described all libertarians as "fascists" at a party, I replied that I found myself sympathetic to some libertarian positions. I could shrug indifferently at the rejoinder: "Well, that makes you a fascist bitch." After all, I am getting used to being called a fascist and a reactionary by the anonymous phone-calls and the signed and unsigned letters. This all goes with the territory, and the territory is big enough and comfortable enough to more than compensate.

It is only this that disturbs me: Mistaking the impulses that guide me for fascism means that Orwell's "Slavery is Freedom" has all but arrived. Harsh words can't hurt *me* but, contrary to the doggerel of old, they can be more damaging to a society than sticks and stones. Harsh and inaccurate words are moulding and confusing public opinion. Legislation is being passed with terrifying ease and rapidity that is changing this free society into a coercive society. Although there is a great deal of vague talk about there being "too much government", I do not believe that the Canadian people are properly informed about the nature of the changes taking place in their country, or the consequences of these changes. If I believed that they fully appreciated the consequences of the laws, by-laws, and regulations that the numerous levels of government are passing with such alacrity, then I would throw up my hands, grant a people the right to enslave themselves, and leave.

I am a wandering Jew. I always have my toothbrush handy. My allegiance is not to any piece of earth or particular set of rock outcroppings. My allegiance is to ideas, and most especially to the extraordinary idea of individual liberty. That idea is still there in the North American landscape, a landscape I have come to love. I do not wish to leave. But my suitcase is packed. I do not feel bound to any country or any popular will more than to my own conscience. I would leave here as easily as I would have left Germany when its people elected Hitler to power.

My few years in journalism have given me many privileges. They have allowed me to talk with Cabinet ministers and policy-makers. They have given me the time to study the causes and *causes célèbres* that are at issue in the development of our society. My views have created, it seems, some small alarm in such places as the offices of our various Human Rights Commissions. Let me now explain to them what I am alarmed about.

CHAPTER THIRTEEN

Cows, Sacred and Liberated

WHERE TO BEGIN: Perhaps, in the editorial offices of *Chatelaine* magazine in 1974. I have been called in for a meeting with then-Editor Doris Anderson and Managing Editor Jean Wright. This is the first time I have met Anderson, an imposing woman who sits in a small office behind a desk fiddling with a large string of beads she is wearing. The purpose of the meeting is to propose a story idea to me. The magazine would like a story on women "ripping off" unemployment insurance. I am a little taken aback. "Are they doing that?" I ask. "Well," says Wright, "I have a number of girlfriends who all quit their jobs in the summer so they can spend time with their kids at the cottage." Doris Anderson pulls at her beads. "Should we single out women?" I ask. "It seems a little odd just to nail women. Maybe we could look at the system in general." Anderson speaks. "W-e-ll," she drawls in her distinctive flat voice, "I'm not sure about the story myself. But if women are doing it we ought to clean up our own house." I remain silent. I am still a beginner in journalism and this is an important step – to be called in and *offered* a story rather than scrounging work with lists of ideas xeroxed to different magazines hoping one will say yes. Anderson fiddles again with her beads and then there is a large pop. The beads scatter all over the floor, flying in a thousand and one directions, and there the three of us are: Wright, Anderson, and myself, on our knees, foreheads bumping under the small desk as we grope to pick beads up.

I have a premonition: this is not the place for me to be working. When I leave the office I have agreed to research the story for a couple of weeks and hand in a report on whether or not I think it is a valid idea. I should have stuck to my premonition.

Much time is spent on the piece. I hand in a report that says in effect, yes, a small number of women do appear to be abusing the Unemployment Insurance Commission. Their number is insignificant; I expect it is no greater than the number of men. The only reason it is important, I theorize, is that it casts aspersions on the majority of women who genuinely need help in periods of legitimate unemployment. I am told to go ahead and do the story, making sure I have good examples of abuse.

The story is handed in. It is meticulous in pointing out that abusers among women are a small minority and that they must be weeded out to forestall harsh rules that will penalize legitimate hardship cases. Wright loves the piece. I get a letter by return mail praising it and the following week my cheque for payment-in-full arrives.

About four days after I have handed in the manuscript I visit the Ontario NDP offices to interview Stephen Lewis for a cover story for the *Canadian* magazine. Lewis has just been elected Leader of the Opposition in Ontario. His campaign manager, Gerry Kaplan, has tried to block the story because I am a "slanderous, reactionary journalist". Lewis, however, is prepared to talk to a journalist of any persuasion and has given me an early appointment. While I am waiting, Lewis's assistant, Ellen Adams, walks into the office. On hearing my name she turns an interesting colour of purple and begins to berate me about the "awful, distorted piece you have just written on women and the UIC." I listen with some interest as she quotes my article. When she has finished I inquire how, since the piece is not yet even typeset, she has managed to see it. Adams becomes scared and evasive. She leaves the office.

The article is never run in *Chatelaine*. I ask Jean Wright if *Chatelaine* is in the habit of submitting its articles to the NDP for ratification before publication, since the normal procedure is for a magazine to have its staff researchers check stories. Wright is very embarrassed. She mumbles something about the times not being right for the piece. About a year later, when it is clear that I am not going to stop writing or go away, *Chatelaine* calls me again to do a story. This time Wright is more forthcoming. "I wouldn't expect you to work for us after our inexcusable behaviour with the unemployment piece," she says, "but you know how it is. Politics." I do work for *Chatelaine* again because Wright is a good editor, and, besides, *Chatelaine* has an important audience I want to reach. I also know how it is: politics.

I mention this incident for two reasons. The minor reason is simply to illustrate that women in power or politics are not governed by impulses superior to those guiding men. History has made this fairly obvious, having given us the notorious Romanian leader Anna Pauker in the same century as Israel's relatively moderate Golda Meir. Nevertheless, some spokeswomen for the Movement still try to pull out the superiority of Rule by Women Who Lack the Instinct for Aggression Found in Men, as if this were (a) a guarantee of a world without aggression, which it certainly is not, and (b) true, which it clearly isn't either. But the major reason for recounting the story is that this particular little article of mine was a victim of the need of (socialist) women to launder or suppress reality.

Ever since I first stumbled on to the literature of the Women's Movement in North America, I have been aware of this need, shared by many other philosophies at various times, to distort history and reality in order to promote their ends. My attention was first drawn to this by a phone-call I received in the mid-seventies from a woman identifying herself as an employee of the Ontario provincial labour department.

"Would you," asked the voice, "please tell me how you have been discriminated against as a woman in your career?"

I thought about it. "Sorry," I replied, "I really can't say that I have."

"Well, could you please give me the names of career women you know who have been?"

I thought again. My closest friend was currently heading up the Queen's Park Bureau of the *Toronto Star*, where she supervised several men; another friend had just returned from unemployment in the States to a $25,000 job as an officer in Manpower and Immigration in Ottawa; my sister had recently been appointed associate head of the in-patient psychiatry department of New Mount Sinai Hospital, a precedent-breaking appointment that had to be approved by the hospital board, not because she was a *woman*, but because she did not happen to be a doctor. I knew these jobs were not at all typical, but I couldn't even think of a stage in my employment history from fruit-picker to salesgirl to steno to TV journalist where sex had been a barrier to advancement.

"I'm sorry," I said, "I'll give you a couple of names, but I don't think they can personally help you."

"Well, you're no good to me," the voice said indignantly, without a trace of humour. "Don't you want to help women?"

The problem with the Women's Movement in North America is that it is based on a totally false understanding of history. Its members see history as a male conspiracy to suppress women, and a conspiracy, moreover, that was carried out with force – both physical and economic. The falsity of this view could have been revealed by the most cursory examination of history. Until the last stages of the industrial revolution, societies had one major and vital central issue in common, and that was the propagation of their members. A woman often had to give birth to ten or twelve children to have a couple of them survive. Women had to be either pregnant or in labour for most of their lives because without this it would have been very difficult for the tribe to stay alive. Society was arranged in its own best interests for survival. This resulted in a perfectly natural division of labour.

The introduction of push-button labour-saving devices is also a fairly recent development. In the past, most of the tasks required to ensure a society's survival required a certain physical strength. And while it is true that in actual physical terms the difference between a man and a woman may be nothing more than five to ten per cent of upper-body strength, in marginal economies this is enough to make the difference between survival and extinction. I have always been amused at the interpretation given to the familiar paintings or photographs of stooping peasant women in harnesses pulling along a plough held by a solitary man. "Look," I have been told by story editors at the CBC and feminists at various meetings, "this indicates how women were exploited. Four women in the harness and one man just holding the plough." The truth, of course, was that it made sense to put as many women in harness as necessary to get the required combined strength to pull the plough. But only one person could hold the plough at a time, and that person had to have the physical strength to push it as deeply as possible into the soil, since a half-inch difference in depth could make the difference between next year's sufficiency in crops or starvation.

Similarly, the very slight edge that men seem to have in the perception of spatial-geometric relationships could mean the difference between a stag shot and a stag escaping. Or between killing and being killed in hand-to-hand combat. Society has never been overly ideological. It organized itself in the best way it could to survive. And clearly patriarchies *used* to be the best way.

It is also clear that those women who were not needed by society for breeding and taking care of the family – and this generally meant upper-class women – could be, and often were, given immense power. This has been true since Cleopatra of Egypt and the high priestesses of antiquity. Even in the Catholic Church, while a woman could not become a priest for theological reasons, the prioresses of the great or-ders wielded far more power than the parish priests. Women from Margaret of Navarre to the inheritors of feudal estates occupied positions of enormous influence. In the fourteenth century, for example, as Barbara Tuchman's brilliant book *A Distant Mirror* points out, in the upper classes it was the women who were educated and could read and write and often went to universities. The men of that period were schooled in how to ride a horse, how to hack and hew with a broadsword, how to perform at a tournament – and then sent off to fight in some Crusade or other. Society – or men – never assumed that because a woman could not joust, shoot, fell trees, or plough as well as a man, she couldn't judge or govern.

One of the great problems, in short, of North American feminism is that it extrapolates the history of women solely from the example of middle-class post-industrial America, where indeed women tended to wield less direct power. But in the hierarchically developed societies of Europe or Asia, women who were not needed for specific survival functions were always recognized and given both direct and indirect authority.

But, curiously enough, in North America for the first 150 years of its existence, civilization returned to a lower form of organization. The task of clearing the land, fighting the Indians – indeed, the very pioneer existence – brought back a primitive set of values that were, for women, a step backwards. Once again they were needed in the almost neolithic roles of the hunting-agricultural society. It is from this experience that North American feminism has painted its picture of a world that has forever been organized to repress women. And it is this perception that they now use to try and justify the abandonment of justice and equality in the marketplace in order to make up for these past wrongs to women.

This is not to say that women do not suffer certain handicaps. It would be sheer ideological blindness to pretend that women do not continue to face difficulties in the advancement of careers in certain areas. For example, though the CBC has had female directors and producers since its first days (in spite of the comments made by Status of Women Minister Marc Lalonde in a Toronto visit in 1977, when the presence of a female director sent him into a flurry of "look how far we've come"), it has *not* given women the same opportunity in management areas. Similar examples can be found in boardrooms right across the nation. The other obvious area of discrimination, for which no excuse – historical or otherwise – can now suffice, is the problem of difference in pay for the same job. Though independent and individual qualifications may make one person more valuable in the same job than another (experience, talent, versatility, etc.), all too often it is simply the question of gender that accounts for the smaller pay packet.

In 1967, when I was working for CBC public affairs as a story editor, a male trainee was assigned to me. Cameron Smith, I discovered, in the course of trying to explain to him the use of A and B rolls in filming, was being paid $45 more a week as a trainee than I was as a story editor. I stormed into producer Ross McLean's office. (Stormed, actually, is not quite accurate. I took a cup of tea and two Elavil pills. I was so scared by the encounter that, having got my complaint out and heard McLean's response "Cameron has a wife and child to support," my throat contracted, trapping the pills. In a flurry of confusion I had to be sent to Wellesley Hospital to have the pills dislodged.) Smith, who, having learned the difference between A and B rolls, was clearly not impressed with the distinction, returned very shortly to the *Globe and Mail*. Producer McLean decided, when my contract came up for renewal a few months later, that he would give me an equivalent raise. In retrospect, of course, though McLean cited Smith's family responsibilities, a stronger argument was available. Smith had a law degree and several years' experience in journalism. All the same, he still couldn't tell an optical track from a double system on the day he left.

And, on second thought, perhaps Smith's family status was not so irrelevant after all. Had I been married at the time, I would have been under no legal obligation to contribute one penny of my earnings towards my husband's support or even the family budget. As a woman, I could have spent it all on my clothes or at the race-track. But as a man Smith was obliged by the provisions of the Criminal Code of Canada to "supply the necessities" to his wife and child, as he would be to this day. My money belonged to me; his, by law, didn't belong to him. Infuriated as I was, I could not in good conscience find the disparity between our salaries entirely unjustified or cite it as an example of discrimination to the lady from the Ontario government.

Still, Equal Opportunity and Equal Pay are the legitimate problems facing women. And in these areas the women's movement has been of real help in focusing public attention. If it were a case of simply pursuing these ends, I would be at the barricades waving placards next to Doris Anderson and – even – Marc Lalonde. But the logic of the feminists has spilled over into dangerous and deceptive areas. Equality of opportunity is now muddled up with *parity*. Women constitute 44 per cent of the labour force, say the feminists, but only .5 per cent of managerial positions. The problem here is obvious: the fact that there are more women than men in clerical jobs and fewer women than men in, say, engineering jobs may not be entirely due to inequality of opportunity. With complete equality of opportunity it may be that the distribution of women in engineering jobs may increase from 1 per cent to 5 per cent or even 15 per cent, but it is ludicrous to suggest that the goal ought to be 44 per cent because that is the distribution of women in the labour force.

What feminists seem unable to realize is that while most executives are men, most men are not executives. They, too, occupy dreary, routine, low-level jobs. It would be just as foolish to demand that occupations such as nursing, now dominated by women (while men, incidentally dominate the lowly ranks of orderlies), should have a 50 per cent quota of males in them. There may be all sorts of reasons why certain groups – racial, sexual, and ethnic – dominate certain jobs, and these reasons may have only partially to do with inequality of opportunity, or, sometimes, not at all. But in so far as inequality of opportunity has prevented a capable woman from becoming a jet pilot or playing on a hockey team or becoming a welder, then that particular bit of discrimination should immediately be replaced by equal opportunity for the *individual*.

There is a world of difference between this and parity for the *group*. What you cannot do is create instant parity in the form of job quotas and preferences for women. To do this is to bring about a condition of inequality for another group and set society on the dreadful road of serial injustice or reverse discrimination, with committees deciding which group is to be preferred this year. Equality of opportunity becomes Russian roulette while society decides whether handicapped, female, homosexual, or short people are this year's in-group. Reverse discrimination, of course, is heartily endorsed by the women's movement and by those "professional" women in branches of government like the Women's Labour Bureaus, whose job empires are immeasurably expanded when they can run around monitoring quotas and setting goals.

It is here that it becomes important to view history correctly. If a past disparity – or even bias – is viewed as an injustice, rather than as the logical outcome of what a society required to survive, then you have the inevitable temptation to "hurry things up" with the reverse injustice of affirmative-action programs. If it is not viewed in this false light, then it becomes what in fact it is: a matter of accommodating society's new needs, which will take a normal amount of readjustment time.

In recent years in the United States and Canada there has been a tentative movement to organize a women's political party. This sums up to me the extraordinary patronizing view many middle-class feminists have of women. The arrangement of a political candidate's reproductive organs are of far less interest to most women than the everyday – and even nocturnal – emissions of the candidate's cerebral cortex. Or ethics. It is interesting that the Women's Movement should promote the differences between men and women in such a spurious area as politics, where the difference is probably next to nothing – for I believe that women can politically represent men, and men, women, with equal ease – but demand that the real differences that may exist between the sexes in psychological-emotional-sexual areas be expunged from discussion or depiction. They demand, furthermore, that our schools should teach children that these differences do not exist in ludicrous programs that call for "the elimination of sexual stereotyping". It may well be that it is to the advantage of the left-leaning women's groups to confuse or set up an adversary relationship between men and women in our society. Why? Because anything that puts a stress on the free-enterprise liberal democracy strengthens the argument of those who wish to replace it. One does not know whether it is stupidity or complicity that puts our educators in the vanguard with them. Given the quality of schooling children now receive, and the abominable prose of the educational bureaucrats' guidelines and curriculum reports, one suspects that it is mere stupidity.

What seems to be beyond the grasp of the Women's Movement and their trendy followers in the educational systems and the media is that the legal status or equality of women in economic, political, and intellectual spheres does not rest on there being *no* differences between men and women. When the Egyptians accepted Cleopatra as their queen, nobody tried to pretend that she was the same as a man. They accepted her rule not because they were liberal, but because they knew that the difference did not matter. The true spirit of liberalism, in an even more sensible way, simply judges everyone on his or her own merit. There may well be thousands of individual men who would like to do nothing better than put on an apron and look after children. But it does not follow, and would be ludicrous to suggest, that when nature divided up biological roles between genders it was not generally women who were imbued with the maternal spirit. Nature would defeat itself by not giving women a slightly different emotional make-up, suited to their natural needs. And on its own grounds nature does not choose to defeat itself, as people discovered a long time ago – and are forced to rediscover time and again. To put out the kind of programs that the Ontario Ministry of Education is currently pushing in its 88-page booklet titled *Sex-Role Stereotyping and Women's Studies* is dangerous, false, and a total laundering of reality – as well as an arrogant waste of time that could be spent on the real business of education. Consider some of the following examples from the Guidelines:

> Have students take pictures of men and women. Compare with photographs used in commercials. Have students discuss their findings in relation to stereotyped views of male/female hands/feet.

> Rewrite the lyrics of a song, eliminating the sex-role stereotypes of the original; e.g., You're Having My Baby (Paul Anka); The Girl that I Marry (Frank Sinatra).

But it doesn't end here. We recently had Secretary of State David MacDonald preparing to monitor television commercials to prevent the "stereotyping" of women. We have already had feminist Laura Sabia complaining about the tellers in bank commercials always being women. Well, most tellers in banks *are* women. What David MacDonald and Laura Sabia and all the other would-be-commissars want *is to depict reality not as it is but as they would like it to be.* This is the definition of "socialist realism" or propaganda. But forcing artists or advertisers to lie will not build a better society. Mind you, the women's movement never worries about having it both ways. When a judge in Ontario made a remark that a woman's confusion in the witness-box might be the result of her "change of life" he was picketed, publicly rebuked by the Law Society, and forced to apologize. But where were the picketers when a woman in Hamilton pleading guilty to shoplifting cited menopausal depression as an extenuating circumstance, and was granted a suspended sentence by the judge?

Three issues sum up to me the philosophical shortcomings of the women's movement.

(1) Matrimonial property law. Women have pushed reforms that see marriage as an economic partnership with all the assets of a marriage to be split down the middle without reference to who amassed them. This, of course, is legislation for the well-to-do. For lower-income families there are virtually no assets to split. The legislation rewards dependency. The higher the husband's income, the less a wife generally has to do in terms of housework and home labour, yet the more highly she gets paid for it in the event of a divorce. In recent cases involving multi-millionaires who had made their money in architecture, banking, and real estate, the wives received settlements close to a million dollars based on "their contribution as homemakers". The services of a highly skilled homemaker can be bought for a few hundred dollars a week, and the professional homemaker does not require a wardrobe and the necessities of life to be provided for her, or a standard of living to match her employer's. Wives are not liable in law to provide the necessities of life for husbands. Husbands can go to jail for failing to do so for wives. Wives do not pay rent, taxes, or grocery bills. To suggest that the income of an architect is dependent on his wife is ludicrous – with the very rare exception of, say, a wife whose single-handed entertaining skills were directly responsible for securing new clients for her husband, which could be judged on merit in individual cases.

But most importantly, while the division of assets may have been a more humanitarian approach to old-style marriages, it has little to do with the realities of contemporary marriage. The new generation of businesswomen may have to sign contracts with their prospective spouses or they too will become the victims of a matrimonial property settlement that clearly is weighted in favour of the less productive spouse of either sex. If playing golf or canasta and giving instructions to the gardener gets you half, why bother going to work?

It may be a positive step to make spouses responsible for financing the transition period necessary to put a non-working spouse back into the labour force. It is better than forcing the taxpayers to do so. But it is a step backward to suggest that people do not deserve the fruits of their own labours, or to deny that while both husband and wife may be responsible for their children, ultimately we are all responsible for ourselves. That is not callous. *That* is liberation.

(2) Abortion. His name was Dr. Smolling and his office was a store-front on Toronto's Danforth Avenue. I was twenty-four years old, a script assistant at the CBC, had been assured by doctors that I could not get pregnant, and had had intercourse with a man only once in the previous six months. I was close to five months pregnant when Doctor Smolling gave me an abortion in his back room. He wore a black rubber apron and the pain was excruciating. Later, in hospital after haemorrhaging, I was told that I escaped never being able to have children only because of the massive doses of antibiotics Smolling took care to prescribe.

The issue of abortion gives me a great deal of moral concern and, frankly, in the long run I cannot support it with much enthusiasm. I believe it to be morally wrong. At the time I had my own abortion I believed it to be morally wrong. I expected, knowing little of the laws of the land then, that if I were caught I would go to jail. (In fact it was Dr. Smolling who was eventually charged over another case.) I was in too much of a hurry with life. I couldn't wait the extra four months and then, if a child was "inconvenient" for me, put it up for adoption. I chose murder instead.

Because, of course, it *is* murder, and all the nice distinctions made in the stages of the development of the fetus – when it is conscious or when it acquires a separate identity from the mother – are simply nice distinctions. But as I would not shrink from murder to protect my vital interests, I would not shrink from abortion – except I prefer to face what I'm doing. And in most cases the interests aborting mothers protect are not remotely vital. But if public policy is to come down clearly in favour of abortion on demand for reasons of utility, then the least society can do is to make that policy equitable. By this I mean very simply that if "convenience" is sufficient cause for abortion, then it should be operative for both the mother *and* the father. If a man does not wish his wife or his girlfriend to have a child because the financial burden will inconvenience him – for considerably longer than nine months – either the mother should be required to have an abortion or, if this is not acceptable to her, the man should be released from financial responsibility for the child. Convenience is not a one-way street. If it is an excuse for the mother, fairness and equity demand that it be an excuse for the father.

There are few other issues that have disturbed me as deeply as abortion. The prospect of unwanted children fills me with unhappiness. In the end it is not particularly pleasant to find oneself in the world unwanted or without parents. People *can* get pregnant through little fault of their own, unless one views intercourse itself as a "fault", which I do not. The social inconvenience can be a heavy burden. But it is the use of "convenience" as a justification for ending someone else's life that worries me. It may seem a giant step to extrapolate from this and suggest that in the same direction, only a little further down the road, lies the extermination of the mentally ill, the chronically ill, and so on; and to suggest that convenience is an excuse that can bring tragedy and bloodshed to a society. But I do fear it, and see already with some apprehension the growing movement for euthanasia. Nine months is not so inconvenient a length of time in the human lifespan to give up so that a human being can live. I have no sentimental feelings about the child I killed. But I find my reasons morally reprehensible.

(3) Work benefits. Women claim they want equality in the work-force, but they demand special privileges such as maternity leave and the guarantee of their job when they return. An employer faced with the choice of hiring a man or a woman for the same job would not be "discriminating" if he chose the man, because the man will present no problems by requesting fifteen weeks' maternity leave during which the job, or its equivalent, must be held open for him. If we were

faced with a too-small labour force *and* a population survival problem there might have been some basis for this encouragement of women to straddle both worlds at the taxpayers' expense. But neither condition exists.

Libbers argue that the apparent unfairness of maternity leave, subsidized by fifteen weeks of unemployment insurance, can be easily rectified. Give men paternity leave. The trouble with this is that at some point it all has to stop. It is already clear to financial analysts that our provincial and federal governments have been spending Canadians' pension contributions with abandon to cover the cost of all the programs they so ambitiously promote. God alone knows how that incredible mess will sort itself out, or whether, indeed, as reputable analysts have suggested, the Canada Pension Plan will simply collapse.

Our society cannot now afford to help the truly indigent to a proper extent. The old-age pensions paid to the really needy are scandalous. We do have orphans and the handicapped to consider. Our economic problems are compounded by our country's low productivity and mounting government debt. Productivity is not simply a question of how hard each worker works. It is the sum of the goods and services we produce compared to what they cost. The staggering cost of our social services and our subsidized industries – is there a country in the world where provincial and federal governments become so warm and moist and generous at the sight of a crippled industry? – have taken their toll on our productivity. We simply cannot afford now to create another social scheme of UIC-sponsored paternity leaves.

In summary, the women's movement in North America has become a marvellous con-game. Give us equality, they ask, when what they mean is give us preferential quotas, maternity leave, child care, and promotion based on sex. The difficulty with con-games is that you can fool all of the public some of the time and some of the public all of the time, but in the end no one will be fooled. For those many women who can compete on equal footing with men in the labour force the attitude of the Women's Movement has become a source of embarrassment. "No," said the female vice-president of a brokerage firm when being interviewed by a *Maclean's* journalist, "I damned well was *not* an International Women's Year appointment."

CHAPTER FOURTEEN

Goldfish, Fin-Back Whales, and Other Fishy Matters

"No, no!" said the Queen. "Sentence first – verdict afterwards."

"Stuff and nonsense!" said Alice loudly. "The idea of having the sentence first!"

"Hold your tongue!" said the Queen, turning purple.

"I won't!" said Alice.

"Off with her head!"

Alice had it easy. Her fears were only dreams that disappeared at tea-time. But no matter how I blinked, said "pardon", or reread the transcripts of the interviews I was doing for my work, the nightmare would only reveal itself in a new form. The issues piled up one after the other: foreign policy, the environment, education, multiculturalism, Canadian identity, etcetera, etcetera, etcetera, with all their reports, studies, ministerial pronouncements, and public reaction. The pattern seemed clear. Sentence first, verdict next, and then maybe some evidence. But why? How did Alice in Wonderland become the public policy of the liberal West? Sometimes, now, I look at my notes and play the cassettes of various interviews with a feeling that what I lack is a sense of humour. Because I still feel like weeping when I listen.

We are sitting in his car, Marc Lalonde and I. The subject is the Crippled Olympics. The federal government withdrew the promised subsidy to the Crippled Olympics after the organizers announced that an integrated team from South Africa would take part.

Marc Lalonde: "Yes, that was my decision and I might say that I am very proud of it."

Amiel: "Why?"

Lalonde: "Well, it indicates that we will have nothing to do with a country that practises discrimination and violates human rights."

Amiel: "All right. But what about the Soviet Union and countries like Nigeria that all but wiped out several million people on the basis of their tribal affiliation? Will we stop playing sports with them?"

Lalonde: "Well, no, of course not. The Soviet Union has a constitution guaranteeing human rights to everyone. It is written down. You can read it."

Amiel: "I have. It does not seem to stop the persecution of the Ukrainians, the Jews, the Baptists, and so on."

Lalonde: "Well, these things are deplorable and I'm not suggesting they aren't. But they don't discriminate on the basis of race. Or at least they haven't put it down in writing like the South Africans."

I make no reply and ask no further questions. What is there to ask or to say? I recall a CBC radio talk show between the Canadian nationalist writer David Godfrey and my husband George Jonas (the interview took place before we were married). The subject was nationalism; the time, 1971 or 1972. Godfrey opened with the statement that he was not so much pro-Canadian as anti-American. I'm quoting the conversation that followed from memory.

Jonas: "Let's define our premises. How would you describe the ideal society?"

Godfrey: "I guess a society that puts the greatest value on ordinary human beings, and where power is distributed most equally among all the people."

Jonas: "Fine. And which society, of all societies past or present, comes closest to that ideal?"

Godfrey: "That's easy. China."

Jonas: (after a pause) "Just so we avoid any possible misunderstanding, did you say that your ideal was a society where the premium is on ordinary people, and power is distributed most equally among all individuals?"

Godfrey: "Yes."

Jonas: "And of all human societies, past or present, you believe Mao's China comes closest to that ideal?"

Godfrey: "Yes."

Jonas: "Well, then, perhaps we should move on to the next subject. How do you feel about goldfish?"

Now the point about someone like Godfrey – co-founder of the Toronto literary press The House of Anansi, which published such Canadian authors as Margaret Atwood, Dennis Lee, and George Grant (also, incidentally, my husband's first three books) – is that he is a man of solid academic credentials who would probably score higher on any I.Q. test than ninety-nine per cent of the population. He is not seeking power; he could not be discounted on these grounds, the way a politician like Lalonde could be. Yet he said what he did and presumably meant it, adding later that it would be difficult to *distribute* power among ordinary people if you did not *concentrate* it first, like Mao. You can't give away what you haven't got, said the Queen. If Alice doesn't see it she'll have to go without her tea.

When I am in Toronto I wake up to read the *Globe and Mail*. This puts me in a proper frame of mind for harassing

innocent bystanders like taxi-drivers and elevator compan-
ions who become the brunt of my "did-you-read-about-it-in-
this-morning's", etc. The November 9, 1977, edition, for example, has an account of the suspension of swimming-coach
Deryk Snelling from national and international competitions
for three months by the Canadian Amateur Swimming Association because he took a vacation in South Africa during the
summer, paid for by South African swimmers. Mr. Snelling,
who is acknowledged to be one of the best coaches in Canada, says of his visit: "I did it at a bad time." Phone-calls to
various amateur sports people reveal that Snelling's suspension is being carried out not because of conviction but because of fear of reprisals by the Minister of Sport, the Honourable Mrs. Iona Campagnolo. They refer me to her
October 1977 speech to the House of Commons.

*The Hon. Iona Campagnolo (Minister of State, Fitness and Ama-
teur Sport)*: "This new Canada of ours has responsibilities
beyond our borders, however, and one such responsibility
concerns sport relations with South Africa. . . . I should
like to reiterate, for those who have been concerned about
our policy, a very clear and succinct understanding. The
government of Canada will not underwrite with public
funds, or provide moral support for the participation of
Canadians in sporting events involving South Africa, in either South Africa or Canada.

"From as early as 1970, Canadian government invest-
ments in South Africa have been removed. Canada no
longer sells defence goods to South Africa. That is our answer to the heinous policy of apartheid. . . . Politics is an
everyday part of life, whether in this historic chamber or
in teaching your children a value system which is consistent with your own free beliefs. In turn, sport is part of
politics. . . . Do any Hon. members here think that the
head of the IOC, Lord Killanin, would be negotiating now
to bring China back into the Olympic family if Canada and
our Prime Minister had not stood firm and the Prime Min-

ister had not remained adamant on the issue last year of Taiwan's bid to attend the Montreal Olympics?"

Some Hon. Members: "Hear, hear!"

Mrs. Campagnolo: "Our young people [are competing] against the United States, Cuba and Mexico, but also in the USSR, in Japan, Poland, in Hungary, in West and in East Germany. . . . They are representations of human contact; they are a very fine example of the Helsinki accord."

Less than a year later on the front page of the *Globe and Mail* there will be Mrs. Campagnolo's announcement barring all sports visitors from South Africa. *On the same page* a reader with a sense of irony will find the report of more Christians and Jews being hustled off to the Gulag for asking the Soviet government to observe the Helsinki accords.

I loathe the concept of apartheid in any form, but especially as it is practised by the South Africans. At least Idi Amin (for so many years every contemporary leftist's favourite "Look, I condemn black dictatorships, too") had the consistency of practising apartheid of the cutting-off-my-nose-to-spite-my-face kind. He kicked out the Asians because he (a) was nasty and (b) wanted Uganda for his own tribesmen, even at the price of removing with the Asians his primary source of revenue and business acumen. The South Africans haven't even that kind of honesty. They talk about separate development, but so long as the blacks want to stay in South Africa (or come in to work there in large numbers from other black African countries where working conditions, salaries, and political freedoms are even worse) they let them. What white South Africans might do, with far more moral consistency, is to declare South Africa their own tribal homeland (it is; there were no native inhabitants in it before the Boer settlers) and send everybody else packing. But they just can't give up all that nice cheap labour – yet.

More of Africa – this time the part we like – or used to.

It was only a sudden shortage of funds that stopped the

proposed three million dollars of CIDA money going to Emperor Jean-Claude Bokassa's Central African Republic. Canada had agreed, a Brussels senior official of the European Economic Council explained to me, to give the money to Bokassa for the purchase of boats. The Chairman of CIDA, Michel Dupuy, cautiously denied it: "We have not given it. I have no knowledge of it at this time." After that interview, I telephoned Brussels again:

EEC Official: "Oh yes. I have the file in front of me. You have agreed in a series of meetings, some of which I attended in Ottawa, to give this money.

Amiel: "Why?"

EEC Official: "Well, you seem to have a very curious situation there. The French-Canadian branch of CIDA wants to support and prop up these dreadful ex-French regimes. The English don't. It all gets very tense."

Amiel: "Does Bokassa need the boats?"

EEC Official: "Well, it's hard to see why. The river has been blocked for God knows how long with the wreckage of the boats we gave him before. They don't service them and there's no point in sending them parts any more. And the economy is so bad they don't seem to have anything to put on the boats. All the money is going on the coronation."

Amiel: "The what?"

EEC Official: "Bokassa has a touch of the 'royals'. He is going to 'coronate' himself. The throne is made of hundreds of pounds of gold. The Empress has been shopping at Cartier's and her gown is being made at Dior's. It is said the affair will cost $6 million. That's where your money will go, of course."

Maybe. Fortunately for Michel Dupuy, first the publicity surrounding this proposed grant to Bokassa delays the funds, and then the big squeeze on money dries them up complete-ly. Later, even Amnesty International, whose myopic vision is notorious, will be forced to mention (in May 1979) that Bo-kassa is killing hundreds of children. Perhaps it is the fact he has become an Emperor, just like the old colonialists, that persuades Amnesty to finger him. They remain relatively quiet about the People's Republic of China and most African third-world countries. They are very concerned about Chile and Argentina. A Martian (or the average politically naive American student) reading their reports would conclude that in the last quarter-century the overwhelming majority of torture, killing, and repression in the world has been the work of a few right-wing military dictators.

Of course, it is easier to get facts and figures from the worst fascist regime than from the most enlightened country of scientific socialism. In the Ayatollah's Iran, executions are semi-public and dead bodies are photographed for press re-leases. Tass or the New China News Agency prefers workers pouring steel and happy children playing in nurseries. Lest anyone should misunderstand – I do not quarrel with Am-nesty International for pointing out the nasty ways of the colonels. I quarrel with them for failing to point out the nasty ways of the comrades with equal diligence.

But then what is there to say about the moral acuity of an organization which regards the guillotine execution of a rape-murderer in France and the incarceration of a dissi-dent in a mental asylum in the USSR as equal violations of hu-man rights; which objects to the solitary confinement of ter-rorists in the West as much as to the solitary confinement of journalists in Czechoslovakia? Perhaps Amnesty says it best about itself:

"Our impartiality is not always appreciated or even understood. . . ."

Right. It is not easy to understand "impartiality" based on strict neutrality between good and evil.

Rummaging in the files.

Globe and Mail, September 26, 1974.

"Prime Minister Pierre Trudeau is determined to give

Canada a strong new activist role on the left wing of international affairs," Ivan Head, Mr. Trudeau's special foreign affairs advisor, said yesterday.

Mr. Trudeau will make three foreign visits by mid-winter and welcome several foreign leaders here this fall.

Among them will be Swedish Prime Minister Olof Palme who, Mr. Head said, has greatly impressed Mr. Trudeau with his outspoken left-wing approach to international problems.

The Swedes, with their denunciation of the Vietnam War and the military revolt in Chile, have become "the cutting edge of the left – very active, outspoken and moral," Mr. Head said.

Later it is reported that Mr. Head and Mr. Trudeau deny the Canadian Press story. I don't understand why; it is no worse than shouting "Viva Castro" in Cuba, which Trudeau had never bothered – and would have been hard put – to deny. (But he did explain it by saying that it was simply the "custom in Cuba". It is lucky, I suppose, that we did not have him as Canada's prime minister in the 1930s, when a state visit to Germany would no doubt have produced a similar shout, one very much the custom in the Third Reich.)

But, since we are talking of Hitler it is just as well to remember that in the 1930s the pundits of the West were, until the very outbreak of the Second World War, not really as alarmed about fascism, proto-fascism, and extreme right-wing politics as they are today. Why? The evils of Nazism and its sub-varieties were no secret – indeed, a quick reading of Hitler's *Mein Kampf* would have amply revealed them. What is more, unlike today, international fascism was a real power, an acute threat to the vital interests of Western democracies. Why did our statesmen equivocate, try for "peace in our time", seek to employ milder words against the spreading power of German-Italian-Japanese jackboots and bayonets than they are employing now against South African whites or Chilean generals who – whatever they may do to their own unfortunate subjects – have no power or desire to hurt us?

I believe the question contains its own answer: it is precisely because the extreme right used to be a real power and a real threat that we in the West, through our government, our media, tried to close our eyes and seek accommodation with it, right up to that unavoidable day in September 1939. Far from banning the sportsmen and sportswomen of racist Germany, we travelled to play with them all the way to the Berlin Olympics, with the Canadian team in the march-past politely giving Hitler the fascist salute. It is not any new-found moral enlightenment that causes us today to ban the South Africans or restrict trade with the Rhodesians, but the comfortable knowledge that we can be ever-so-principled with impunity. We put no pressure whatever on Lord Killanin or his predecessors to expel from the Olympic family of nations Formosa or Taiwan or whatever you call it where Chiang Kai-shek was trampling on every conceivable human right, *while he was actually doing it*. Only long after he was gone, when all the evil he had ever represented was superseded by the equally abominable though far more efficient Red Guards, could our Sports Minister Campagnolo stand in Parliament and boast that our Prime Minister had "remained adamant" in refusing "Taiwan's bid to attend the Montreal Olympics". For moral reasons? No: in order to accommodate the new, the better, the more efficient, more dangerous murderers of Mao's China.

Is it mere coincidence that our strongest stance against the evils of communism – indeed, our unjustifiable and shameful Red-baiting, witch-hunting days – occurred when the Soviet Union was not yet armed with atomic weapons or delivery systems to rectify the clarity of our moral vision? I think not. If anything, we knew *less* about the horrors of the Great Socialist Fatherland in the Truman-McCarthy-Eisenhower era than we have learned since: the handwriting may have been on the wall, but there was no Khrushchev speech, no Twentieth Party Congress, no Solzhenitsyn yet to take us all the way down to the final circles of the communist hell. But it was not in those days that we were talking *détente*. Have our morality, our social conscience matured since the 1950s? I believe not: only our fears.

Just as in the thirties we were ready to suspend our judgement against everyone with tanks, aircraft carriers, and U-boats, so today the possession of nuclear submarines and Intercontinental Ballistic Missiles seems to atone for any number of sins. Yet we wax more and more indignant against the few small beleaguered villains of the political right. I shed no tears for *them* – only for us. It is not our morality that is growing, only our cowardice and hypocrisy. Our left-libbers may think they are practising realpolitik – but it will profit us no more than the realpolitik of the Chamberlain Tories did a couple of generations ago.

But on with the issues.

Of all the sacred cows in Canada the most sacred is the caribou. It was a lucky day for the caribou when Mr. Justice Thomas Berger was appointed to head the inquiry into the proposed Mackenzie Valley oil and gas pipeline. Justice Berger, of course, did not pretend to be a specialist in the habits of the caribou. But he is a man who knows what their habits ought to be.

Justice Berger's inquiry, though predictable enough from the day of his appointment, still managed to be intriguing both in the way in which he chose to interpret the evidence presented to him and in his conclusions. In Canada (unlike the United States, where the hurly-burly of judicial election is a great leveller) the most sacred cows next to the caribou are the members of the Bench. It is considered extremely bad manners to do anything but tiptoe backwards out of their presence, so all-powerful are they – unless, of course, a judge happens to do something truly terrible, like get his name in the address book of a prostitute or make a reference to behaviour in his courtroom which offends the Women's Movement. Then no power on earth can save him. But the case of Mr. Justice Berger is interesting, because it indicates the silence greater than the grave which falls on Canada's vigilant gladiators in the press when the issue actually is of some moment to the country's future.

Bearing this in mind, I was most careful in my muted comments about the appointment of Justice Berger in a short article I did for *Maclean's*. In fact it was a book review–article, which reviewed, among other volumes on our North, a book by the then *Globe and Mail* reporter Martin O'Malley, who covered the Berger inquiry for Canada's national newspaper. I did not have space in that review to quote from Mr. O'Malley's book but I will do so now. Of particular interest to me was Mr. O'Malley's biographical picture of Justice Berger. O'Malley is an emotional and skilled writer, and minces no words in letting you know where he stands. His sympathy is for those native activists in Northern Canada who wish to prevent development. He speaks of them as "challenging today's economic religion that mindlessly pursues growth and consumption." He points out that Alaska's Alyeska oil pipeline has provided high-paying jobs but has sent "rents and prices skyrocketing" and "has made whores of Eskimos." (This last statement is particularly intriguing. If it means that taking jobs of an industrial nature equals prostitution, there are a lot of whores in the world. If it only means prostitution for Eskimos, one would wish for elaboration on this fine ethnographic discovery. If it means neither, what does it mean? I dare say not all working Eskimos look at themselves as whores in any case, and those who don't might rightly be irritated by Mr. O'Malley.) However, back to Justice Berger. Writes O'Malley: "Five years after he graduated he was setting legal precedents. He became British Columbia's leading native rights lawyer. He defended Indian bands over reserve rights to timber, hunting and fishing. He represented Métis and Indian trappers of the Athabasca Delta in a dispute with B.C. Hydro over muskrat hunting grounds. He defended aboriginal rights of Nishga Indians all the way to the Supreme Court of Canada, pushing his case that the Nishga Indians had aboriginal title to their land when white men arrived and still have title to it. A split decision of the Supreme

Court went against him but the judgement remains a major legal basis for native rights in Canada."

O'Malley goes on to more folksy stuff about Justice Berger, most of it quoted from columnist Allan Fotheringham. Details include tales of animated discussions between Berger and a Vancouver couple named Tom and Maisie Hurley on the subject of "underdogs and the law". Maisie Hurley founded the first Indian newspaper in Canada and was a spirited crusader for Indian rights. The Hurleys, we are told, were very influential in Berger's life. Maisie was also very important to the British Columbian Indians, who called her Chief Sim-Klux, or Mother of the Fin-Back Whales of the House of Gooksan. There's a bit more of this and then O'Malley goes on to Berger's political career culminating in his brief stint as leader of the provincial NDP party, and concludes with one or two less complimentary remarks suggesting Berger lacked a sense of humour (not necessarily a political handicap in Canada) and that some saw him as a "ruthless socialist".

Thus we have, presiding over an inquiry into the basic issue of technological development versus native and environmental claims, a man sprung full-blown out of the circle of Mother of the Fin-Back Whales of the House of Gooksan, and one whose record shows a consistent advocacy of aboriginal "rights". Now, it may be wise to make several things clear before I continue with this line of thought. First, I think it is important – indeed crucial – that every group in society should have skilled advocates to represent their causes. Justice Berger is clearly an advocate of much skill and genuine commitment to a native people who, in spite of current government funding to support their causes against the government, may often in the early days of their grievances have been completely without resources to hire adequate spokesmen. In this capacity Berger is a pillar of the democratic process.

Furthermore, I am as moved by tundra and caribou as the next nature-lover. I confess to a doubt that it is in the long-term interests of the native peoples to maintain a paleolithic culture in the twentieth century and, personally, I'd prefer to see more of my tax money spent on helping Indian and Eskimo individuals to enter the mainstream of the dominant culture of this country. Historically no group has managed to retain a stone-age culture within a more advanced society, except as some sort of anthropological curiosity that delights sentimental writers who have read too much Rousseau when young. (And if some are offended by the value-judgement the word "advanced" implies, so be it.) Still, if our native peoples wish to continue a life of extraordinary hardship and limited lifespan, there seems to be plenty of frozen tundra to go around without depriving the rest of us on this continent from access to the resources of the North. Of course, simple justice demands that native people share in the benefits of these resources, and no native individuals should be denied a chance to any opportunity available to other Canadians.

My single complaint was the appropriateness of a judge of such a clearly partisan background to head an impartial inquiry. Writing in *Maclean's*, I suggested that, though Justice Berger was no doubt a man of "great personal integrity", it seemed unfair to put him in a position where he might do irreversible chiropractic damage to himself by having to bend over backwards to be fair. I suggested that if the government had appointed a man to head the inquiry whose record had shown a similarly consistent *opposition* to native land-claims and a consistent pro-development position, people like O'Malley would (very rightly) have objected to such an appointment. I myself would have. It is more than a question of the appearance of justice. It is a question of justice itself.

Still, the *Globe and Mail* reporter on this landmark issue didn't quite see it this way. He wrote a letter ostensibly in response to the question I raised about the appropriateness of Justice Berger to head such an inquiry, but in fact not addressing himself to it in any but the following way:

"Berger alas, has 'impeccable credentials' for the job and 'great personal integrity' but did you know that before he was appointed to the Bench he was one of the country's leading native rights lawyers and a card-carrying member of the New Democratic Party? Gotcha! Another Canadian folk hero bites the dust."

I raise this, not out of any animosity to O'Malley, whom I've never met, and whose writing skills are undeniable, but because as the reporter for Canada's most influential newspaper on one of the most significant inquiries in our history it is interesting to see the way his mind works. The question I raised, though I believe valid and important, was not unanswerable. In fact, I could have come up with several arguments against it myself. (An examination of the past courtroom stance of several members of the Bench during their days at the Bar would reveal attitudes about issues or the rules of evidence and procedure that are in no way reflected in their current judicial decisions. An advocate's theories in the courtroom, where his job is to argue as forcefully as possible for his client, do not necessarily give a forecast of his future judgements. And so on.) But O'Malley did not choose to actually deal with the question I raised. In this, his was similar to the hundreds of left-lib letters of disagreement that I received in my career. Generally, I would have learned more – or changed my mind more quickly – by arguing with myself than by reading one more rebuke about how my views must be shaped by the fact that I probably have always had a dishwasher or have never had to go to bed hungry or that I am 5'8" tall – of which, incidentally, only the last assertion is true.

But back to the Berger inquiry. The conclusions of Mr. Justice Berger could (and ought to) be the subject of an entire book. Still, two or three of them might illustrate my point.

• Berger quotes the evidence of a marine biologist who pointed out that the arctic ecosystems are so fragile and conditions so tough that, for example, out of 23,000 species of fish only 25 live in arctic waters, out of 3,200 species of mammals only 9 are found in the high arctic, and so on. Now, two inferences can be drawn from this. The most logical would seem to be that, as a matter of policy, given the limited amount of wildlife able to survive these gruelling conditions, the benefit of technological development to the country and its population might outweigh the cost of harm to nature, since there is so little nature to harm. Berger chose to interpret it as indicating that so fragile an environment should have extra-special care and protection.

• *Trapping*: Conflict between figures on the number of natives actually engaged in trapping emerged at the hearings. The Arctic Gas study, prepared by Gemini North, came up with only 96 people out of a study area of 23,600. The Indian Brotherhood of the Northwest Territories came up with 1,075 actively engaged in trapping. Berger decided in favour of the Indian Brotherhood figures in the following manner: "A man who is working for wages with a seismic exploration crew (and who would, therefore, enter Gemini North's figures as a wage employee) might still regard himself as a trapper (or hunter) because he intends to use part of his wages to buy a new snowmobile, a new boat, new traps or a new rifle. In his own eyes, therefore, he is working at 'a job' to support 'his way of life' as a trapper."

In advancing this argument in favour of the Indian Brotherhood figures Berger seemed to put himself in a most peculiar position. What he was saying was that trapping alone is not a viable occupation for most people without the subsidies of industrial jobs. This comes as no news to anyone who has read the gripping and tragic stories of the terrible hardship of native life. But it is a curious position to advance in favour of blocking further development. And to put those who do part-time trapping or hunting into the full-time figures on grounds that it is "a way of life" would, by extension, make my psychiatrist friend in Toronto "a fisherman" since he works in order to be able to afford to go back to his native island in the Maritimes to fish as his Acadian ancestors did hundreds of years ago. In his own mind he certainly lives and works for no other reason than this, and would be ready to so testify in court.

Still, I read the account of the Berger hearings and then the Berger Report with mixed feelings. I even read O'Malley's book with mixed feelings. It is always sad to see the end of a way of life. I am, to put it mildly, no technology buff. I *prefer* hunters and trappers to computer-analysts and accountants. But our attempts to prop up hunting and gathering societies in the twentieth century have produced nothing but terrible human waste and tragedy. I shall not forget the weeks I spent up north filming for the CBC, recording a proud and independent Indian people caught between two cultures and reduced to debris.

I repeat, we can learn from history. It may have been possible for the Tasaday rain-forest people to survive in their primitive state: a happy, sharing, warm people – with the good fortune to find themselves in a forest filled with food and cut off from civilization. But once in contact with the outside world, they must be reduced to curiosities for guided tours and photographs in the *National Geographic* or, eventually, will have to assimilate into modern society. The only other option is to suffer from all the maladies of the majority culture and none of its benefits.

Meanwhile, our resources go untapped and our situation grows more desperate. We need natural gas, oil, and power dams. In the end, we will be forced to build our pipelines with the kind of haste that could lead to true ecological disaster for all.

Only one question remains. We now have the conclusion of Justice Berger: no pipeline in one area; no construction anywhere till all native land rights are settled. We do not yet have the reasons that motivated the Trudeau government to select Justice Berger to head this inquiry in the first place.

CHAPTER FIFTEEN

The Cult of Multicult

ONE MORNING IN MAY 1979 the phone rang. "Damn," I thought. However, it turned out to be a propitious conversation. The caller wished to draw my attention to a curious situation down at Toronto's new multicultural television station. It seemed that a certain Hungarian lady had worked very hard in the soliciting of funds, support, and organizational back-up for the winner of the MCTV licence competition, and had, according to her, been given to understand that in return for this she would head up the station's Hungarian-language programming. This sounded logical, since the lady in question, an ex-journalist, was very active in putting on performances of various Hungarian poets, playwrights, musicians, and authors, and had done so fairly successfully. But multicultural rivalry had reared its multiheaded visage. The lady's name was not popular with a rival Hungarian organization and they had been down to the station to present their point of view. According to the caller they suggested that she was a communist. The station, for this or whatever reason, had decided to put one of the rival nominees in charge of programming instead of her. "It's really not fair," said my caller.

Fair or not, the lady, it seemed, was not about to take it lying down. She had sent off fifty letters to various members of Parliament accusing her rivals of being Nazis. Another blow for the wonderful world of multiculturalism, I thought.

"You will write about it, won't you?" our caller said. "After all, you know that she's not a communist. This simply isn't fair."

In fact I had no idea whether the lady was or wasn't a communist, any more than I had any idea whether her rivals at Hungarian House were or weren't Nazis. Furthermore, I didn't care. I loathed both, but in Canada it was not against the law to be either. What interested me far more was the illustration it presented of the evils of multiculturalism.

The Multicult bandwagon is very much a growth industry. The Trudeau government probably regards it as a useful antidote to Quebec nationalists – lest for one minute they think that being one of the two founding races of this country gives them any special status over the dozens of other people who speak strange languages. Of course, it also helps soften the backlash to the careful elevation of French everywhere in Canada. When Ukrainians in Manitoba, for example, started to protest that they were a founding people, too, and more people were able to speak Ukrainian than French in their area, the Multicult people in Ottawa solved the problem by giving them money to be as Ukrainian as they could – or as Icelandic, or German, or Italian, and so forth. It also gives the Liberals exclusive drawing rights on that large ethnic bloc of votes in Canada. It's a lesson the Liberals probably learned from the Democrats in the U.S., where things have been so managed that the blacks have no choice but to vote for the Democratic party if they want to keep the funds for minority programs coming. It provides employment for a number of people whose main skill is a native ability to speak the dialect of Hercegovina or paint Easter eggs or process applications. It has provided us with federal and provincial ministries and concurrent powers of patronage. It is also one of the more dangerous cults in Canada today.

Dangerous on two levels. First: what happened down at the multicultural television station illustrates an important if minor aspect of the problem. When the government gets into the business of encouraging ethnic cultures it has to turn to the high-profile ethnic organizations in the community. Governments, after all, in spite of their SIN files, codes, and computerized information on all of us, do not *yet* know who among their citizens knows the most about gypsy violins. But in any ethnic community the population breaks down into two groups: the great majority, who are to all intents and purposes assimilated into Canadian society, and a minority who, instead of merely speaking their native language or enjoying their native cooking on an informal basis at home, prefer an organized community association. Many of these community associations are highly politicized – especially those of Eastern Europe, but also some of the West European and Asian groups. They may represent the left or the right; they generally loathe one another.

All this is no problem. The problem begins when the government turns to these unrepresentative organizations and, probably unknowingly, fosters with taxpayers' money the feuds and hostilities of the Old World. They may even do more than that. There *are* ethnic organizations in Canada that are strongly supported by *extreme* right-wingers and *extreme* left-wingers. The pattern of their beliefs most likely will be reflected in the programming they choose for a television station. Thus, the extreme right may choose the old movies of the immediate pre-war era with their implicit celebration of fascist ideals, while the left will mount productions of socialist writers and poets, thus supplying a forum for socialist propaganda. The government will have little control over this (nor should it) and probably, since even the most bilingual civil servant rarely speaks Serbian, Hungarian, or Polish, will not know what that nice tall blond chap with the striking carriage and firm chin is saying in that old black-and-white movie to that smiling girl carrying the young child and a bunch of wild flowers.

The second level on which multiculturalism is dangerous is in its need for utilizing "objective truth" or the Big Lie.

Three years ago I was doing the research for an article on

education. I began sitting in on classes in various Toronto high schools. This was my first encounter with official multicultural studies. The school that most intrigued me was Agincourt Collegiate in a suburb of Toronto with a very mixed ethnic population, where a particularly bright history teacher was trying to do his best with the new – but not yet solidly entrenched – government guidelines on multicultural studies. "With the Irish potato famine," the teacher was saying, "we got strong Irish immigration to the New World. Old feuds between Protestants and Catholics were transported overseas. Do we perpetuate such attitudes by encouraging people to keep up the old ways?"

The discussion that followed was instructive. Knowledge of events surrounding the potato famine or the Serbo-Croatian disputes of the Old World were in short supply in the classroom, but personal opinions were not. Educational egalitarianism teaches that the student who knows nothing is just as good and worthy of a hearing as the one who knows something. This is the logical offshoot of the egalitarian thrust which preaches not that all people deserve equality of opportunity but that all people are equal in achievement. It is one of the most spiritually and mentally debilitating diseases of our time. It is not so much that it diminishes appreciation of people with special talents – talent is its own reward, like virtue – but that it debases taste and discourages the pursuit of excellence by society in general. It is, of course, the disease of choice in any society based on the politics of envy. Instead of teaching history, the helpless educator was opening floodgates and allowing – as he had to – his students to sit through waves of their own illiteracy and ignorance.

"I think if people come to Canada they should turn into Canadians. There should be a law or else they go back."

"How can you make a law for people who don't talk English? My mother doesn't speak anything but Croatian."

"Then she should go back to Croat [*sic*]." But that was three years ago and the educational multicultural boom was just beginning. To teach the appropriate form of multicultural studies – i.e., that every immigrant's culture is just as good as everyone else's – required considerable sanitizing of history. But that, after all, was the pace set by Trudeau in his call to Canadians to "forget the Plains of Abraham." (The French Canadians on the other hand, who understand the value of history, put "Je me souviens" on their licence plates.) The Ontario Ministry of Education (the most "progressive" in Canada) became, as it had earlier become with the trendy Hall-Dennis report, the instrument of enforcement in the agitprop of Multicult.

In 1977 it issued new History and Multicultural Heritage curriculum guidelines, which made a mockery out of both history and education, and even of any fleeting value multiculturalism might have. Grades Seven and Eight added some new core curriculum content such as "Social Reform: Trade Unionism and Women's Suffrage". Grades Seven to Ten were now to "develop a sympathetic understanding of the problems facing Third World Nations" and to fill out charts discussing the "bias" and "prejudice" immigrants face in Canada. The basic content of both the history courses and the multicultural programs affiliated with them was to develop "the concept of multiculturalism as a modern approach to dealing with cultural diversity which establishes each group's rights to cultural uniqueness, responsibilities for cross-cultural understanding, and full participation in building the Canada of the future." *Sic.*

The immediate result was the elimination from the approved textbook lists of fourteen textbooks condemned by the South Asia Origins Liaison Committee of the Toronto Board of Education as "negative and prejudicial". The books made reference to the caste system in India, among other things, which was not considered helpful in depicting Indian society in a "positive" manner. Such matters as historical accuracy were apparently not a consideration. A textbook co-authored by the distinguished Canadian historian Professor John Saywell was condemned for "patronizing Indians" by mentioning the English clothing that Mahatma Gandhi sometimes wore. It was ludicrous, of course, but it was chilling. History was being rewritten in order to please the pressure groups the multicultural industry had created.

By 1979 the major Canadian textbook publishers (known as The School Group) had sworn fealty to Multicult – and its multidollar textbook contracts – and had published their own abominable little handbook called "Textbooks Are For Everyone". According to the handbook, "All publishers and educators are alert for bias, and all learning materials are scrutinized carefully for any evidence, however inadvertent, of invalid racial, sexual, ethnic, religious, occupational and class assumptions. Various guidelines are used, but all have a common objective – to treat people as people in every context and to present every element in society as fairly as possible."

I have no idea what a textbook author would have to have lurking in his inner being to make an "inadvertent invalid sexual assumption" or a class, racial, or religious one for that matter. I'm prepared to bet that it would be less harmful to any normal child than the conscious assumptions of the bureaucrats scrutinizing the books. No betting is required, however, to see that while the aim of this approach may be to present "every element in society as fairly as possible" – since "fairly" is a relative term – it is clearly not to present every element as *truthfully* as possible.

The handbook has several full-page coloured illustrations. One is a kitchen scene with parents and a child. It is captioned "Showing parents sharing home chores helps very young children overcome unconscious sex role bias." The three figures in the painting are either native Indians or Orientals. The kitchen is clearly furnished by Karelia or one of those nifty kitchen boutiques and comes complete with a good selection of the electrical appliances known to man. A smiling dad is doing the dishes. A smiling mum is relaxing with a cup of something. A smiling young male child is sitting on the floor feeding the cat who, incidentally, is also oriental. A bright-coloured drawing of a smiling kitty-cat under a beaming sun is taped on the fridge door just below a little note "Don't forget the bread!" – probably written by dad, and attached to the door with a smile button. On top of the fridge, indifferent to inflation or class assumptions, is a huge bowl of fruit overflowing with grapes and bananas. It is a kitchen large enough to shoot a sitcom in and larger than any kitchen I have ever been inside. On the next page is a picture of five children playing together. The caption on this picture reads: "The multicultural character of Canada's population is reflected." Well, maybe the wishful-think Canada of the Multiculs. Two of the five children are white. One assumes (though one is not allowed, of course, to make assumptions) that one of these two white children is also ethnic, or else the substantial Polish, Italian, German, and the-rest-of-us will have lost out completely. One assumes this because European ethnics clearly can't be represented by the three black and yellow members who by proportional representation in this illustration give a completely false picture of Canada's racial make-up.

The point about all this, of course, is not that one disapproves of pictures with blacks or Orientals in them, but that one does disapprove of the attempt to depict Canada as a predominantly black or oriental country. It simply isn't true. Nor do I particularly disapprove of dad doing the dishes (though not in my house, thank you); I disapprove of presenting dad's doing the dishes to children as the norm when it clearly is not the norm. Or morally desirable when, at best, it is morally neutral. In the end one disapproves of the schools' spending time on these matters at all. They are questions to be dealt with according to the culture of the home and best dealt with, anyway, after the child has learned to read and write and think. But what teacher will have time to bother about reading and writing and thinking when they first have to concentrate on eliminating all the nasty unconscious stereotypes from their pupils' minds so he or she can concentrate on non-stereotypical studies of Third World Problems or The Trade Union Movement or The Meaning of Multiculturalism?

Though some politicized teachers embraced the Multicult approach to reality with much enthusiasm, most of those I interviewed seemed unhappy about the distortion and emphasis of the revised history and social study programs. Finally the discontent of academics bubbled into the open. Three eminent University of Toronto professors, J. M. Beattie, J. M. S. Careless, and M. R. Marrus, criticized the guidelines in a scathing letter to the *Globe and Mail*, after the entire history department requested them to do so. The professors wrote of the new curriculum: "A collection of moral tales to serve political ends. To put it bluntly history is being turned into propaganda. History done in this manner uses (or rather abuses) the past to teach a moral lesson, selecting historical content at will, sifting through the centuries without regard for patterns of development."

CHAPTER SIXTEEN

Glazed China

THE OCCASION WAS a book-launching party, and among the guests were journalist John Fraser and his wife, Elizabeth McCallum. Fraser was deep in the middle of his Chinese lessons and reading all about the Third Civilization in preparation for his imminent departure for China to replace the *Globe and Mail*'s Ross Munro – whose series on human rights in China had won world-wide recognition.

Fraser was enormously enthusiastic about going to China and was working harder in preparation for his assignment than any journalist I've ever known. He was describing in much detail the history of the various dynasties. I interrupted.

Amiel: "Have you read Simon Leys' *Chinese Shadows?*"
Fraser: "No, I haven't. What is it?"
Amiel: "It might interest you. It's among the first dissident literature to come out of the Chinese experience. Not *the* first, of course. Have you read Jean Pasqualini's (Bao Ruo-wang) *Prisoner of Mao?* That came out in paperback in '73. Or Lai Ying's *The Thirty-sixth Way?*"
Fraser: "No, I must do that."

Of course, Fraser knew considerably more about the difficult and fascinating history of pre-revolutionary China than I. My understanding of ancient China, simplistic no doubt, is of a people who managed to develop one of the highest, most complex cultures in the world and one of the cruellest. In spite of my disagreements with Edgar Snow over various interpretations of Mao's ambitions, goals, and methods, I could not deny the singular unpleasantness of life for hundreds of millions of ordinary Chinese under the previous regimes. Slavery, starvation, and subordination to warlords. Or foreigners. But as I listened to Fraser's rapturous accounts of the intricacies of the mandarin tongue, I couldn't help recalling two scenes from the recent past. The first was a walk with Marc Lalonde.

We are outside Toronto's Royal Ontario Museum. As we walk up Avenue Road, Lalonde asks me if I have seen the recent Chinese touring exhibition.

Amiel: "Yes, but I was a little sceptical."
Lalonde: "Of what?"
Amiel: "Well, I'm not sure that some of that paint-work could have been quite as early as they claim." (I was swimming totally out of my depth. If there is one thing I know less about, if possible, than particle physics, it is the characteristics of early Chinese artifacts.)
Lalonde: "But you know the Chinese are incredibly concerned about preserving their heritage. Under Mao they have taken great steps to bring the old art to the people."
Amiel: (choking) "Is that why they revised the Chinese language so the works of most philosophers and classicists would be inaccessible to the new generation unless translated by the state? *Chinese Shadows* is filled with accounts of the wanton destruction of the old temples and relics."
Lalonde: "I don't think I know this book *Shadows*. Is it by Edgar Snow?"

New York: circa 1970.
I am in an East 56th Street apartment for a small reception

for Maoist apologist author Han Suyin (*A Many-Splendoured Thing*, etcetera). There are about a dozen people there. I am clutching one of Suyin's books which I want her to autograph. As often as I try to speak to her she will pay no attention. I can't blame her. She is an exquisite woman, surrounded by men who are hanging on every word. And every word is about China. Suyin is explaining how she has just returned from witnessing an operation (an appendectomy, I think) on a young woman who had no anaesthetic but acupuncture. Everyone oohs.

One man: "My God, the Chinese."
Another man: (a trifle sceptically) "Speaking as a doctor, I'm inclined to think that maybe it was hysterical amnesia."
Suyin: (drawing a cloak of 3,000 years of civilization around her) "In my country we have methods you don't understand."

I manage to reach her and spurt out my uncle's name. Instantly she melts. *You* are Bernard's niece. There is much warmth and effusiveness – at a good arm's length. She autographs my book very affectionately. I ask, timidly, about the talk of labour camps. Han Suyin smiles. "Re-education farms," she says. I try again. There is no answer. In an interview in 1975 she will admit to 90,000 killed in the Cultural Revolution in Szechuan province alone. Even that figure will be considered a fraction of the real cost.

Along with Sweden, China becomes the great untouchable subject in the Canadian press. With the exception of the remarkable series of articles by Ross Munro on the repression of civil liberties in China, the standard Canadian media commentator will always be someone like the diplomat Chester Ronning, whose obeisance to the party line is nothing short of flackery. In one revealing passage in his book *A Memoir of China in Revolution* Ronning relates how, on returning to his childhood village in China, he discovers that instead of the barbaric punishment of being spanked and sent up to one's room for a childish misdemeanour, communism has brought in constructive self-criticism sessions at which little tykes stand up and confess to the community. It takes a truly totalitarian impulse to believe that going from a slap on the bottom to the psychological humiliation and emotional destructiveness of a group-encounter session is progress.

As new reports are coming out of China via John Fraser and other leading journalists of America and England, I begin to wonder if they've all gone stark, raving mad. Though as yet there is no Chinese Solzhenitsyn, there *is* sufficient data accumulating to indicate that in terms of mass murder, Mao Tse-tung, Chou En-lai, and their heirs are the world champions. Have we no concern for the Chinese people, I wonder, or do we lose all perspective in the presence of power and victory? I think of all the Sinologists: Franz Michael, George Taylor, George Backmann, with their estimates of twenty million to sixty million murdered. Even the conservative and cautious historian J. Guillermaz in *Le Parti Communiste Chinois au pouvoir* comes up with the figure of five million executions for the land reform program of 1949-52. The Russians put the cost of establishing Mao at twenty-five million (a calculation about which the wicked pen of William F. Buckley wrote: "The Soviets are very skilled at estimates of this kind").

Finally I can stand it no longer. I write a short column in *Maclean's* suggesting that all the visitors returning from China to tell of the absence of flies, venereal disease, poverty, and unhappiness are victims of the Potemkin Village syndrome, and see only what their hosts want them to see. My jumping-off point for this is a spare and powerful collection of short stories by a Chinese woman living in Vancouver named Chen Jo-hsi, who has spent six or seven years in Mao's paradise.

Chen Jo-hsi is the sort of person who gives Sinophiles acute attacks of speechlessness, which is perhaps why she is not included on their reading lists. Chen was educated in Taiwan, where she grew increasingly restless with the constant anti-Mainland propaganda of Chiang Kai-shek. She came to the United States to do graduate work at Mount Holyoke and Johns Hopkins University and ran smack into the early days of the China Syndrome. The rosy reports of all the marvellous things Mao was doing on the Mainland – reports which had been censored in Taiwan – confirmed Chen's scepticism of Taiwan's endless diatribes. She and her Chinese husband became true believers. They both returned to the Mainland and lived there for seven years, a period which included the Cultural Revolution. After that, they managed to leave. Her experiences became the material for short stories, articles, and a novel. What distinguishes her accounts of the dreadful Mainland regime is an intelligent love of and genuine compassion for the Chinese people; it is a love that never fails to note the dignity and pathos in the smallest action. The stories in her book *The Execution of Mayor Yin* cover the period of the Great Proletarian Cultural Revolution – as the Chinese people saw it. I was moved beyond description by her writing. It was not simply that it confirmed all my suspicions about the monstrous regime of Mao Tse-tung; it was that her stories gave flesh-and-blood actuality to the suffering. It was the flesh-and-blood of a simple old man trying to buy a piece of fish for his sick wife or the suffering of a lonely widower trying to get permission to remarry. It was *ordinary* suffering – not the drama of a Solzhenitsyn talking of life and death in the Gulag which you can begin to glimpse, Chinese-style, in Bao Ruo-wang's book, but suffering rooted in everyday experiences.

And so, I write my column on China. It is a small cry of pain at the future indignity to be visited upon the Chinese people: the indignity of free Westerners approving the enslavement of the Chinese. The reaction at *Maclean's* is one of general unhappiness. One of our editors is particularly unhappy and is reported to demand the magazine give equal space to an item about the "real" China. This is scarcely surprising. The same editor has also told me, on the occasion of the flare-ups in the Middle East, that the only country with a genuine desire for peace there is the Soviet Union. Incredulously, I ask him again, "Do you mean the *Soviet Union*? That biggish place on the map from what used to be Poland to Vladivostok? *They* don't want to keep things unstable and bubbling?"

Affably, firmly, in impeccable English liberal tones, he replies: "God no. They are the only ones with any decent instincts." Our super-liberal it seems, is untouched by the enmity of the Sino-Soviet giants and retains an equal sympathy for both – which would probably make him a prime candidate for a long period of re-education in either. Later, at the time of the Iranian crisis, he will say that the Russians have no interest in that part of the world, and reassign a story on Iran when he discovers that the staff writer originally assigned does not share all his views on that country.

My Chinese column attracts a fair amount of reader mail. All of it is unfavourable. Readers write to tell me I don't understand the nature of the Chinese revolution. Some say they haven't been there, but they know it is better. Others have been there and they know it is marvellous. One letter, on a National Film Board letterhead, particularly intrigues me. Ms. Phyllis Berck has written from Calgary to upbraid me. Writes Ms. Berck: "I have recently returned from a trip to China and I was impressed by what I saw. The reason I was impressed was because I had prepared myself by reading a great many books about China by pundits of many perspectives. This is what I feel your article lacked. . . . some awesome achievements have been accomplished since 1949 and you must not sell those short either. The praise for that belongs to the chinese [*sic*: capitals are either too capitalistic or too elitist for Ms. Berck or her secretary] themselves for the elimination of epidemic diseases, improvements in the status of women, elimination of prostitution, begging, selling of daughters for food, etc. . . . What it made me wonder about, is whether democracy with its inherent rights and freedoms could have done so much so soon."

My curiosity gets the better of me. What "great many books about China by pundits of many perspectives" are our NFB Sinophiles reading? I reply to Ms. Berck requesting her reading list. It is quite intriguing. The books and television programs listed are all rapturous accounts of the New China and include Shirley MacLaine's *You Can Get There From Here* and Han Suyin's *A Many-Splendoured Thing*. There is a post-script to Ms. Berck's reply. It seems that her perspectives on China are much appreciated. She has sold several pieces now on her experiences there and "while I don't expect a Pulitzer yet, I'm on my way."

The one reaction to the article I get at *Maclean's* that I am grateful for comes from senior editor Michael Enright. "I disagree with everything you say," he tells me straight, "but I'm glad there's room here for you to say it." This stops me for a moment and makes me reflect on my responses to John Fraser who, having rapturized his way through the Xidan Democracy wall, is now having a second look. The point about such bourgeois-trained journalists as Fraser is, of course, that – leaving aside voguish leftist sympathies, tren-diness, and even power-worship – they cannot quite get rid of their bourgeois reverence for *facts*. That is what Marx was being ever so sarcastic about over one hundred years ago in the Communist Manifesto. Fraser, like a good many other professionals of Western print, still labours under the delu-sion that there *is* such a thing as the simple truth – as op-posed to the "objective" or "class" truth of Marxism or pres-sure groups – and that his job as a reporter is to see as much of it as he can and then call it as he sees it. Even if he wishes it weren't so. Even if it doesn't "objectively" serve the Great Helmsman's cause and, consequently, the People's. No: obeying their as yet unre-educated bourgeois instincts, the John Frasers of our world must record it if they happen to observe it. They can't help it, like Pavlov's dog. Facts make them salivate.

And so it happens that, as often as not, a pretty accurate picture of the dreadful oppression that is China emerges from Fraser's reluctant pen. And that is why *Maclean's* senior editor Enright is glad – genuinely – that there is room in his magazine for a column with which he profoundly disagrees. It is a bourgeois habit and he can't quite shake it. And this is the reason the *Globe and Mail* will run the Ross Munro series casting a cold eye on China – side by side with its inane editorial celebration of the late Mao as a "great humanitarian", but run it nevertheless. And it is this peculiar bourgeois custom of running a great many diverse opinions side by side, attacked, belittled, steadily diminished, but not yet extinguished by the regulatory spirit of left-"liberalism"; this idea of liberty, which Marx sneeringly, unhappily, but I think quite accurately identified as a mere "outgrowth" of private enterprise; this liberty that permitted Marx himself to publish the view that it is not an "eternal law of nature" but something that would vanish under a different economic system, such as Marx's own – it is this liberty that I, and better people than I, are trying to hang on to. It is precisely the "inherent rights and freedoms" Ms. Berck fears might have held China back from stamping out epidemics, beggars, or prostitution that I would like to retain. Even if it means a slower rate of "improvements in the status of women" which Ms. Berck holds out to me in exchange. As a stubborn bourgeois, I think Ms. Berck's is a bad bargain, an offer women can and should refuse.

And beggars should refuse it too, I think, and prostitutes, even if the arbitrary equation were not as false as I believe it is. For if *lack of freedom* is indeed all it takes to wipe out epidemics and poverty and starvation and female servitude, old imperial China ought to have been rid of all these ills ages ago. Or old imperial Russia, or the great Indian sub-continent. It is the West, with its long tradition of ever-increasing individual liberties, that ought to have been, by the turn of this century, the sickest, poorest place on earth. Yet even left-libbers might concede that it was not.

Still, for some unfathomable reason we keep insisting that if others reject the freedoms that helped us to create our own standards of productivity, hygiene, and welfare – long before we started flirting with planned economy or the Welfare State – they will somehow reach our standards *sooner*. For heaven's sake, Ms. Berck, why?

CHAPTER SEVENTEEN

Freedom of Speech (When I Like What You Say)

THE PHOTOGRAPH in the March 14, 1974, *Globe and Mail* summed it up. I had been following the issue for a few days by then, but until I saw that picture I had not made a decision to write about it. Then there was no choice.

In the front stood Professor Edward L. Banfield of the University of Pennsylvania, hands clasped behind his back, staring rigidly off to infinity, a man well into his middle years, thin, balding, bespectacled, and besieged. Behind him on a platform, hands in pockets, legs akimbo, with tinted aviator glasses and Afroed hair, was the pudgy figure of Bill Shabas, leader of the Students for a Democratic Society, and several supporters standing around a table to which a sign had been attached:

"No Academic Freedom for Racists! Ban Banfield!"

Banfield, a highly respected conservative urbanologist, author of several books, including *The Unheavenly City* and *The Moral Basis of a Backward Society*, had been invited to speak at the University of Toronto by a group of professors. His visit was the high point of the year-long "find a racist" romp that had been sweeping the Toronto campuses in imitation of a similar American witch-hunt a year or so earlier. Banfield was the tail-end of it all, the last stand of the SDS, but after the fuss and moralizing and blood-letting subsided, the Banfield incident would mark the beginning of a far more serious witch-hunt respectably incorporated into our educational and government institutions.

Banfield's own case was very simple. Between 1954 and 1955 he took his Italian wife and their two children to live in a desperately poor village in Southern Italy. They stayed there for nine months. Banfield's purpose was to try and understand the cycle of poverty and despair that seems endemic to much of Sicilian peasant life and, if possible, to recommend practical ways of breaking the cycle. His conclusions appeared in the book *The Moral Basis of a Backward Society*. According to Banfield, the sole concern of each family in the Southern Italian village he studied is their own day-to-day survival, with the natural result that there are no organized community efforts to improve life as a whole. Being an academic and a sociologist, Banfield coined the term "amoral familism" to describe this syndrome. (One can only wonder what the connotations of "amoral" may have been to barely literate left-wing students whose grasp of "morality" seemed to extend only to the clichéd areas of free love and the right to do as they please. This word, so easily confused with "immoral" by those with a shaky grasp on letters, would not be a fortunate choice for Banfield in the days ahead. Still, the failings of his detractors could scarcely be put at Banfield's door.) It would be difficult to change these conditions, Banfield concluded, but after discussing the various alternatives he suggested massive aid to improve educational facilities for the village (with incentive programs to get the best teachers) which "would have the interest and support of the villagers . . ." and the use of public television and newspapers to foster community awareness. It was this book, astonishingly, that earned Banfield his racist, anti-Italian label.

Some years later, in 1978, the eminent Italian author and journalist Luigi Barzini would describe a conversation with a Neapolitan taxi-driver lamenting the forced resignation of Italy's southern president, Giovanni Leone, for gross corruption. "The taxi driver," wrote Barzini in *The Spectator*, "enumerated Leone's sins: he protected and helped his friends, ingeniously utilized all tax loopholes, saw to it that all his relatives enjoyed all possible advantages in the struggle of life, etc. When he travelled on official business and state visits abroad, he took along extra planes filled with freeloading friends, clients, relatives, relatives of relatives, electors, courtiers and retainers, including his wife's hairdresser. Were these sins? the taxi driver asked. He wanted me (a foreigner from North Italy) to explain why the poor president had been condemned for performing admirably only what, after all, are considered a man's absolute duties in Naples." It would be hard to illustrate the accuracy of Banfield's earlier study and his thesis of "amoral familism" in a more telling way.

To summarize Banfield's other book, *The Unheavenly City*, in a few paragraphs would be to risk the kind of distortion the media displayed. Banfield's book is a complex, highly original study of urban life that is head and shoulders above most sociological works and shows why Banfield was recommended for the Chair in Urban Studies at Harvard University. Just to quote Banfield is to misquote him because he attaches special meaning to certain common words (such as "lower class" or "inner city"), which he carefully defines in the book, and without his definitions the sense in which he uses these terms is lost. His theses include the idea that *relative* poverty, meaning the material well-being and lifestyle of a group being lower than that of another group, cannot be eliminated by the reduction of poverty as such. He makes a distinction between social classes on the basis of their relationship to the "present" and to the "future". (Living for the present is more likely to be a "lower-class" mode of life, but would also be found among the well-off. Similarly, planning and sacrificing for their children's future would be a hallmark of middle-class values that may well be found in financially impoverished homes.) He outlines how certain social legislation, such as the minimum-wage laws, may actually perpetuate the very problems it sets out to solve (an idea that was endorsed recently by a coalition of blacks and labour leaders). And he concludes that the measures necessary to eliminate quickly certain urban problems would be acceptable to a totalitarian society but are rightly unacceptable to ours. This complex analysis of the problems of urban society was summed up by *Toronto Star* reporter Ellen Roseman as Banfield's view that "American blacks are responsible for their own poverty . . . mired in the ghetto not because of white discrimination – but because of their own culture."

Until the SDS forcibly prevented Banfield's lecture, very few Canadians either on or off the campus knew his name. Within hours of the incident a large number of them were describing him as "racist". The *Globe and Mail*'s editorial page struck a pious note about the behaviour of the SDS two days after the cancelled lecture, but couldn't resist describing Banfield as "a ridiculously reactionary American professor". There was no reason given for this description, and no evidence in the editorial of the slightest familiarity with Banfield's work. Perhaps they had cribbed from Miss Roseman. A week later the *Globe and Mail*, quite endearing in its haphazard honesty, described the editorial conference they called at which the text of Banfield's cancelled speech was read. The column proudly noted how the massed editorial staff fell asleep listening to it.

Around Toronto the reaction of many who hadn't read Banfield, and had difficulty with words of more than two syllables in any case, was similar. "Sure Banfield's a racist. Anti-Italian, no question," Dan Ianuzzi, editor of the Italian-language paper *Corriere Canadese* (and now licence-holder of the Toronto Multicultural TV station), told me in a telephone conversation. "But the SDS should have let him speak and hang himself," he added in a burst of generosity.

One week later in the debates room of the University of Toronto a public meeting would be held, organized by the Students for a Democratic Society. At the speakers' table a group of concerned citizens sit smoothing their hair and fiddling with papers as the television crews and reporters line the walls and the rows of chairs quickly fill up with students and civilians alike. The SDS spokesman, Bill Shabas, is in charge of the meeting. Next to him sits Charles Roach, counsel for the National Black Coalition of Canada. A handicapped immigrant worker sits next to Gianni Groho-vaz, editor of the Italian community paper *Il Giornale di Toronto*. The meeting is being held to organize the fight against racism, and the room is pulsating with the excitement of brushing close to the terrible germ that infected the world of Hitler and the Third Reich. The room is very aware of this because references to Hitler and the Third Reich abound in the rhetoric. Delicious little shudders go over the white-haired matrons and their long-haired daughters. It seems such a terrible waste that these people of apparently very decent instincts have fallen into the oldest trap of the extreme left: The Front.

Lawyer Charles Roach gets up and delivers himself of two sentences wherein lies the basic approach of left-wing pressure groups: "The right to know, the right to freedom of speech, the right to freedom of assembly, are rights only so far as they secure our basic right to equality. If that means you can't have books, you can't have statements, you can't have meetings, that's how it must be . . . and we've been trying to remove [Banfield's] books from the libraries." Charles Roach is described by the media – then and today – as a "civil rights" lawyer.

At the back of the room is a table piled high with pamphlets and leaflets, now being perused by press and those spectators unable to get seats. As Bill Shabas reads the telegrams of support for his anti-racist drive from the National Black Coalition of Canada, 100 Canadian National railway workers, 100 postal workers, members of the Portuguese Democratic Association, and the executive of the Canadian Union of Public Employees, Toronto Central Library local, I go over to the table. The names in the leaflets of those academics being accused of racism are familiar: Arthur Jensen, William Shockley, Hans Eysenck, and so on. In addition are the local racists about to be paraded in effigy: Dr. R. Ian Hector, Associate Professor in the Faculty of Medicine, University of Toronto, and Psychiatrist-in-Chief at the Wellesley

Hospital; and Dr. Carl Bereiter, educational psychologist at the Ontario Institute for Studies in Education.

What follows is their story. It is an account I was never able to publish in Canada because the magazine for which I was writing, *Saturday Night*, suspended publication for a year just before the issue containing the story was to be published. I condense it here and alter it slightly because then, in 1974, I thought that we were coming to the end of a long night and that the example of what happened to these men would serve as a reminder to prevent another darkness. I was wrong. In the fight between the ideas of men like Charles Roach and liberal democracy, it is Charles Roach who seems to be winning. Only his ideas are no longer the shrill rhetoric of the outside fringe, but are being institutionalized – quietly, respectably, euphemistically – by our government. In 1974 it was still the SDS's thugs who were breaking, albeit successfully, the law. By 1979, as I will try to show, the lawbreakers might have been Banfield and the professors who invited him to speak.

"Racism", meaning the concept that one race or group of humans is inherently superior to another, is a noxious and patently false doctrine. Of course, even if a group were found to be superior, it would still not reduce the concept of equality before the law or the concept of equality of opportunity, the legal and social concepts that we choose to live by in liberal democracies. They do not have to be earned and they cannot be lost, and no statistical distribution of ability can invalidate them. They are – or ought to be – entrenched axioms that do not address themselves to questions of merit. Even if the group to which we belong were scientifically proven to possess some special qualities, or to be deficient in some, it would and should confer no special privileges or place no special burdens on us. In our society we agree on the assumption of equality precisely to free us from the necessity of constantly determining whether, in fact, we are equal or not. In any case, the best available evidence suggests that we probably are.

Denying these assumptions *is* racism, and it is true that, even in liberal democracies, many individuals and sometimes entire regions have been known to deny them. But in the 1960s "racism" began to be used in a different sense. It began to refer to the reason why certain groups, or certain individuals from *any* group, were socially and economically different from others. Welfare mothers, unemployed youths, convicts, and any group of non-English-speaking Canadians or Americans were said to be victims of "racist" policies. If some members of these groups also happened to be black, brown, yellow, or anything but white, the "racism" from which they suffered was doubled.

This up-dated definition of racism was based on the belief that human rights included membership in the middle class, regardless of ability or effort. All the problems facing people at the bottom of the socio-economic scale started to be covered by the umbrella of "racism". The Canadian government quickly got into the act, following the leadership of the by now feeble-minded and blatantly "racist" – in the oldest and purest sense of the word – United Nations. Canada dutifully convened seminars across the country thoughout 1974 to celebrate the beginning of the United Nations' Decade to Combat Racism. They included representatives from welfare groups and Convicts' Rights Associations and every other bandwagon going. (The Homosexual Rights movement hadn't really peaked then, so they missed out on most of the conference fun.) It was tricky going for the federal find-the-racists squad. There were no obvious targets in Canada, since we had virtually no slavery, and no whirlwind to reap. (Perhaps the only legitimate target might have been the Department of Indian Affairs; it administers the Indian Act, which insists on treating native peoples differently from the rest of us, to the extent of pressing for their conviction on charges which could not even be laid against other Canadians – at least until the Supreme Court of Canada overturned the conviction of an Indian caught drinking on the reservation. But no one, least of all the native groups themselves, were going to finger Indian Affairs so long as they

had all those grants and projects to hand out.) So the delegates on racism cast around for more vulnerable targets.
And with the help of the SDS and other far-left organizations
they came upon the work and ideas of medical and social sci-
entists Banfield, Bereiter, Jensen, and Hector.

It was, initially, the work of Arthur Jensen of the University of California that caused all the fuss. In 1969 Jensen
published his controversial essay "How Much Can We Boost
I.Q. and Scholastic Achievement?" The SDS had the issue of
racism on its waiting hands.

Large-scale social programs to fight urban problems in the
U.S. had been a failure. The liberals and the socialists
blamed the programs for the failure, and of course blamed
society for the problems the programs were to have solved.
Jensen was concerned with the specific failure of compensatory education. His essay, based on an impressive body of
evidence, hypothesized that heredity may be as powerful in
determining intelligence as environment, perhaps even
more powerful. He called for research into that part of the
human intelligence which exists before the social environment has any chance to act upon it.

I have no idea, not being remotely trained in this area,
how to evaluate the evidence. That, however, is beside the
point. The point is that Jensen wished to research an area
and that area was designated off-limits. Jensen pointed to
statistics indicating that *blacks as a group* scored lower than
whites even on the so-called culture fair tests and suggested
that, in addition to the environmental factors which he did
not dismiss, there may be a more powerful factor of heredity. He emphasized that the hypothesis was nothing but a hypothesis to be tested and researched. Its aim would be to
provide compensatory education that would take into account different patterns of ability, when – or if – these patterns were revealed by research. He pointed out the limited
meaning of "intelligence" as measured by I.Q. tests, and
clearly stated that it was not synonymous with the sum of an
individual's mental abilities, although it was linked to traditional scholastic achievement.

Liberals and socialists were outraged. They had vast sums of money and patronage tied up in the environmentally oriented programs they supported – environment in this sense meaning, of course, the social environment in which an individual develops. Egalitarians were apoplectic. Here was someone wanting to *research* the invidious idea that human beings may have individual differences in their innate abilities and that, far worse, there may be patterns of mentation more characteristic of one racial group than another. (God knows why this upset anyone. It seems fairly evident that certain groups show a higher percentage of achievement in certain fields. Which doesn't prevent the artistically blessed Italians from giving us some of the greatest engineers or mathematicians, or the scientifically inclined Germans from coming up with Beethoven or Thomas Mann. These things may excite actuaries, but are of little concern to the rest of us.) Jensen was called/"a notorious white supremacist"; his essay was referred to as "academic manure". An advertisement in the Sunday *New York Times* in October 1973, signed by assorted faculty members from Canada and the United States, described his work as "unscientific" and "socially vicious". The ad went on from there:

> Nevertheless, the generators of this new racism persist in their bigotry. Their theories, despite their academic garb, do not differ in their scientific character or their social effects from those advanced by American slave-owners, the Nazis, or advocates of apartheid in South Africa.

Only the occasional voice of reason prevailed. Of this attack on Jensen, D. O. Hebb, Chancellor of McGill University, wrote in a letter to the *American Psychologist*:

> Jensen is not immoral, or unethical, or antisocial to make his argument, even if he has made errors of interpretation. . . . I am appalled at the quality of criticism from social scientists. Their reaction is dogmatic and emotional, and to hell with logic.

The research of Banfield, Jensen, *et al.* had involved minority and disadvantaged groups. What the SDS, the Italian-language newspapers, the delegates to the government seminars I attended, and the National Black Coalition of Canada failed to see, as they railed at and abused these men, was that only through the work of academics of intellectual curiosity, coupled with courage and integrity, was there any real chance of understanding or solving the problems about which they claimed to be concerned. If the interests of the people they presumed to represent had really been paramount in their minds, the names and ideas of Banfield, Bereiter, and Jensen would have been discussed, not necessarily with agreement, but with respect. But then it is the existence rather than the solution of these problems on which the power of leaders of special-interest groups is based.

Dr. R. Ian Hector is a man who wishes to be left in peace. In 1966 he was appointed Psychiatrist-in-Chief at the Wellesley Hospital in Toronto. By 1970 he was also a consultant to the Ontario Workmen's Compensation Board and on staff at the University of Toronto. His reputation among students and professional associates was excellent. But by 1974 the University of Toronto would be evasive about his status there, the Ontario Workmen's Compensation Board would de facto relieve him of consulting work, and the Wellesley Hospital would re-route calls endlessly, and finally replace him as Head of Psychiatry. Dr. Hector is a man who has been harassed, maligned, and professionally damaged. He deserves to be left in peace. Regrettably, his story is of some importance.

In 1970, in the course of his job for the Workmen's Compensation Board, Dr. Hector wrote a report on an Italian worker who claimed to be disabled because of a back injury. Somehow a four-page extract from the report found its way into the hands of the SDS and the Communist Canadian Party of Labour. They seized upon it as "racist", and so Dr. Hector became fair game.

The four-page extract from the report is quite unremarkable, except perhaps for its thoroughness. After a physical examination of the workman, Hector concluded the injury had no apparent physical origin (a fact not contested by Hector's detractors). As the man was nevertheless totally disabled, he concluded the ailment was probably psychogenic in origin, as opposed to physiological. Hector suggested causes for this condition. The patient, in Dr. Hector's words "a poorly acculturated Italian", had a Grade Five education and a limited knowledge of English. He had moved from Calabria to Milan to Stuttgart to Cologne to Barrie, Ontario, to Toronto, employed as a general construction worker. Other personal factors in his life indicated possible dependency needs. By believing himself ill he had an excuse for a situation that was just too much for him to handle. Dr. Hector recommended a partial disability pension, attempts to help the patient improve his English, and welfare assistance. It was the report of a conscientious and thorough physician.

Nowhere in the report did Dr. Hector make any causal link between the patient's nationality and his illness. Those wondering how the SDS could possibly interpret the report as "racist" are forced to conclude that, by identifying the workman as Italian, Dr. Hector was *ipso facto* guilty of racism. All in accord with that popular school of thought which insists on ignoring *any* differences between people at whatever cost to fact and logic.

The one ray of enlightenment cutting through the gloom of all this came in an impassioned speech made by a Dr. Anthony Cecutti to the Governing Council of the University of Toronto. Dr. Cecutti, an obstetrician, was a member of the Governing Council in 1973-4 when an SDS-organized petition was presented to it urging Council to fire the "racist" Hector from the Faculty of Medicine.

Cecutti pleaded for the right of a doctor to acquaint his students with community and cultural traditions. Italian women, he said, *may* scream and cry in childbirth. Members of the family *may* cry with them. If we aren't allowed to tell our students about the different cultural attitudes to pain and such events as childbirth, explained Cecutti, patients will not get the understanding they require or medical students

the knowledge they need to become first-class doctors. Cecutti's point was well taken. It is clearly easier to assist, diag-
nose, and determine the needs of patients if the doctor
knows the customs of their culture or their likely reaction to
unpleasant stimuli. In certain oriental cultures, for instance,
an overt reaction to pain is considered such poor form that a
patient could literally be on the threshold of death before a
Western physician would suspect there was anything seriously wrong with him or her. Mediterranean people generally suffer from no such reticence – though of course individuals may significantly differ from the norm in any
culture.

Left-lib reaction to Dr. Hector's report was neither conscientious nor moderate. In a letter to the University of Toronto's student newspaper *Varsity* the report was grotesquely
distorted. The letter was signed by seven faculty members,
headed up by Professor J. D. Kaye of the Centre for Linguistic Studies (Dr. Kaye is now at the Université de Québec à
Montréal). Wrote Kaye:

"In *The Moral Basis of a Backward Society*, Banfield writes
that southern Italians are poor because of their culture –
their laziness, their 'amoral familism'. Dr. Ian Hector of the
Medical School puts Banfield's ideas into practice by accusing Italian workers from the same region about which Banfield writes of being 'culturally predisposed' to 'play a sick
role'." The out-of-context quotes from Hector's report were
doubly false. They not only concealed the doctor's sympathetic approach to the individual case he was reporting, but
they also managed to turn his assessment of one man into a
slander on *all* Italian workers.

Professor Kaye was not about to stop at this. He was a
member of the Teach-In on Racism about to be held at the
University of Toronto's Convocation Hall and so his interpretation of Hector's remarks appeared on the Teach-In
posters glued up all around the university. It was an interesting comment on the use to which linguistic studies could be
put.

But mau-mauing can be very successful, when it comes

from the left. (I have yet to see, in postwar years, a single successful example of it from the right.) Michael Starr, then newly appointed Chairman of the Workmen's Compensation Board, met with the SDS-supported "Committee for Just Compensation" and announced, "I have spent my whole life fighting to stamp out discrimination. Suffice it to say that I am not in agreement with the approach of Dr. Hector."

Well, not quite suffice. Apparently Mr. Starr hadn't actually read Dr. Hector's report at that point – perhaps he had just read about it from Ellen Roseman's nifty little précis in the same article that summed up Banfield. A couple of months later (and subsequent, I believe, to Dr. Hector's hiring a solicitor), Mr. Starr blithely announced he had now read Dr. Hector's report and did not find any evidence of racism or discrimination in it. "Dr. Hector's services," he proclaimed, "if necessary, will be retained by the Board in the future." Subsequent telephone calls to the Board indicated that such future occasions were not about to arise.

Dr. Carl Bereiter, a highly qualified educational psychologist, was the first to feel the tickle of the left-wing campaign against academic freedom when he came up to the Ontario Institute for Studies in Education in 1967. His specialty was designing teaching programs for pre-school children from disadvantaged backgrounds. Seen passing in the street, Bereiter would have been indistinguishable from the flower-generation gang. Tall, gangling, bearded, and gentle, he had the kind of temperament that could take the spilled food, insults, and tantrums of frustrated pre-schoolers in his stride. He'd keep going because he believed, and believed quite firmly, that there *was* a way to reach out and give ghetto kids a break. What in fact distinguished him from most flower children was the kind of tenacity that is the mark of a disciplined professional.

Bereiter had worked in the States with educator Siegfried Engelmann and developed a highly structured pre-school program that had shown a remarkable success rate. The U.S. Department of Health, Education and Welfare chose his system as one of twenty-one in the nation showing significant academic achievement out of one thousand screened projects. His arrival in Toronto coincided with the release of a five-year study chronicling the failure of our junior kindergartens to help immigrant and native Indian children. Though the *Toronto Star* headlined the story about Bereiter's arrival with "They're Going to Put Tiny Tots in a Pressure Cooker" and described the negative attitude of teachers to Bereiter's two-hour program of tough, fast drilling in language and basics (hard work for teachers), the reporter wrote that the kids seemed to like it.

Bereiter's approach made sense. In trying to help disadvantaged children compete with middle-class kids, most Canadian schools and systems had attempted to copy the *frills* of middle-class life – the excursions to the zoo and the games, music, and finger-painting of family fun – without understanding that it was precisely because children from an educated background received their enriched vocabulary and language skills *automatically* that they could afford to spend time looking at alligators. Underprivileged children were being taken on museum-and-zoo outings by well-meaning teachers while they still lacked the basic academic tools they needed to assimilate what they saw. They didn't go home to rooms lined with books and dinner-table quizzes designed to see if junior could do his multiplication tables. These children, more often than not, went home to alcoholic fights, or parents who were desperately trying to hold down two jobs, or parents who couldn't read a word of English or, perhaps, of any language.

Bereiter was determined to give them the skills they would need to get out of the rut their parents were in. But he insisted on explaining the concepts behind his programs. And that was a mistake. He explained that a major handicap for some children was language: they spoke a sort of shorthand street-dialect that wasn't adequate for expressing and assimilating the ideas and content of school curriculum. Essentially he was saying what George Orwell had said so eloquently in his essay "Politics and the English Language". He said that language influences thought. But Bereiter used a phrase that rankled the egalitarians of the left. He said children who spoke this shorthand English were "culturally deprived". He knew he was on thin ice, and explained carefully that this cultural deprivation referred only to skills necessary for success in school. His system stressed grammar, syntax, and vocabulary, and it worked. But Bereiter had committed the fatal heresy. He had examined factors inherent in a group's culture (in this case the street-English of disadvantaged children) and pinpointed this as one of the reasons for their lack of advancement. The fact that experience seemed to prove him right made things worse. The creed of the times – then as today with the ongoing clean-up of history for Multicult purposes – is that the culture of any group is always equal to (if not more equal than) the culture of any other.

The campaign against Bereiter and the others was initially organized by the SDS and the Canadian Party of Labour. Phrases were lifted from his work and reprinted on posters and pamphlets, their meaning distorted or destroyed. The Canadian Party of Labour printed a particularly unpleasant piece of literature titled *Verbal Deprivation and the Racist Work of Carl Bereiter*. Cartons of the 24-page booklet were stacked up at strategic locations in the University of Toronto. Student groups, particularly those representing minorities, started to demand that Bereiter be fired. And it spread. While a delegation of parents from the Regent Park public housing project was asking that Bereiter's work be continued with their children, the University of Toronto Students' Administrative Council and ten other associations and individuals (including the dreadful Jean-Paul Sartre – will he never leave us? Are we forever to be plagued by this senile and immoral man urging young students to "go out and kill a *flic*" rather than trying it himself and taking the consequences?) were sponsoring the Big Teach-In featuring Ashley Montagu, Charles Roach, and others. Caricatures of Bereiter, Hector, Banfield, and their colleagues-in-crime that would have done *Der Stürmer* proud were plastered everywhere, with out-of-context or distorted quotes issuing in large balloons from their mouths.

No word from the vigilant press in our land. Not a mutter from the Civil Liberties Union, except one cautious letter, after the cancellation of Banfield's speech, pointing out that "the imputation of racism" was not sufficient to justify the abrogation of freedom of speech. Not a peep out of the then University of Toronto president, John Evans, who was busy rushing around assuring community pressure groups that he "regretted" the Banfield incident and making pointedly sure that he did not reissue an invitation to Banfield. All quiet on the Western Front. And when, after a two-year evaluation of Bereiter's program in ten Toronto schools showing positive results, the Ontario Ministry of Education rejected it, it was on the grounds that "the program disagreed with our philosophy."

Bereiter left. There were plenty of offers for him to help the disadvantaged children of America's immigrants and ghetto families. Banfield left. He might be blocked from another platform or two, but he would go on to write and lecture. The people whose problems Banfield and Bereiter were actually trying to understand couldn't leave. They were locked into their poverty and handicaps. But perhaps the voice of editor Gianni Grohovaz of *Il Giornale di Toronto* would comfort them: "Some people came to me with this problem of academic racism and we embraced it right away, because wherever an idea of justice comes from, we embrace it. I believe in freedom, the rights of people, and I cannot accept the idea of academic freedom when that freedom makes slaves of someone else."

A few months later it was all over. The leaders of the SDS were tried in a three-ring circus of a student court for violating academic freedom. The papers talked a bit about the right to academic freedom, though no one bothered to clean up the reputation of the people smeared along the way. That was thought either unnecessary or the responsibility of the injured parties through civil litigation. The ringleaders of the SDS incident were suspended from the university for several years. The SDS itself was denied the right to use the prefix "University of Toronto". There was no mention made of the encouragement of the SDS tactics by faculty members or their promiscuous use of racist slogans. John Evans remained as University President, apologizing to everyone he could find.

Some thought it was all over, as the so-called student conservatism of the mid-seventies set in. These people – myself included – should ponder the last paragraph of Albert Camus's novel *The Plague*.

> And indeed as he listened to the cries of joy rising from the town, Rieux remembered that such joy is always imperiled. He knew what those jubilant crowds did not know but could have learned from books: that the plague bacillus never dies or disappears for good; that it can lie dormant for years and years in furniture and linen-chests; that it bides its time in bedrooms, cellars, trunks and bookshelves; and that perhaps the day would come when, for the bane and the enlightening of men it roused up its rats again and sent them forth to die in a happy city.

It was about a year later that I walked into the office of Ontario Conservative Premier William Davis. As I waited for him, I looked at the books on his bookshelves. There was a copy of Banfield's *The Unheavenly City*. I was astonished. When the Premier came into the room, I asked him what he thought of the book. "Well," he replied, "I haven't had time to read it yet." But he'd heard it was something he ought to take a look at. I muttered something about its being a controversial book that examines the problem of minorities in cities, in order to better understand and, if possible, help in solving them.

"Well," said the Premier as I was getting ready my tape machine, "we are doing something similar about minorities in this province. We are strengthening the Human Rights Commission. To make things better for all the people of Ontario."

CHAPTER EIGHTEEN

A Correspondence Course with the Thought Police

IT HAS COME TO THIS. Issues collect on my desk in great heaps of unopened letters, torn-out newspaper clippings, notes pinned next to my typewriter with phone numbers that I cannot connect to a limb or even a hank of hair. But this letter, here on top, this one matters.

It is a letter that was sent, not to me, but to my editor at *Maclean's*, Peter C. Newman. He has passed it on to me to answer – thank god, since the authors of the letter did not want me to see it. There was no copy for me. After all, it was merely a complaint against my work made by a government organization to my employer without offering me any opportunity to respond. And which government department would operate in this manner? Why, a Human Rights Commission.

I look at the letter again. Ironically, it is not my words against the murderers in the Soviet Union, not my dislike of the moral relativism we show towards the relentlessly cruel and barbaric new rulers of Africa, not my general unhappiness with social democrats, or my complete contempt for Swedish ones in particular, that has aroused the ire of the government. No. The Manitoba Human Rights Commission has accused me of being anti-*German*.

I giggle. But wait. This *is* the logical outcome of all that Charles Roach, William Shabas, Marc Lalonde, Laura Sabia, David MacDonald, Iona Campagnolo, and the other countless would-be commissars want, even if in this instance they would not have initiated it. This is a quick flash of *their* brave new world.

Time to put my foot inside the door. After all, I did not open it.

What caused the fuss was a lengthy article that appeared in *Maclean's* on April 4, 1977. The article was an analysis of Britain's current economic and social woes. I had worked very hard on it, and the interviewing and reading I had done were extensive. In the course of the article I had tried to understand why the British wouldn't pull together to get themselves out of the dreadful economic mess they were in. It was a question most of the world was asking, and no one seemed to be able to answer, except with vague rumblings about socialism and trade unions. I had no clear answers either, of course, but there were important questions to be asked. The North Sea oil was obviously going to shore things up for only a few years. The so-called "Dutch Disease" of spending North Sea oil profits before they were gushing was already being predicted for England. I brought all my folders, clippings, notes, and cassettes back to Canada and wrote for three weeks.

Here is the section that caused the offence – in context.

Diagnosis: Everybody wonders about the reason for the British disease, yet on the face of it it seems the least mysterious of this century's historical events. People work hard when they are propelled by necessity; Britons are not. In fact, they sometimes can make more on the dole – or the "fiddle" – than by breaking their backs at a job. People work hard when the state compels them to work: the British state doesn't – at least not yet. Whatever stands the state may be forced into later because of declining morale and productivity, at this point in the development of benign statism the government giveth to the worker but demandeth relatively little.

People work when they have ambitions for themselves or their country. Individual ambitions can no longer motivate Britons because of increasing disincentives for any kind of achievement, while the glory of the country – which might mean something, say, to a Chinese worker today – would only be greeted with hoots of derision in England.

The British might work, at least in the sense of pulling together, when they feel the enemy is at the gates. But Britons don't seem to feel that at all: the Huns are gone and nobody really believes in the reality of the Russian Bear.

Later on in the article I would mention, with some sympathetic understanding, the political plight of Enoch Powell. I would talk about the clashes between East Indians and the British in terms of a cultural conflict rather than as expressions of sheer bigotry as many observers preferred to view them; I would talk about the abominable National Front, the new statism, the trade unions, the character problems of the British – but the Human Rights Commission would pounce upon none of these.

The letter came to Peter Newman, dated June 30, 1977. Excuse me if I reproduce it in full. Everyone who writes in Canada may soon start to receive such letters; these writers, and their readers, should know about them. Under the imposing letterhead of the Human Rights Commission of Manitoba, it read:

Dear Mr. Newman:
In Maclean's magazine of April 4, 1977, an article was published about the economic and political problems of Great Britain.

On page 32 this article stated:
"The British might work, at least in the sense of pulling together, when they feel the enemy is at the gates. But

Britons don't seem to feel that at all: the Huns are gone and nobody really believes in the reality of the Russian Bear. Under the circumstances you'd have to be a bloody fool to work and, whatever else they may be, Britons are not fools."

This part of the article identifies the German people with the Huns, and this is a very serious insult of a nation that today is an ally of Canada and the NATO.

The Huns were an Asiatic tribe of fierce fighters who, in the fourth and fifth centuries, had invaded Europe and threatened the Roman Empire. They are considered barbarians and merciless killers. Their best known king was Attila, who was called "Scourge of God".

The term "Huns" was widely used in the First World War to stereotype the German people as barbarians. It was, again, used in the Second World War by the war propaganda. The purpose was to make all Germans look like brutal barbarians, whereas in fact only the Nazis and their ss and Secret Police committed atrocious and barbaric crimes – not only against Jews but against a great number of Germans who opposed Hitler and the Nazis.

The article in Maclean's does, however, not refer to the Nazis as Huns but includes all Germans, whether they were Nazis or not.

It thus insults a large number of Canadians of German origin who immigrated after the Second World War and who were properly screened as to their political past before they were admitted by the Canadian immigration authorities.

It is improper and not justifiable to apply the term Huns to them in a Canadian magazine as it exposes them to hatred and may lead to discrimination.

We bring our concerns to your attention for consideration in future publications. We would appreciate receiving a response.

Yours truly,
M. Myers, Q.C.
Chairperson

I was in the middle of a major feature for *Maclean's* with a press deadline of the following week, so I did not reply for about eight days. My response was dated July 13, 1977, and since I had no idea whether Chairperson Myers was male, female, or cabbage, such being the nature of our de-sexed euphemisms, I was forced to address myself to a neutered Myers.

Dear Chairperson Myers:
Thank you for enlightening me on the origin of the word "Huns". It may interest you to know that it was first employed by the late Kaiser Wilhelm to describe his own subjects ("the world will fear us as it once feared the Huns ..." etc.)

You are also right in stating that the word was used in both wars by the Allied War propaganda for the purpose of making all Germans look like brutal barbarians. Presumably this was necessitated by the considerable practical difficulties in telling the difference between Nazis and good Germans in the opposing trenches. In fact, some authorities believe that members of the Gestapo and the ss – who according to you are the only ones who could be accurately described as Huns – were not even present in any great numbers in the battles of England and the mid Atlantic. Much as many Germans may have opposed the Nazis and Hitler, this seemed less than evident to the peoples of the world until the end of the war.

For this reason I don't feel that it is inappropriate to talk of the Huns in the context of the war years, which of course was the context in which I used the expression in my article. I can assure you that I would not use the word when talking about Goethe, Beethoven or my next door neighbour in Toronto – even without a warning from the ever vigilant (and chillingly literal-minded) Human Rights Commission of Manitoba.

Since you saw fit to bring your concerns to our attention

"for consideration in future publications" not as a private individual but as the "Chairperson" of a government organization that, presumably, has some regulatory authority, I wish you to take note of my gravest concern over a government organization arrogating itself the right – even with the best of intentions – to revise history or deliver pronouncements about what terms are "improper and not justifiable" to use "in a Canadian magazine." It strengthens my belief that in our day the Huns at the gates are the ever increasing number of de-racinated, de-sexed Chairpersons of thought police designed to launder reality in order to enforce their own ideals of non-discrimination, non-violence, equal status or affirmative action.

As you can see, this is my personal response. The views of *Maclean's* do not necessarily coincide with mine.

Yours truly,
Barbara Amiel

Naturally I sent a copy of my response to Newman, and together we waited to see if this would still the quivering impulses of Chairperson Myers. Might he now move on to some real problems, such as those facing the native people in his own province?

All was quiet. We were grateful, and went on with the business of getting out a magazine. Then, on August 11, 1977, my telephone started ringing. "You racist bitch," the first words began. Hardly the way to greet a new day, I thought. After a while the friendlier callers got through. "Hi! Have you seen the newspapers?" asked my sister cheerfully.

"No," I said, worried. "What have they done *now*?" I assumed that a law had been passed requiring us all to wear thermal underwear whenever the temperature went over 72 degrees Fahrenheit in case we overheated and cost the provincial medical plan extra money in emergency services.

"It's *you*," she replied accusingly. "You're a racist."

That was my sister's word – not Chairperson Myers', I hasten to add. But her response was fairly typical. It seemed that Chairperson Myers had decided that my letter was not sufficient, and instead of replying to me – or indeed to Peter Newman – he had sent out a release to Canadian Press. At the office we had clippings from newspapers in Ottawa, Vancouver, Thunder Bay, Oshawa, Grande Prairie, and so on. This being a wire story, it was much the same.

The Manitoba Human Rights Commission has protested to Maclean's magazine about a phrase which appeared in the April 4 edition which it says is an inappropriate reference to the German people.

The article in question was written by Maclean's staff writer Barbara Amiel. In it, she noted that the British had united during the adversities suffered in wartime in contrast to their present seeming unconcern despite the economic adversity the country is suffering.

"The huns are gone," the article said.

In the letter to Maclean's, Human Rights Commission chairman Mel Myers said the commission deplores the use of the term "huns" as "a description of a whole people in one word."

The letter explained that "hun" was used during the Second World War to describe the Germans as barbarians. It said the term should at most be used only as a description of Nazis or ss personnel, and not in a way that would encompass the Germans of today.

The letter noted that today West Germany is a member of NATO and is a nation that has regained its esteem in the eyes of the world.

Officials of the Human Rights Commission said their letter was written about a month ago but that they have not yet received an official reply from Maclean's.

At this point Newman stepped in. His letter of August 22, 1977, was brief and to the point. It backed me up, adding only that as one whose family had suffered considerably at the hands of the Germans he could speak with some passion regarding the events *of that period.*

This apparently required Chairperson Myers to gather his wits at length because his next letter was not written until December 5, 1977. But the Chairperson could still not bring himself to reply to my letter, make mention of it, or even send me a copy of his further correspondence about my work. Human Rights, it seemed, especially under Chairperson Myers, went only so far. I began to wonder if he was perhaps related to Charles Roach.

December 5, 1977
Dear Mr. Newman:
Re: Use of the term "Huns" – article "The Collapse
    of Great Britain" by Barbara Amiel, April 4, 1977 issue

Our Commission has considered your reply of August 22, 1977 and wish to advise that we are taking no further action with respect to this matter. We do, however, regret the apparent misunderstanding that has arisen.

Our Commission was not presenting the view that all Germans are good. We were objecting to the likely identification by readers of "Huns" with all Germans rather than strictly Nazis. While it is evident from your letter that this was not the *intended* meaning, the conveyed meaning might be different. Indeed, the Random House Dictionary defines "hun" as:

"1. a member of a nomadic and warlike Asian people who devastated or controlled large parts of eastern and central Europe and who exercised their greatest power under Attila in the 5th century A.D.

2. a barbarous, destructive person; a vandal

3. (derogatory) a) a German soldier in World War I or II
   b) a German"

It is quite evident, therefore, that the meaning of the term, independent from one's intention, does carry a derogatory reference to Germans in general, while this is not the only meaning.

Without belabouring the point, our drawing this to your attention was in response to a complaint from representatives of the German community in Manitoba who were offended by the use of the term in the article. Unfortunately, we omitted to clarify our jurisdiction in our previous correspondence of June 30, 1977. We were not pursuing this matter under our enforcement mandate which sets out various prohibited discriminatory practices (Part 1 of the Act, copy enclosed) – but under our *educational* mandate, Section 13:

"The Commission has power to administer this Act and without limiting the generality of the foregoing, it is the function of the Commission,
(a) to forward the principle that every person is free and equal in dignity and rights without regard to race, creed, religion, sex, colour, nationality, age, marital status, ancestry or place of origin;
(b) to promote an understanding of, acceptance of and compliance with this Act;
(c) to develop and conduct educational programs designed to eliminate discriminatory practices related to race, creed, religion, sex, colour, nationality, age, marital status, ancestry or place of origin;
(d) to disseminate knowledge and promote understanding of the civil and legal rights of residents of the province and to conduct educational programs in that respect;
(e) to further the principle of equality of opportunities and equality in the exercise of civil and legal rights regardless of status."

Our response to this concern is no different than our response to other similar complaints regarding, for example, the use of the term "Jew" in the context of an advertisement placed by a store – "Jew-me-down sale" or the use in general of terms such as "Jap, nigger, kike, hunky, wop, . . . and so on". It is no more our intention to "launder reality" than it is yours to distort or offend.

While doubtless the use of the term "Huns" will have little impact (and understandably so) on those who have suffered bitterly through either the First or the Second

World War, its connotations are nevertheless offensive to many Germans who also suffered, are ashamed of, and opposed the rise of Nazism in Germany. Our concern is with the insensitive use of such terms and how they may inadvertently have a subtle influence on those who do not yet have hard and fixed views.

Yours truly,
M. Myers
Chairperson

Indeed, attached to the letter was Chapter H175 of the Manitoba Human Rights Act. All 39 clauses of it. I immediately drafted a reply.

Dear Chairperson Myers,
Your letter of December 5, 1977, was passed on to me by Peter C. Newman. In responding to it once again I'm presenting my own views and not necessarily those of *Maclean's*.

It is very generous of you to propose to take no further action in connection with my April 4, 1977 article in *Maclean's*, especially as I'm not aware of any further action that might be available to you under the law. In fact, I wish it were otherwise, since nothing would give me greater satisfaction than meeting your challenge in court.

I wish to advise you, however, that I *will* take further action with respect to this matter, and I will do so by every lawful means and in all forums available to me in the Canadian media. But first, using my own mandate as a writer on public affairs to disseminate knowledge and promote understanding of the meaning of freedom and truth, I will undertake to educate you and your Human Rights Commission on my reasons for doing so.

Throughout its history, compared to most other countries in the world, Canada has been a bastion of human rights and individual dignity. For a century before the establishment of Human Rights Commissions it was to these shores that people came from all corners of the earth to escape from the tyranny of governments that were imposing their own creeds, standards and beliefs in them. Canada was, and to a considerable extent still is, a free country because it has consistently rejected the view that it is for the government to decide what is desirable and decent in social commentary or political thought. Before now, no Canadian government has arrogated itself the function of "educating" its citizens, writers or journalists in what is or is not an acceptable sentence or opinion.

The reason previous governments have not acted in this manner, one supposes, was that they understood the difficulty of determining the one correct course in human affairs; the complexity of religion, morals, science and politics; and the dangers of trying to determine the right philosophy by government edict. It is precisely those governments that have not understood this, from the absolute monarchies of Czarist Russia or Prussian Germany to the dictatorships of Franco's Spain or Mao's China, that ended up, regardless of their intentions, with a goodly number of their population in prisons or re-education camps. Though Canada is still far from reaching the end of this road, it is my view that with the establishment of your Commission it has taken the first step.

I happen to abhor discrimination based on race, religion, etc., as much as your Commission presumably does, but I reject the idea that your (or any other) Commission has the capacity and the right to determine what constitutes discrimination. I find it highly debatable that you can and should do so even in judging deeds – such as hiring or housing – but I find it especially dangerous and distasteful that you should presume to do so *vis à vis* words and thoughts. Your reaction to the words "the Huns are gone" in my article, minor as the example may be, is a perfect illustration of the chilling world we will enter if we ever accept your, or any other government official's, judgement in such matters.

The German enemy was commonly referred to as "Huns" by Britons during the war years. I reiterate that the term actually originated with the German Emperor who used it with reference to his own people. The word was by no means restricted in application to members of the Nazi party or the Gestapo: it was used to describe *the enemy*, and it was used by everyone from Churchill to fighting soldiers, like my own father, battling Rommel's tanks in the African desert. It was a proper and accurate word in the context of the times. Today, when used with reference to those times – as I very clearly did in my article – no Human Rights Commission should try to consign it to some Orwellian memory-hole.

It is ludicrous to suggest, as you do in your letter, that you were "objecting to the likely identification by readers of 'Huns' with all Germans rather than strictly Nazis" and that "while it is evident from [Peter C. Newman's] letter that this was not the *intended* meaning, the conveyed meaning might be different." First, the intended meaning was evident from the article itself to any reader, with the possible exception of German pressure groups or Human Rights Chairpersons. Second, even if it were not so, does the government propose to interfere not only with intended meanings but also with "likely" or "conveyed" misreadings by biased, superficial or ignorant readers?

Third, it is clear from your letter that you still don't understand that "Huns" *did* refer to all Germans, whether they happened to be card-carrying Nazis or not, during the two German wars of this century, and that this designation was entirely accurate and proper. It is not up to the Manitoba Human Rights Commission to re-write history, and history between the years 1914-1945 consisted of two barbarous wars conducted largely for the sake of the aggrandizement of the German state. This, at least, is my view, and coincidentally the view of innumerable highly respected historians. If you have a different view you are, of course, entitled to it; but you are not entitled to try to outlaw or "re-educate" mine.

And this brings me to my final point: the gross imperti-

nence of a branch of the government trying to educate me
or any other citizen. This would be presumptuous even if
you understood better than I or the average Canadian the
history of the war years, or the meaning of context, or the
meaning of plain English. Your letter, however, makes it
evident that your understanding of these matters is no
more infallible than the understanding of those who have
no mandate to educate others, and it may be less. In fact, I
even question if you fully understand your own mandate.

The article in *Maclean's* did not make the remotest reference to residents of the province of Manitoba of German or any other origin. The article referred exclusively
and unmistakably to the German belligerent in the historical period known as the Second World War, in the sole
context of Britain. The most careful reading of the Human Rights Act that you are charged with administering
does not reveal to me any legitimate interest that your
Commission might have in regulating *or* educating journalists in their description of the enemy as viewed by any
foreign country in this or any other period of history.

Sincerely yours,
Barbara Amiel

After a few radio stories on the "slurs at *Maclean's*" against
the German people, I settled down to think about what had
occurred. On one level, of course, it was extremely minor.
But it clearly had an ominous underpinning. I had never
looked into the Human Rights Commissions very seriously,
but I made a note that it might be worth while seeing what
they were up to. If they had so much energy to expend on
the fate of the Huns, God alone knows what they might be
doing with more contemporary phenomena.

But, time passes quickly when you're working in the real
world, and so the Human Rights Commissions were put out
of mind until I received word that, yes, the *Ontario* Human
Rights Commission had been having little chats with my edi-

tor-in-chief, Peter C. Newman, again, without mentioning this warm concern to me. I was beginning to wonder if this attitude was general or manifested only to persons like me, who did not appear, by virtue of skin colour, name, or socio-economic position, to be part of a minority group. I wondered if I should send them my bank statements and thus get on their endangered-species list.

Soon enough, courtesy of Newman, a copy of the latest missive appeared on my desk. Newman, understanding the game, was not satisfied with "telephone chats", and had requested the minions of the Thought Police to put their frank comments onto paper. Their comments appeared somewhat toned down by this request.

Dear Mr. Newman:

Re: "The Collapse of Britain" by Barbara Amiel,
      Article in April 4, 1977 issue of Maclean's

This letter confirms my telephone conversation with Ms. Helen McLachlan, Assistant to the Editor, on Monday, November 28, 1977, regarding the above-stated matter. Per your request, as advised by Ms. McLachlan, please find enclosed a copy of correspondence received from the Trans-Canada Alliance of German-Canadians regarding their concerns over the use of the term "Huns" in Ms. Amiel's article.

As you may know, the Commission, through its community relations role, endeavours to promote a climate of mutual respect for all residents in Ontario, regardless of ethnic or racial background. It is in this capacity that we are bringing the concerns of the Trans-Canada Alliance of German Canadians to your attention, as it is their perception that the use of the term "Huns" has reflected negatively on the German-Canadian community.

We would appreciate any action you might deem appropriate to assist in the clarification of this matter, which might accommodate the goals of all parties concerned. Should you have any questions regarding this matter, please feel free to contact us, as we would be happy to discuss it with you further.

Yours sincerely,
Mark Krakowski
Human Rights Officer

The attached letter read:

The Ontario Human Rights Commission
Ministry of Labour
400 University Avenue
Toronto, Ontario
M7A 1T7

Attn. of Dr. T. H. E. Symons

Dear Sir,
Re: Article in Maclean's of April 4, 1977,
    "The collapse of Britain".

Enclosed please find copy of said article.

We consider the following words in this article extremely offensive: "But Britons don't seem to feel that at all: the *Huns* are gone. . . ."

In our opinion, it is a serious insult to label the German nation as *Huns*. The Federal Republic of Germany is an ally of Canada and NATO. During the first world war, the Germans were frequently called huns, in order to mark them as barbarians. This expression was used again in war propaganda during the second world war with the intent to signify the Germans as brutal barbarians, although in reality there were only a few criminals in the Nazi-party and in the secret federal police, who committed barbaric crimes, not only to Jews but also to any Germans who were against the Hitler regime.

However, this article in which Germans are generally called "huns" is not with regard to war criminals, but includes all Germans whether they were for or against the regime.

This article was published in Canada in a Canadian

magazine. Therefore, it is an insult to all Canadians of
German origin, who immigrated to Canada with the hope
of a better tomorrow. The danger exists, therefore, that
signifying the Germans as "huns" in general, in a Canadian magazine yet, creates hate, subsequently ending in
discrimination.

For this reason, we, as umbrella organization for all
German-Canadians in Canada, protest against the term
"huns" with reference to all Germans.

We would appreciate very much if you would take necessary steps in this matter.

Yours very truly,

TRANS-CANADA ALLIANCE OF GERMAN-CANADIANS
Erhard Matthaes,
Secretary General

I noticed that the attached letter of the Trans-Canada Alliance of German-Canadians was dated August 5, 1977, and
the wording sounded remarkably similar to the lines of my
old pen-pal, Chairperson Myers. Since one could not suspect
the Chairperson of being himself a member of the Alliance,
it was more likely that he had cribbed his "arguments" (without acknowledgement) from a form letter sent to all Human
Rights Commissions from the Trans-Canada Alliance of
German-Canadians.

A conflict of interest (my own) began to gather on the ho-
rizon. Now I was dealing with the Human Rights Commission of my own province, and instead of faceless bureaucrats, I was about to take up cudgels with people whom, even
if I didn't personally know them (such as Judge Rosalie
Abella), I rather liked by reputation. Others I did know
(Rabbi Gunther Plaut), and I found that I had an instinctive
taboo against pummelling the rabbi who married me. Such
things matter to a nice Jewish girl.

Just to exorcize any such feelings I crossed the street from
my office at *Maclean's* and went over to the Human Rights
Commission offices located in one of the spanking-new-
high-rise-fast-elevator-rude-personnel buildings that governments so favour today. Everything – provided it was ina-

nimate – worked exquisitely, quietly, and with the kind of su-
per-cool efficiency designed to calm frazzled nerves. The
moment I came into contact with the first government-issue
humanoid sitting at the reception desk I knew why it was
necessary to have a Human Rights Commission – or, more to
the point, a Criminal Code. She was blonde, long-haired,
and having a swell time on the phone with her friend. She
wouldn't, not for any one of the three of us waiting to have
our rights looked after, acknowledge our presence in any
way.

After about eight or nine minutes of this, during which
she switched the buttons over and over on the call director,
without pausing to look up while ritually intoning "Just one
moment, please", I was the only one of the three left. That, I
supposed, was one way of cutting down on government services. Eventually I walked behind her desk into the main
office area. This action seemed to cause something of a stir
because several people popped up from their offices, and
the blonde receptionist, suddenly alert, disentangled herself
from the call director and came breathlessly around the
room divider. "You can't go in there," she said. These words
did not go down well with me. This, after all, was *my* strip of
broadloom. My taxes helped cover the floors and put in all
those colour-coordinated filing cabinets. My use of historical
phrases had provided several good sessions of work for a
number of employees. Like a shareholder, I wanted to see
what my labours were producing.

The ostensible purpose of my visit was to pick up a copy of
the Ontario Human Rights Commission book *Life Together: A
Report on Human Rights in Ontario.* It took only a couple of
minutes for the little huddle of Human Rights Persons to
find me a copy of their 139-page plan to remake Ontario in
their own image. With the Little Green Book in my possession it took only another minute or two of gentle scanning to
realize that – personal friendship and distant respect aside –
the Huns were still very much at the gates when it came to
establishing a large, arbitrary empire all over again, only
now here in the green and pleasant vistas of Ontario. I
marched up to my office and drafted a reply to the furtive

telephone caller of the Ontario Human Rights Commission –
Mr. Mark Krakowski.

Dear Mr. Krakowski
Re: The Collapse of Britain by Barbara Amiel
    Maclean's April 4, 1977

Thank you for your letter of recent date. I used the term
"Huns" in the above article in a context that was, in my
opinion, not capable of being misunderstood. The full text
reads:

> The British might work, at least in the sense of pulling
> together when they feel the enemy is at the gates. But
> Britons don't seem to feel that at all: the Huns are gone
> and nobody really believes in the reality of the Russian
> Bear, etc.

In this context the term so clearly does not apply to residents of Ontario that I question whether the Ontario Human Rights Commission has any jurisdiction to ask for as
much as a clarification in this matter. . . . I find it perfectly
accurate and legitimate to use the word with reference to
the war-years and, should the occasion arise, I intend to
do so in the future.

While I appreciate your desire to "accommodate the
goals of all parties concerned" I'm afraid the apparent
goals of the Trans-Canada Alliance of German Canadians
cannot be accommodated without falsifying history. It was
clearly not "a few criminals in the Nazi party and in the secret federal police" who crossed the Czech and Polish borders, bombed London and Rotterdam, or cheered Hitler
at his various mass rallies. Whether the Canadian-German
Alliance likes it or not, the Nazis were one of the few totalitarian parties in this century that were freely elected to
power by the voters of their country. While there was no
doubt some internal opposition in Germany, few nations
in recent history were so united behind their leaders and

their policies as the Germans were behind Hitler and his group, at least while they seemed to be winning the war.

Though I'm certain you are calling this matter to my attention in good faith, I find it disturbing that you should clothe with any apparent legitimacy an attempt by a special interest group to censor the press. It is my view that the various Human Rights Commissions are coming dangerously close to interfering with public and private opinion and free speech even when operating within their mandate, and should be especially reluctant to act, even in their "educational" capacity, when the matter complained of does not pertain to Canadian residents and is as far outside their jurisdiction as my reference obviously is.

You may, if you wish, pass on this reply to the complainant. It expresses my opinion and not necessarily *Maclean's*. I trust you will extend the courtesy of sending me a copy of your reply to the Trans-Canada Alliance.

Sincerely yours,
Barbara Amiel

Unlike the Manitoba Human Rights Commission, the Ontario commissars could see that at least as far as this particular issue was concerned, the traditional tactics of behind-the-scenes "talks" and "moral suasion" was probably not going to do the trick. Accordingly they promptly sent me a copy of their reply to the Trans-Canada Alliance of German-Canadians. I was interested to see that my case had now been passed from the hands of Human Rights Officer Mark Krakowski into the files of Mark Nakamura, Manager, Comunity, Race & Ethnic Relations. I hoped this was a promotion for one of us.

Dear Mr. Mattheas:
Re: "The Collapse of Britain" by Barbara Amiel
    Article in April 4, 1977 issue of *Maclean's*

This letter is pursuant to the receipt of your correspondence which outlines your organization's concern with respect to the term "Hun" appearing in an article published in the April 4, 1977 issue of Maclean's.

As you may know, the Commission through its Community Relations mandate endeavours to foster a climate of mutual understanding and self respect amongst all residents in this province regardless of their racial or ethnic background. It has been our experience that oftentimes problems which arise amongst and between groups find their origins through misunderstanding. In this regard we brought your organization's issue to the attention of Maclean's and specifically to Barbara Amiel, the author of the article in question in the hope that a resolution might be made manifest.

We have enclosed a copy of her response to the concerns your organization has raised. We hope the points contained within her response will be of assistance to you in clarifying the issues at hand. One particular point she has stressed is that the article was not intended in any way to reflect upon residents of Ontario who might be of German ancestry.

We hope that this information is of assistance to you and we wish to thank you for bringing this matter to our attention.

Yours sincerely,
Mark Nakamura
Manager
Community, Race & Ethnic Relations

On January 7, 1978, the Trans-Canada Alliance of German-Canadians replied – *directly to me*.

There was no reply to be made to their letter. Mr. Matthaes and I were climbing different mountains when it came to understanding history. But I was particularly taken by his closing sentences: "Canada consists of various ethnic groups who work together in friendship and unity for a beautiful future in their country Canada. The use of improper names for an entire nation, that are not specified, causes friction among the various ethnic groups." Yes. And never more so, as I discovered, Mr. Matthaes, than when there are Human Rights Commissioners to whom you can turn in the hope that they might enforce *your* view of history. This, you see, only highlights the great gulf between us: I, too, believe that *my* view is correct, except I'd never try to use the state to re-educate you. That is what really distinguishes (or used to) a free people from Huns.

CHAPTER NINETEEN

Reverse Discrimination and Other Human Wrongs

THE ACTION OF THE Ontario Rights people had pricked me into action in turn. Since I was now being asked to function as an after-dinner, during lunch, and around tea-time speaker, I decided that the ambitions of these regulatory agencies ought at least to receive a little publicity and some public scrutiny. I began boning up on their literature to find out just what they were after.

My first run-in with them had come during a live television interview I did for *CTV Reports* in the fall of 1977. My guest was the newly appointed federal Human Rights Commissioner, Gordon Fairweather. I was nervous, wondering how to get around to the question of quotas in job programs and other tricky subjects. Fairweather was ebullient, and was not about to mince words. I mentioned my apprehension about "affirmative action" programs that gave preference to women in jobs. Might that not be a violation of the great ideal of equality? Fairweather smiled expansively: *"Reverse discrimination*, you mean, Barbara. I'm not afraid to use the phrase. Reverse discrimination. Sure I favour it, and it's going to be around for a while." Barely concealing my gasp, I inquired how long.

"Oh, probably till the year 2000," said Mr. Fairweather.

Later I calculated that any young Canadian male of nineteen would have to wait until he was at least forty-five years old before he could be guaranteed his equal rights in the Canadian labour force. But by the time my husband and I got around to writing and talking about this particular aim of the Human Rights lobby, Mr. Fairweather had discovered the fine political art of dissembling. In a column in the magazine *Canadian Lawyer* my husband had referred to Fairweather's affirmative-action policies as reverse discrimination. A letter came to the magazine by return mail.

"I have spent a great deal of time trying to clear up the confusion surrounding the concept of affirmative action. Mr. Jonas is not the first person to mistakenly refer to affirmative action as reverse discrimination, and I fear that he will not be the last." The letter was signed "Gordon Fairweather". My husband had to dissuade me from inviting Mr. Fairweather to a private screening of his own "mistaken reference".

It was during the same period that the researcher at CTV handed me a report on the South Asian Community in Toronto written by a Dr. Bhausaheb Ubale and submitted to the Attorney General of Ontario, Roy McMurtry. Everyone at CTV was very "high" on the report. The Toronto media were salivating over it. Several wretched incidents involving brutal physical attacks on East Indians in Toronto subways by hooligans had rightly aroused the wrath of the media.

The prison sentences later meted out to the youths were severe, reflecting, in my opinion, a very proper exercise of judicial discretion. Though a person may be guilty of assault no matter what motivated him, it is right that he should be punished much more severely when his lawless passion was aroused by the mere sight of a person of another race than, say, when being insulted himself or witnessing a child or a dog being kicked.

But Toronto seemed still to be smarting from a case of New York envy. New York had Real Urban Problems, and one of them was racial tension. Now we, too, had Real Urban Problems – if Dr. Ubale was to be believed. Mingled with the

justified outrage, there seemed to be a collective sigh of re-
lief that we had finally come of age and could quickly start
forming committees and study groups and maybe even new
laws to correct the situation. I decided the Ubale report
should be looked at carefully if I was to take up the fight
against the Human Rights Commissions on the speaking-
circuit.

It was a gem. Never had so much damage been done to
the cause of Mr. Matthaes's "various ethnic groups who work
together in friendship and unity" than in the study of Mr.
Ubale. Only readers who had managed to avoid any basic
history could have swallowed the report. But Dr. Ubale was
not altogether careless. Given the parochial thrust of the
Canadian educational system and the distorted lens placed
over the third world by the media, he could expect his version of history to go unquestioned, as it did.

A sampler:

- "Racial prejudice as it exists in the world today is almost
  exclusively an attitude of whites and had its origins in the
  needs of European conquerors from the sixteenth century
  on to rationalize and justify the robbery, enslavement and
  continued exploitation of their coloured victims all over
  the globe."
- "Over the years, Western historians have projected a
  wrong image of South Asians presumably to preserve a
  colonial mentality. . . . If [a Westerner] happens to visit the
  sub-continent, no doubt he sees the evidence of poverty as
  it is projected through the media, but he soon realizes that
  it is the result of past colonial economic policies."
- "In this sub-continent the Western observer witnesses the
  peaceful co-existence of different people in a multi-racial,
  multi-cultural and multi-lingual society, both in the urban
  and in the rural areas." (Reading this particular section my
  mind turned to Bangladesh, Pakistan, the Karachi riots,
  the caste system, and the extraordinary hierarchy of the
  sub-continent; I really wondered if this was pushing things
  even for Dr. Ubale's doublethink. Again, I was wrong. Not
  a peep from the analysts of the report.)

a peep from the analysts of the report.)

Then Dr. Ubale stated his main thesis. The time had come, he said, "to make Canadian society accept the fact that it is no more a predominantly Anglo-Saxon society." Well, I thought. There's the rub. Being a wandering Jew myself I have never had much sympathy for the idea of the nation-state. But whatever my own sympathies, the fact remains (Dr. Ubale notwithstanding) that Canada was founded by such West Europeans as the Anglo-Saxons, the French, and the Celts. Its majority institutions and language remained – at last count – English. Its general culture, inasmuch as it re-sembles anything, clearly resembles an Anglo-Saxon culture more than, say, a Hindu culture. People of other cultures have come here to share in it, often because they found it preferable to their own. My husband's secretary claims to be a full-blooded Cherokee, and my private secretary happens to be an East Indian, and the receptionist at *Maclean's* ap-pears physically to be an Oriental, but none of them could be said to share anything – apart from their femaleness – except their successful assimilation of Anglo-Saxon culture. I have no idea what religious or cultural practices they may enjoy privately, like my own private struggle to learn Hebrew. The point is we're all as proud as hell about our roots, but we're not trying to change Canada. Roots are a private question, and not a matter of public policy.

But having stated his determination to re-educate Cana-dian society, Dr. Ubale listed the ways in which this could be done once and for all. And it wàs here that I saw the Thought Police loom, not as shadows on some paranoid ho-rizon but palpable and real, needing, like the Golem of Jew-ish legend, only a master to breathe life into them. And Dr. Ubale started breathing. His recommendations included:

- Compulsory in-service multicultural training of teachers to ensure a racially just society.
- The re-writing of school textbooks on Asia with the "ob-ject of giving a correct picture of their socio-cultural and economic development." "Power should be given to the

Human Rights Commission to both monitor and investigate suspected cases of discrimination on its own initiative.
This would require the creation of an inspectorate within
the Human Rights Commission which would undertake
investigative work in the same manner as is done by other
government agencies such as the U.I.C., income tax, customs and excise offices, etc. Politically such a move may
appear unpopular at the initial stages, but this should not
deter policy makers." (It hasn't.)
Deliberate policy measures to appoint qualified South
Asian Canadians and other non-white individuals to strategic positions. . . . When a non-white person is employed
or promoted to a senior position, he should be given initial
backing from the top management (presumably regardless of how well he functions) until his position and authority are firmly established in the company.

Included in Ubale's recommendations were various censorship procedures to screen university professors, and media and government employees. Worth noting was his advocacy of the British National Union of Journalists' code of
ethics in reporting racial matters. Said Ubale: "To monitor
this code, it set up a Race Relations Subcommittee. It would
be worthwhile to do the same in Canada."

Since I had read the horror with which papers as disparate
as *The Observer* and *The Economist* had greeted this racial code
of ethics (said *The Economist*: "It is non-journalism . . .") I decided to write to the British Union and get a copy. I discovered that the 1975 guidelines were the beginning of the
problem. Journalists were being turned into a special-interest lobby group. What was this code recommended by
Ubale? One example might suffice: said an NUJ circular in
May 1976, "In the last few weeks there has been an increasing number of stories connected with immigration, and the
black and Asian communities living in England.

"The Union's Race Relations Sub-Committee is concerned
that the way these stories have been reported may be positively contributing to the evident worsening of community
relations.

"In turn certain political forces with a racist or anti-immigrant policy are using these news stories as proof of a revised public interest about so-called 'immigrant problems'." The NUJ did not – and could not – claim that the spate of stories concerning problems between immigrants and the majority culture were fictitious. They just thought that perhaps they should not be talking about this at all. But by April 1977 a leading branch of the NUJ was quite clear about its tactics. Stated the North London Branch in a new series of rules:

1. Where stories about racist organizations are being published, write critically of their anti-social stance and actively seek rebutting comments from their opponents.
2. Don't "respectabilize" racist organizations and accord them the status of a bona-fide political party by straightforwardly reporting their statement.
3. Don't shirk from confronting your management even if it means taking industrial action, when it means establishing a constructive policy to race reporting.

At the time I had hoped that, after the initial interest in the Ubale report, the excitement would die down and Ubale-ism would return to its appropriate place in the subterranean corridors of our new Thought Police. It was not to be. The report precipitated the censorship of textbooks mentioned earlier. In an astonishing move a few months later, Premier Davis appointed Ubale to the Ontario Human Rights Commission. At the time, Ubale, who had been in Canada only two years (thus undermining his own complaint that "Canadian experience" was a major, though unjust, requirement for work in Canada, but confirming my suspicion that maumauing is the most effective technique to use on the dispirited, disheartened, and frightened majority), was conducting courses at a police college on how to police a multicultural society.

This course was the result of the report of another pioneer in the race-relations industry, Dr. Walter Pitman, whose scenario of a biased and racially explosive Toronto could only have been discovered by a well-meaning socialist in desperate search of injustice. (I shall never forget Dr. Pitman coming up to me at the CFTO studios after watching a screening of a short report I had done on "racism" in England which explained the problem as a clash of cultures rather than sheer white bigotry. "I think that's so true," Pitman had said, effusively shaking my hand. "It's not racism at all, and we need to emphasize that." I looked puzzled. "But didn't your report . . ." The floor director called Pitman to take his seat at the round table on camera next to Roy McMurtry. "So true, so true," and he nodded off into the merciful oblivion of the one-question round-table interview.)

It is perfectly true, of course, that in his report Dr. Pitman mentioned culture and cultural difference as a factor of tension between different groups. However, the thrust of his report could have been taken verbatim from Dr. Ubale's "the white vice of racism" theory.

But the real impact Ubale (now promoted to Ontario's Commissioner for Race Relations) would have on policy-making was in the pamphlet under my arm as I walked out of the Ontario Human Rights Commission on University Avenue in Toronto. In that green book were plans for a Thought Police that exceeded even the wildest dreams of Dr. Ubale. Or surely even his wildest fantasies. And yet, to this day, I wonder just how many of his distortions were wishful thinking or deliberate. After all, what can you make of a report that emphasizes the Indian sub-continent as a mecca of multicultural harmony in Chapter Five, but then, in its concluding recommendations, points approvingly to the racial commissions of the U.K., where "the British Government and the BBC have both taken special care to appoint one member from Pakistan and one from India in each of their commission and committee, wherever applicable. This helps to prevent intergroup conflicts. In Ontario, three members from the South Asian community – one from Pakistan, one from India and the third representing South Asians originating elsewhere – should be taken on the Commission. . . . one needs to move away from the present practice of lumping together people from India, Pakistan, Bangladesh, etc."

Ah, yes. Orwell would have understood Ubale-ism. The trouble is that today's politicians don't. All they hear are the shrillest voices, the best-oiled bandwagons and – perhaps – the faintest pulsing of their own decent impulses. For who among us would not want a society that ignored such a spurious quality as the degree of pigmentation in a person's skin in favour of his intrinsic qualities? Instead, we are creating a society that will determine all according to the colour of skin or the degree of hair wave or the arrangement of sexual organs. It is the intrinsic individual qualities that are to be ignored. Such is the price to be paid for those in a hurry to create absolute equality in defiance of the basic principle of equality before the rule of law. It's no bargain.

For my first speech on the Canadian Club circuit I spent a week cramming up on what the various Human Rights Commissions in Canada, the United States, and England wanted. It was a fairly simple task. The Human Rights Commissions were consuming enormous amounts of paper in their various publications describing and illustrating "mock hearings" into charges of discrimination with Human Rights officers playing "complainant" and "witness". There were reports on "sensitivity workshops for the Ontario Housing Corporation's community relations workers on intergroup relations in a multicultural setting." The abominable "newspeak" of the various publications aside, I was reminded of Malcolm Muggeridge's adamant conviction that all sociologists and their kith and kin should be banned from existence. The Human Rights publications made it perfectly clear that if there were no problems yet, with a good dose of consciousness-raising we could be sure to provoke some wretched little swine into "interracial tensions" in an "inter-city multicultural setting", and then an army of counsellors, psychologists, mediators, conciliators, and officers could move in and re-educate them. Frankly, remembering my own experiences as the local "kike" kid in a Devonshire community with its share of nasty British bullies, I felt a good fist-fight would probably be faster, cheaper, and much longer-lasting in its results. (I lost mine, but another little kike won hers, and since no one in authority took us terribly seriously, we had some difficulty recognizing these affairs as major threats to ourselves or the fabric of society. The devil has to be *named* before it appears – which is understood by folk-wisdom but not, alas, by modern sociologists.) Still, in Canada what real examples there were of racial tensions were dealt with firmly in community meetings – and from what I could gather from the reports, with about a five-to-one quotient of Human Rights officials per alleged racist. If nothing else, we could always smother them to death.

The Human Rights Commissioners were quite explicit about their role in promoting awareness of racial tensions lest anyone should fail to notice them. In its 1975 annual report the Ontario Human Rights Commission – regretfully, it seemed to me – noted that on a strictly numerical basis there was "a drop in total cases" (though a 75 per cent increase in inquiries and referrals), but pointed out to any disappointed readers that "the drop in the total figure was due, not to decreased activity, but to a more precise definitional system and to the changed nature of the activity. Community projects took on larger dimensions, became more time-consuming and used the services of as many as five officers for individual projects." Proclaimed the report:

> We sought to aid this movement by making our primary community relations effort the playing of a catalytic role. The Commission repeatedly made public pronouncements to alert the community to racist activities as an indicator of community evolution and to reassure minority groups who were being attacked. The most explicit expression of this effort was a campaign of letters to urge community groups and concerned citizens of all racial and religious backgrounds to speak out on the issues involved. . . . A gratifying number of copies of letters sent in response to this request were forwarded to the Commission.

By the time it published its 1976-77 annual report, the Ontario Human Rights Commission could draw up a chart showing that Canada was beginning to set the pace in anti-discrimination regulation. In a comparison of prohibited grounds of employment in the U.S.A., Britain, and Canada, we were in the lead. Sure, grounds like Political Opinion and Belief or Physical Handicap were still only effectively prohibited in three or four provinces (and in the pending federal bill C-25) but we were getting there. Certainly, we still hadn't made *mental* handicap an insufficient reason for an employer to refuse to hire someone, as the United States had, but we would soon alter that. And the report was also showing the new impatience with "legal remedies" in cases of discrimination. The Commissioners wrote:

> Legal remedies are necessary but not sufficient tools to eliminate institutional discrimination in employment. This is because the evolution of law and legal principles is a slow process. . . . Enforcement powers of the human rights commissions in Canada could be expanded to include strategic investigation or company-wide and industry-wide investigation to eradicate job discrimination inherent in the industrial relations system in this country. . . . Class-action suits could be encouraged by the human rights comissions in order to both enlarge the scope of the investigation and the remedies. . . .

They were on the move.

By 1977 they were out in the open. The report of the Ontario Human Rights Commission (mild compared to provinces like Manitoba and Saskatchewan) was calling for expanded powers that would set it up as an independent investigative authority. They asked for a tripling of their budget, and powers of search and seizure without warrant of all company correspondence and records they deemed pertinent when a complaint was made. They asked for affirmative-action programs for those places that have a disproportionate number of "non-Canadians" on their staff to seek out or prepare "Canadians to redress this imbalance". (This meant Americans, of course, given the current political climate. Who knows, next year it may be Lithuanians.) They recommended that political belief be outlawed as a ground of discrimination. The Commission further demanded that a criminal record be a prohibited ground of discrimination in employment. An employer might ask "oral questions" about a criminal record – but that was it. Sexual orientation would also be prohibited – a cherished progressive move that was to have its built-in backlash revealed when a Toronto gay bar would try to hire – quite legitimately, in my opinion – a gay waiter. The bar would be told this was "discriminatory".

The report was quite hideous in its bureaucratic ambitions, and the scope of the monitoring powers it asked for were truly astounding. What the Commissioners did not seem to understand – or perhaps they did – was the wholly illiberal nature of their proposed intrusion into areas of private morality and liberty and the polarizing effect such intrusions would have on the very communities they sought to bring together. Curiously enough, a hideous murder in Toronto halted – temporarily – the implementation of the report. The death of shoeshine boy Emanuel Jaques in a homosexual rape-torture and murder case made the Ontario Cabinet balk at the implementation of the report. "Wait till things cool down," one supporter of the new Human Rights Act said; "then Cabinet will be able to bring it up again. Right now with that provision about no discrimination on the basis of sexual orientation the whole bill could be killed." It was ironic; of all the distasteful provisions, sexual orientation was probably the least dangerous. It would at least not have affected the nation's economy, unlike blanket provisions about criminals or mental defectives.

But the atmosphere was becoming heated. The Commissions had done their work. Incidents began piling up.

At the *Financial Post*, a book called *Bended Elbow* on the Indian problem in Kenora was reviewed by a Catholic schoolteacher, Paul Fromm. The book, poorly written and clearly

the work of an incensed Kenora housewife, shed little light
on how to solve the very real problems of Indian drunken-
ness and sexually explicit behaviour in public places. It was
not a thoughtful or a scholarly book and the review by Paul
Fromm neither praised nor condemned it. It simply stated
the problems which the book outlined. Still, the *Financial
Post* soon received one of the Human Rights Commission's
discreet phone calls, suggesting that they ought not to be re-
viewing such things – and certainly not using reviewers of
such political persuasion. They did not elaborate on what
they meant by "such". The Advisory Council on Multiculturalism got into the act by sending the *Post* a letter informing
them that the book "ought not to have been reviewed" and
most certainly "not by a reviewer outside your staff". This
was a new role, it seemed, for a government multicultural
committee. Interestingly, the letter seemed to be an official
version of the perfectly legitimate – if, in my opinion, erro-
neous – editorial on the same theme in the black community
newspaper *The Islander*, which appeared nine days before
the letter was written. Certain phrases of the multicultural
letter and the editorial were identical.

Private individuals and the press itself got into the act of
censoring or of trying to censor other people's views, encouraged by the spirit of our Human Rights Commissions.
Various journalists, ranging from the *Toronto Sun*'s Peter
Worthington to the *Vancouver Sun*'s Doug Collins to CTV's
Henry Champ, found themselves under attack – usually indirectly, by means of letters to their employers or their
Board of Directors – accusing them of "racism" or "bigotry".
In Toronto, so-called civil-rights lawyer Clayton Ruby got
right into the spirit of things when, in attacking a *Toronto Sun*
editorial of which he disapproved – his right as a citizen and
a reader – he wrote a letter to each member of the Board of
Directors of the *Sun* on his law firm's letterhead suggesting
that the editorial (which had been critical of the Anglican
Church for supporting Marxist terrorists) was "akin to living
off the avails of prostitution". Suggested Clayton Ruby: "I
would ask you to take steps to see that the journalism of the

Toronto Sun is raised to a respectable level." Ruby, of course, had a perfect right to express his approval or disapproval of published opinions. But, infected by the witch-hunt spirit of our times encouraged by the Human Rights Commissions, he did not see fit to send a copy of his complaint to the editor of the newspaper. Ruby only invited the Board of Directors to "take steps", which in plain language means fire or censor under the threat of firing. Said the editor-in-chief of the *Toronto Sun*, echoing the views of a number of other editors (who lacked Worthington's courage in allowing their names to be used): "Boards of Directors run scared at this sort of thing. They're respectable, decent businessmen. They don't want to be accused of bigotry or living off the avails of prostitution. They can be terrorized by this sort of behind-the-scenes attack. And I have to wait and hope that someone will show me the letter so I can at least offer a defence. You'd think he [Ruby] could at least have had the guts to send me a copy." But at least Ruby mau-maued in his own name and not as a government official. Unlike the Human Rights Commissioners, this is still a long step away from using the State's power to enforce one's views.

In 1979, *The Body Politic*, a Toronto homosexual newspaper, was acquitted (I thought very properly) of obscenity charges arising from its publication of a fairly mindless and silly piece called "Men Loving Boys" which told all about the joys of sex between men and under-age children. *Globe and Mail* columnist Dick Beddoes celebrated this acquittal as a triumph of free speech. Now, one could have pointed out that men loving boys (or indeed little girls) *is* a criminal offence. But to use this argument as a censorship device raises such a hideous spectacle that the court rightly rejected the Crown's case. Still, only a week or so later, Beddoes was frothing at the mouth over another magazine. The object, this time not of his affections but of his wrath, was a staff association magazine of the Toronto Metropolitan Police. The magazine, which had no official status, apparently contained some perfectly idiotic (if the excerpts are any indication) articles on the cultural traits of Jews, Italians, women, homosexuals, and just about every group that moved. Now that the issue of race was involved, Beddoes was calling not only for the censure of the magazine but for the firing of those associated with it, and the cancellation of the pension of the retired police officer who had written the articles in question. This seemed not only to contradict his fearless stand on free speech, but to display a rather vindictive attitude to an elderly ass writing away in his waning years. Speaking as a member of *several* of the groups maligned (I leave the reader to assume which ones, and will guess that Beddoes belongs to none of them), I was perfectly prepared to let the Police Staff Association magazine say what it did. My attitude to the police and other public servants is very simple: they are *not* to be judged on the basis of "thought tests" designed by socially conscious or Freudian or any other kind of psychologists, or by the opinions they may express in private publications. They are to be judged by their actions and their actions alone. It is a right I would expect our system to extend to any citizen. If a police officer contravenes the Criminal Code or his own department's rules and regulations, then he should be dealt with firmly and publicly. He should not be the special selective target of the selective morality of newspapermen inflaming the public. (Policemen, Mr. Beddoes, much as this may dismay you, also have civil liberties and human rights.) In spite of all the hubbub there was no movement by the Human Rights Commission, however, to come to their aid. Nor should there have been any: Mr. Beddoes should be perfectly free to express *his* views, without the state holding a club over his head.

Marching briskly to the music of the times, the Attorney General of Ontario, Roy McMurtry, decided that outlawing hate messages would be a good idea. This was directed at the scurrilous little telephone messages the Western Guard had placed on a telephone line they had purchased from the Bell system. When the Western Guard was effectively broken up, a new anti-immigration, anti-black party was formed called the Nationalist Party. In order to register it as an official party, the election rules required ten thousand signatures.

When this seemed a distinct possibility, ominous rumblings came out of the Ontario legislature. First, it was announced that handwriting experts would determine the authenticity of the signatures. Then Premier Davis issued a statement saying that if this was not enough, "other measures" would be considered to ensure that parties like the Nationalist Party would be stillborn.

I hold no brief, to put it very mildly, for crypto-Nazis, neo-Nazis, or any of their distant relatives. My brief is for the mainstream parties of liberal democracy. It is as clear to me as it is to Premier Davis that groups like the Western Guard or the Nationalist Party have only the destruction of liberal democracy in mind. But what our politicians and media seem unable to grasp (as in the ferocious editorials of the *Toronto Star* demanding the outlawing of the Western Guard's telephone messages or the *Globe*'s stance against the Nationalist Party) is that you cannot protect liberal democracy by breaking its rules. The *means* do have an influence on the *ends* when it is the fragile procedures of the rule of law which you are considering. To outlaw "extreme" parties at either the left or the right is to court the very end of that liberal democracy you wish to preserve. Racial hatred and class hatred are not restricted to neo-Nazis; they are equally the province of the Communists, Maoists, Trotskyites, and all their associated splinter groups. They preach it and print it and, when given the chance, will practise it. But so long as we refrain from banning the Communists we must refrain from banning the Fascists. And, God help me, my bourgeois instincts won't be held down. I don't want to ban the Communists. I don't want to stop the Maoists chanting their hatred. I don't want to see the black groups unable to print their violent denunciations of WASPS, whites, and Zionist racism. And yes, I confess, though it is *me* that the Nationalist Party wants to send back to Israel or the re-education camps, I don't want to stop them spewing out their messages on telephone lines or the ballot forms. I don't have to dial their number. I have faith in the people of Canada. I don't think they have to be protected from this or any murderous nonsense lest they go on rampaging pogroms in the streets of Sydney, or Etobicoke, or Brandon, or Prince Rupert. It is liberal democracy that may well need protection from the "other measures" of bandwagoning Roy McMurtry and his sidekick Bill Davis, and all the other provincial governments apparently watching Ontario's "progressive" example with keen interest.

And so I began to speak about these issues. I spoke in Ottawa, Vancouver, Calgary, and London. I spoke on radio, on television (as the house "conservative"), and in the columns of *Maclean's*.

But being regarded as the house conservative has its peculiar moments. Much of this has to do with the fact that I am *not* a conservative, and that by now, given the peculiar pragmatism of our politicians, who'll jump on any vote-bandwagon, irrespective of party affiliation, most Canadians wouldn't know a conservative from a cucumber. Anyway, there I was, the handy home-grown reactionary. The telephone would ring. "Hello," said the cheery voice, "this is Cross Country Check-up calling from CBC radio."

"Yes?" I replied, wondering what we were checking up on this week.

"Well," said the voice, "you know all about this business with the RCMP and the burning of barns and the charges about their illegal wiretapping."

"Yes," I replied cautiously. A Royal Commission was looking into the affairs of the Royal Canadian Mounted Police.

"Of course, they have a very difficult job to do," the voice carried on cheerily. I began to sense that she wanted me to feel that she understood the difficult job she was about to ask me to do. "And Elizabeth [the hostess of the show] thought you'd be the ideal person to explain that."

"Explain what?"

"Well, that the RCMP ought to be allowed to take certain liberties. You know, the conservative position."

I explained the "conservative position". I explained that contemporary conservatism resembled classic liberalism – at least my brand of it did. That I took the side of the individual against the state. That I did not believe in one law for the RCMP and one for the ordinary citizen. Not only did I not believe in it, but I would fight such an impulse with my last breath. That the words of Prime Minister Trudeau, "If it's illegal for the police to open private mail, well, we may have to make it legal," was the epitome of the spirit of illiberalism and authoritarianism. There was a pause.

"But you're supposed to be a *conservative*," she said desperately.

And so it went. I was asked to *defend* censorship laws, alimony, and laws prohibiting homosexuality. I refused. When TV Ontario needed a one-minute debater to argue that maybe more money to third-world governments was not the answer to the problem of the impoverished people of Asia and Africa – they called me. I was grateful in one sense, and astonished by their surprise on meeting me that I did not seem to eat little black children for breakfast. My experience with TV Ontario was in fact the happiest of my house-conservative career. While the programs tended, by and large, to be twenty-seven minutes of unrelieved tripe about the exploitation of the third world by the rich first world (us), the people on the show had some humour, much honesty, and left my one minute of flapping around in the liberal (conservative) morass entirely alone. One day I sat in the dressing-room waiting to tape my rebuttal to Laurier LaPierre, who was urging us to love, finance, approve, and learn from the third world and through this solve the problems of crowded political prisons, tribal genocide, famine, and years of a backward and undeveloped civilization. I turned to the writers of the show: "How did you get interested in the third world?" I asked. "Oh," replied one of them, "we didn't. But the regular people who were to write the show fell through so we had to do a rush job."

One day, when the British government announced that the third world was spending approximately three times the total foreign aid they received on the purchase of arms, I phoned up the show.

"Don't you think that today's report may be relevant in your discussion of foreign aid?" I asked.

"Gee," producer Barbara Barde said. "That's fascinating. But we really don't have time to cope with that. We're doing the problems of the third world's cultural-identity crisis."

My part-time private secretary became apoplectic as she typed out my speeches. An extremely pretty girl by the name of Dia, she had come from East India, and while taking acting lessons at night and two part-time jobs in the day had carved out a decent life for herself in Canada. After an evening typing one of my speeches she came into my workroom brandishing a reference I had made to the Human Rights Commission.

"You know these people?" she asked.

"Yes, I know them," I replied.

"Well," she said, "I went for a job interview today. The woman in personnel was very nice. When the interview and tests were over – and you know my typing isn't so terrific – she leaned over the desk confidentially to me and said, 'If you don't get the job you can go to the Human Rights Commission and complain on two grounds. First, that you're a woman and were discriminated against because they like men for executive assistants, and secondly because you're an Indian.'"

I looked at Dia. "So?"

"Well, damn it. I've never been turned down for a job in my life because of these reasons. I never even thought about it before. She humiliated me and I wanted to slug her. Then she smiled nicely, as if she had done me a favour. If you ever see those people tell them what I think of their damn programs."

After about the third speech I made, I received a telephone call at my office in *Maclean's*. It was Rabbi Gunther Plaut of the Ontario Human Rights Commission.

"We've discussed you down here at the Commission," he said, "and I think it would be useful for all of us if you and I and George [my husband] got together to iron these things out."

Later, another member of the Commission would tell us: "I thought it was *awful* – suggesting a meeting with journalists to lecture them. But it was well meant. I argued against it at the meeting we had about you, but there was nothing I could do."

OK, I thought. Dia, I'll give them your message.

Epilogue

You see, rabbi, after all these words I still don't think you understand. "A different opinion," you say, spreading fine, delicate fingers and smiling benevolently. "We both want the same thing," you repeat to me – and I know what you mean because in one sense we do – but now, after all these words, I have come to realize that, in another, deeper sense, perhaps we don't.

The description of your society is so easy. It sounds like a good liberal camp for the children this summer. A happy, free society in which men and women can stand equal in dignity and opportunity before the law. But not only do you want to arrange that society so it is perfect and happy and equal, but you want to manage it, to monitor it, to see that the daily quotas of love and freedom are always shared and redistributed and kept in circulation. You want a place in the scheme of things for moral referees. Without them you simply won't be happy. The end of your scheme *is* the planned society, if not economically then morally. The end of my society is a free one which, through what I believe to be the essential commonsense and – yes – *practical* value of liberty, will be (no: has been) a more decent one than yours. Coercion does not create goodness. It creates at best apathy and at worst the Gulag.

Here I sit, privileged, well-paid, blessed in a free country, but sitting nevertheless at this restaurant table being informally called to account by the state for the unorthodoxy of holding and defending views on which the entire Western liberal civilization has been built. Views that are no less true for their lack of originality. Views that reflect my profound belief in the value of individual accountability and responsibility, and in freedom – freedom not only in the nation's bedrooms but in the nation's boardrooms and boarding-houses. Freedom that includes and accommodates, as a matter of course, some regulation under a rule of law – alas, we *do* need traffic lights and a social contract to protect our persons and property – but a freedom of the open court rather than regulation by your commissions and committees and faceless apparatchiks. I want my accuser to face me in the daylight. I do not like this new brave society which Kafka foretold, where I can never see my censors; where day by day new regulators accountable to no one, unelected and often unknown, decide what I may watch on television, read in history books, see in public parks, do in the maintenance of my business, hold in my political opinions, or say to my husband and children.

I hold no views that do not reflect the *best* elements of Western civilization. (I cannot embrace classic conservatism because it calls again on me to put the idea of the public good before individual liberty.)

I have examined and discarded the theory and application of democratic socialism with a morbid despair at both its economic inefficiency and its crushing of the human spirit. And now, after six or seven years, I have watched Canadian and North American society bloat itself with undigested ideas and trends and fat, mindless schemes till the body politic can barely function.

We all want clean air – as clean as possible – but not, as the workers at Ontario's Reed Paper Mills pointed out, at the price of jobs and a decent way of life for their families.

We all want to preserve as much nature as possible – but to prevent a power dam because of the darter-fish, unknown till the demolition experts came? To prevent – or delay by a decade or so – the construction of an oil pipeline because of the presumed habits of a few caribou herds or the total preservation of a stone-age culture? Are we to be held hostage in our land by a herd of animals or by 15,000 people who want – understandably – all that is in the shop windows of modern civilization and all the civil liberties they are entitled to, but without (at least according to their political leaders) allowing this civilization to go on creating what they wish to share? How many Canadians have given up their homes or land, expropriated for expressways, power plants, and construction, for much less benefit for all Canadians?

We all want the right to retain our roots – if this pleases us – but what is the enforced program of multiculturalism costing us? Ethnic group against ethnic group, one country fragmented into a thousand consciousnesses.

We all want equal opportunity for minority groups, but is it to follow the example of the telephone office located in New York State, so hastily staffed with unqualified minority workers hired on affirmative-action decrees that when service went into a complete state of disarray, the whole office became more or less a "front" while actual local calls were rerouted through New Jersey?

Must I be called to account for refusing to sanction the mau-mauing of society by special-interest groups?

Must I defend myself for upholding the freedom of academic inquiry wherever it may lead?

Must I explain again the essential fairness of male and female equality and the unfairness of creating newly disadvantaged groups?

Is it wrong to want to know the truth about China as well as South Africa, or, worse, about Mozambique, Kenya, and Zaire as well as Chile, Brazil, and Argentina? Must I again fall into the doublethink that took the words of Thomas Jefferson "And nothing is more sure than that one day this people [Negroes] shall be free," carved the stirring phrase on the walls of the Jefferson Memorial in Washington, D.C., and placed another moving sentence directly after it, neglecting to mention that this fine sentiment of Jefferson's was only *half* a sentence. The concluding half of the sentence, expurgated by the Thought Police, reads: "and nothing is more surely written in the book of fate than that these two people shall never live under the same government." That Jefferson was probably wrong, maybe on both counts, is beside the point. Must we too have our sentences and thoughts laundered to suit your wishful view of reality?

I am not a philosopher, only a journalist. The liberalism I care about was explained a century ago far better than I could ever hope to do in the work of John Stuart Mill, or, more recently, in the books of Nobel Prize winner Friedrich Hayek. If you wish to understand what it is that moves me, the thoughts are there, sharp and honed, inside such books as *On Liberty* or *The Road to Serfdom* or, indeed, Hayek's essay "Why I Am Not a Conservative". But Rabbi, here I am, trying to uphold the basic values of the Western world – an imperfect world, a world that has not found the magic solution to pain and poverty and disease and misery – but a world that has so far done the very best with the system called liberal democracy. You seem baffled by my opposition to your new world of quotas and commissars and special interests. I am opposing the callous new values I see all about me where accomplishment *is* judged by the sexual preference of the artist, or the colour of her skin, or the arrangement of his or her chromosomes, and I am accused of fascism.

What can I say? If my voice sounds shrill, it is because there is so much to lose. If I sound hysterical, it is because there are so few places left to which one can flee. Because I have upheld these values and deeply believe in them I have been invited to enter the vestibule of Kafka's house. Not the torture chamber; no, no, that is still far away. But the door of the vestibule is open, and you hold it open politely in your position as an (unpaid) servant of the state. And now among the potted plants and the nouveau riche pleasantry of the ing the next project on Norman Bethune (tell me, Rabbi, would Bethune have been so honoured if he had worked his blood transfusions for the soldiers of the Third Reich? Do we care that Mao's Great Revolution cost more in lives than the entire population of Canada?) you are asking me to account for my views.

I don't know whether to be relieved or horrified that it is a man such as you, wise, civilized, and, as it were, one of my own. The quiche is good. The expression on your face, your handshake, are warm and genuine. But the breath of the Thought Police is colder than liquid air. I confess now, as I did that warm summer day in the Courtyard Café, that it would be an awful presumption for me to re-educate you. Except, unlike you and your fellow Commissioners, I'd never attempt that. As a writer, I'm merely setting forth my views and submitting them, in all humility, to you in the hope that you will consider them. But that is all I invite you to do in return. It is all I permit you to do. You, and the Human Rights Commission. You cannot outlaw my prejudices without trying to outlaw my judgements, nor can you tell me the difference with sufficient clarity to warrant any action in law. (Nor could I tell yours, of course, which is why I wouldn't try.)

But if you do, you might as well abandon all pretence of civility, potted palms, Mozart being played on the piano, salmon mousse and orange sherbet. The honest instruments of coercion are there, beyond this vestibule of the Thought Police, in the deeper caverns of the self-righteous state. You won't drag me in there without a fight though, and today is as good a day as any to begin.